Poverty
Social Exclusion
and Microfinance
in Britain

BEN ROGALY, THOMAS FISHER,
AND ED MAYO

Oxfam
in association with the New Economics Foundation

First published by Oxfam GB in association with the New Economics Foundation in 1999

Available from the following agents:
for the USA: Stylus Publishing LLC, PO Box 605, Herndon, VA 20172-0605, USA;
tel. +1 (0)703 661 1581; fax +1 (0)703 661 1501; email styluspub@aol.com
for Canada: Fernwood Books Ltd., PO Box 9409, Stn. A, Halifax, Nova Scotia B3K 5S3, Canada;
tel. +1 (0)902 422 3302; fax +1 (0)902 422 3179; email fernwood@istar.ca
for Southern Africa: David Philip Publishers, PO Box 23408, Claremont 7735, South Africa;
tel. +27 (0)21 64 4136; fax +27 (0)21 64 3358; email dpp@iafrica.com
for India: Maya Publishers Pvt Ltd, 113-B, Shapur Jat, New Delhi-110049, India;
tel. +91 (0)11 649 0451; fax +91 (0)11 649 1039
for Australia: Bush Books, PO Box 1370, Gosford South, NSW 2250, Australia;
tel. +61 (0)2 4323 3274; fax +61 (0)2 9212 2468; email bushbook@ozemail.com.au

For the rest of the world, contact Oxfam Publishing, 274 Banbury Road, Oxford OX2 7DZ, UK.
tel. +44 (0)1865 311 311; fax +44 (0)1865 313 925; email publish@oxfam.org.uk

Typeset in Sabon by Garth Stewart; printed by Information Press, Eynsham
Published by Oxfam GB, 274 Banbury Road, Oxford OX2 7DZ, UK
in association with the New Economics Foundation, Cinnamon House, 6-8 Cole Street, London SE1 4YH

Oxfam GB is a registered charity, no. 202 918, and is a member of Oxfam International.

Front-cover picture: © Shelter.

Contents

Oxfam and the
New Economics Foundation

Oxfam has supported community organisations around the world in their fight against poverty since 1942. In 1995 it launched a programme of research, action, and advocacy in the United Kingdom, in recognition of the growing reality that here — as in other countries where Oxfam works – the benefits of economic growth were not reaching all sections of the community. Oxfam believes that poverty is more than the absence of material goods or basic services. It is also a state of powerlessness in which people are marginalised and excluded from society, and unable to control many aspects of their own lives.

Oxfam's anti-poverty programme in the UK is underpinned by the principle of empowerment. Oxfam supports people living in poverty, and the organisations working alongside them, to claim the right to be involved in decisions that affect their lives, and to work for improvements in their own living and working conditions.

Oxfam has identified five major priorities for its work in the UK: strengthening social organisation and capacity-building with groups and communities working on poverty and social exclusion; promoting gender awareness and gender-fair development; challenging negative attitudes towards people living in poverty; addressing links between race, poverty, and exclusion; and bringing an international perspective to and promoting mutual learning about anti-poverty practice and policy in the UK.

Oxfam, Oxfam House, 274 Banbury Road, Oxford OX2 7DZ

The New Economics Foundation (NEF) is an independent, UK-based think-tank that is committed to the creation of just and sustainable economies. It was founded by the leaders of The Other Economic Summit (TOES), which has forced issues such as international debt on to the agenda of the G7/G8 summit meetings.

NEF combines research, policy, training, and practical action. It currently concentrates on the following strategic areas: the global economy; the accountability of corporations; the third sector (such as charities and NGOs); community finance; and participative democracy.

In community finance, NEF has been at the forefront of influencing policy in the UK, with reports such as *Small is Bankable*, *Micro-credit for Micro-enterprise*, and *Regional Community Investment Partnerships*. It is developing a range of innovative initiatives, such as time money, venture capital for social enterprises, and community finance for London. NEF is also engaged in a long-term project of capacity-building with leading micro-finance institutions in India.

NEF has taken a lead in helping to establish new coalitions and organisations like the Jubilee 2000 campaign, the Ethical Trading Initiative, the UK Social Investment Forum, and Green Gauge. It is a registered charity, funded by individual supporters, charitable trusts, public finance such as the National Lottery, businesses, and international grant-giving bodies.

New Economics Foundation, Cinnamon House, 6-8 Cole Street, London SE1 4YH

Acknowledgements

My thanks go first to Kirat Randhawa for reading and commenting on earlier versions, for shouldering much of my workload at home during periods of intense writing, and for moral support throughout. She and many of those named below, among them practitioners and practitioner-researchers, are committed to and involved in the reduction of poverty and social exclusion through careful examination of the evidence and consideration of all means available, and I thank them for enabling me to work on this book in the same spirit. In the mid-1980s, James Copestake, the late Douglas Thornton, Steve Wiggins, and Madhura Swaminathan began my training in understanding the social processes involved in microfinance interventions through joint research on credit for rural development in south India. I am grateful to them; to Audrey Bronstein, who initially involved me in an analysis of whether and how microfinance could contribute to reducing poverty and social exclusion in the UK, and who persuaded me to take part in writing this book; and to one of my co-authors, Ed Mayo, for believing that I could do it and giving me the opportunity, despite lack of experience in UK-based work. Thanks also to Aggie Kent, Pat Conaty, and Jim Dearlove for setting up my first UK study with Ladywood Credit Union in Birmingham, to Helen Derbyshire, who did the study with me, and to Susan Johnson, who co-authored the resulting book focusing on microfinance experience in five countries. Some of the ideas for the present book were initially developed with Susan Johnson through that work and other long discussions. I have also learned much, especially about savings-based microfinance, through working with Alfonso Castillo and Cecilia Lopez of the Tequisquiapan Project in Mexico; through regular neighbourly and collegiate interaction with Ruth Pearson, Chair of the Women's Employment, Education and Training Unit, Norwich; and from Chris Roche, my former boss at Oxfam.

I am deeply indebted to Barbara Harriss-White for teaching me how rigorous research can be an effective tool for well-contextualised pro-poor policy change; and to Kevin Watkins for demonstrating the same through his writings. In the production of this book I am again grateful to Susan Johnson, for taking the trouble to read through several drafts and not holding back with her comments; as well as to Ruth Pearson for inspiration. Bethan Emmett worked voluntarily for several months in 1998 to provide research assistance for Chapters 2 and 3, which would not have been possible without her. Fran Bennett and Thalia Kidder also went to great lengths to help, making extensive and detailed comments and responding to continued requests for information. My thanks to them and to the others who have provided support or advice, including Richard Berthoud, Vanessa Clowes, Ann Cullen, Arjan de Haan, Adrian Harvey, Malcolm Hayday, Cecile Jackson, Gian Kaur, Elaine Kempson, Rachel Marcus, Jana Matysova, Joe Rogaly, Susan Rogaly, Jagir Singh, Saurabh Sinha, Erika Watson, and Claire Whyley. Finally, I would like to thank Thomas Fisher, for the considerable amount that I have learned through our discussions, even (or especially!) when we did not see things the same way; and Audrey Bronstein, Sarah Totterdell, and Catherine Robinson at Oxfam, who somehow found time in their already impossible schedules to steer the book through its final stages.

Ben Rogaly
University of East Anglia, Norwich

We thank all those who have contributed to the ideas that we develop in this book. They include, first and foremost, many practitioners, both in the UK and India, who struggle with the ideals and realities of putting microfinance and community finance into practice, and have given us so much inspiration and practical advice: in the UK, we thank Roger Benson and Richard Street (The Prince's Trust), Roger Brocklehurst (LIF), David Brown and Anne-Michelle Ketteridge (GRF), Peter Bussy and Ralph Swoboda (ABCUL), Nicholas Colloff (World in Need), Rosalind Copisarow (Fundusz Mikro and Street UK), Malcolm Hayday (CAF), Martin Hockly (ICOF), Naomi Kingsley (KMC Associates), Bob Paterson (University of Salford), Steve Pilling (Hackney Business Venture), Glen Saunders (Triodos Bank), Steve Walker (ART), Erika Watson and Jane Bevan (Full Circle Fund); and in India we thank Vijay Mahajan, Sankar Datta and Sriram (BASIX), Rama Reddy and Shashi Rajagopalan (Co-operative Development Foundation), Soumen Biswas, Achintya Ghosh and Deep Joshi (PRADAN), and Jayshree Vyas and Rekha Bharve (SEWA Bank). Thomas is especially grateful to Vijay for all his insight, inspiration, and friendship over many years. We also thank the co-authors who have contributed so much to our recent reports on community and microfinance, on which we draw extensively in this book, especially Pat

Conaty, John Doling, and Andy Mullineux; and not least Ben Rogaly, who has given us so many new and challenging insights. We also warmly thank Audrey Bronstein, Catherine Robinson, and Sarah Totterdell at Oxfam for their very significant and constructive contributions, which have allowed this book to come to fruition. Many others have provided valuable ideas and support, particularly Simon Bale, Nigel Bottomley, Tony Colman, John Ellis, Jan Evers, Sue Gillie, Christophe Guene, Peter Hughes, Susan Johnson, Elaine Kempson, Dan Leader, Peter Lloyd, Malcolm Lynch, Theresa McDonagh, Fred Mulder, Sara Murphy, Bert Nicholson, Peter Ramsden, Susan Rice, Andrew Robinson, Cliff Rosenthal, Jane Rosser, Philip Rutnam, Dan Sattar, Penny Shepherd, Phil Smith, Stephen Thake, Gareth Thomas, Geron Walker, Andrea Westall, David Wright, and Claire Whyley. Finally, Thomas thanks Julie. (Most authors write that without their partners their books would never have seen the light of day. I can fairly write that without this book we might never have been partners!)

Thomas Fisher and Ed Mayo
New Economics Foundation, London

Oxfam GB gratefully acknowledges the support of the Calouste Gulbenkian Foundation, which contributed generously to the costs of researching and writing this book.

1 Introduction

BEN ROGALY AND THOMAS FISHER

SINCE the late 1970s, inequality in Britain has steadily grown, and poverty has become increasingly concentrated in certain geographical areas. Many people live in households lacking secure shelter, diets of adequate quantity and good quality, relations with friends and family, or a capacity to influence events in their neighbourhood or more widely. The experience of relative poverty is well documented and, as recent research has shown, can lead to a higher incidence of illness and early death.[1] Analysis of data on trends in absolute poverty between 1979 and 1994/95 showed that the poorest ten per cent became eight per cent poorer in terms of real income.[2]

The change to a New Labour regime in May 1997 signalled the start of a high-level government engagement with the challenge of countering poverty and social exclusion. At the same time, the anti-poverty lobby of non-government organisations and other civil-society groups, who had become used to working with a government which denied the existence of poverty in Britain, has continued to press the current government hard to meet commitments made at the 1995 UN Social Summit in Copenhagen.[3]

One type of policy intervention intended to tackle poverty and social exclusion, with the support of the government[4] as well as local authorities and voluntary organisations, is the provision of financial services, such as deposit facilities, insurance, bill-payment and money-transfer facilities, financial literacy training, personal loans, and loans for micro-enterprises,[5] which for the purposes of this book will be collectively referred to as 'microfinance'. The aim of the book is to explore how poverty and social exclusion might be reduced through the expansion of such microfinancial services.

THE CENTRAL ISSUES

The book addresses three main questions.

First, what are the dimensions of poverty and social exclusion in Britain, and what role can microfinancial services play in combating them?

Secondly, from international experience of using microfinance as an approach to tackling poverty and social exclusion, which lessons are relevant in the British context?

Thirdly, are microfinancial services able to address the underlying structural causes of poverty and social exclusion? Or do they primarily strengthen people's ability to manage the effects of structural change on their own lives?

In focusing on these questions, we try to avoid a technocratic approach to policy and practice. Microfinancial services are often seen as a kind of technical fix. Yet, like other anti-poverty interventions, introducing and operating such services is also a *process* and occurs within a political context. Clearly politics, formal and informal, will determine, in part at least, what is intended and what is achieved.

For this reason, the language of policy is often in dispute. Social exclusion is a contested concept. The meanings of social exclusion used in the book are therefore carefully specified. There is a significant ideological difference between an interpretation which stresses 'inclusion' in order to minimise 'deviance' from a particular norm, and one which emphasises social exclusion as a lack of control over one's own life, including the capacity to influence what it means to be a citizen. We take the second view here.

Our approach is based on a perception of poverty as the product of structural factors within society, as opposed to the view that poverty is primarily the fault of poor people themselves. However, we want to avoid portraying poor and socially excluded people as victims: we believe that people themselves can and do create change.

Our analysis of lessons from the provision of microfinancial services worldwide is grounded in a review of the contemporary British context. Only by examining what poverty and social exclusion mean and analysing the ways in which they are being tackled *in Britain* can we come to any firm conclusions about what microfinancial services may be able to achieve in this country. The success of any intervention aimed at addressing poverty and social exclusion depends upon a careful weighing of the evidence, both positive and negative, and an awareness of its limitations. Interventions promoted without such grounding in complex realities are unlikely to be effective anti-poverty tools.

DEFINITIONS

Poverty is defined here in relative terms as *the experience of living in a household with a level of income or wealth which is below that necessary to purchase the range of goods and services considered by the standards of the majority in a particular reference group to be sufficient for living.*

This definition focuses on material poverty and encompasses vulnerability to a sudden loss of income, or indebtedness in cases where such losses are not underwritten by wealth or job security.

The terms 'social exclusion' and 'poverty' are not used interchangeably in this book. **Social exclusion** is defined here as *the processes which bring about a lack of citizenship, whether economic, political, or social.* (Although we take care in the book to distinguish between poverty and social exclusion, it should be noted that many international bodies, including Oxfam, define poverty in a way that is very similar to the definition of social exclusion used here.) **Economic citizenship** includes access to good-quality employment and to financial services. **Political citizenship** refers to the capacity to influence processes of decision-making that affect one's own life: being able to change the rules. **Social citizenship** includes a sense of belonging, as well as the ability to accumulate and maintain supportive social networks.[6]

Alongside its broad focus on poverty and social exclusion, the book has particular relevance to the challenge of countering financial exclusion. **Financial exclusion** refers to exclusion from particular sources of credit and other financial services (including insurance, bill-payment services, and accessible and appropriate deposit accounts).[7]

Microfinance refers to a range of services: the provision of small loans, savings facilities with no minimum deposit (or a very low minimum deposit), and other financial services such as insurance, money transfer, or bill payment designed appropriately for people who are on low incomes or financially excluded for other reasons. These services taken together are termed here **microfinancial services**.

Chapter 5, which considers the existing record and potential of microfinancial services in Britain, introduces a term which is specific to the British context: **community finance**. This is the commonly used term for initiatives which seek to widen the access of disadvantaged people and neighbourhoods to capital and other financial services.[8] Such services include microfinancial services, provided, for example, by credit unions; neighbourhood regeneration initiatives, such as community loan funds; and loan funds and social banks targeted at relevant sectors, such as small businesses, community and social enterprises,[9] or charities.

Connecting finance, poverty, and social exclusion

The links between finance on the one hand and poverty and social exclusion on the other are complex. Material poverty, by definition, involves managing on little money, and managing money in particular ways. It may mean reliance on family, friends, and informal providers. Such reliance both depends on and influences the nature of social relations. For people in financial difficulty and with limited access to formal financial services, such relations may be critical, and the way in which people prioritise their uses of money when resources are squeezed may reflect this. For example, despite the often extortionate interest rates charged by private unregulated moneylenders, maintaining relations with and repayments to informal lenders may be given higher priority than paying bills on time or paying off a bank overdraft.

For many, 'financial exclusion' is part of the experience of poverty and broader social exclusion. The causes of financial exclusion lie in the changing market strategies of private commercial banks, which have withdrawn from areas identified with low income and large numbers of people receiving social-security benefits. Leyshon and Thrift refer to this as a 'flight to quality', as banks increasingly focus on customised services for high-income fee-paying customers.[10]

Microfinancial services may be relevant and useful to people who are excluded financially or in other ways, but need not necessarily be so.[11] Much depends on what else is going on in their lives, and on which services are being offered, and how. Money — where to get it, how to manage it, including how to avoid debt — is a critically important dimension of the experience of poverty and social exclusion in Britain. Finance is thus of much broader relevance than the issue of 'financial exclusion' alone.

STRUCTURE AND ARGUMENT OF THE BOOK

Chapter 2, written by Ben Rogaly, places finance and financial exclusion in the context of the broader dimensions of poverty and social exclusion in Britain. The chapter synthesises some of the currently available evidence about the meanings and dimensions of poverty and social exclusion, as well as about their various causes. This is a process of clarification. If the stated objectives of an intervention are to bring about change, it is essential to be clear about what it is (in this case poverty and social exclusion) that it is sought to change. The discussion of causes serves to focus on what can and what cannot be achieved through provision of microfinancial services.

Microfinancial services are not provided in a vacuum. Chapter 3, by Ben Rogaly, places them within the broader environment of policies designed to combat poverty and social exclusion at the national and local levels. This inevitably cursory review notes the centrality of national social-security and workplace policies in British anti-poverty strategy. It also reflects on the potential for local action, commenting on the current government's position as set out in the report from the government's own

Social Exclusion Unit: *Bringing Britain Together: A National Strategy for Neighbourhood Renewal*. The scope for action by poor people themselves — as individuals or acting together — is also considered.

In the fourth chapter, Ben Rogaly examines some international experiences of using microfinancial services to tackle poverty and social exclusion. He draws on examples from the USA, Bangladesh, Indonesia, India, and Mexico to demonstrate the diversity of microfinance initiatives in terms of both scale and orientation. In recent years such initiatives have proliferated, and many more people have gained access to certain financial services. Some initiatives have concentrated on savings, others on insurance, and still others on loans. It is emphasised that microfinancial services should not be confused with credit for micro-enterprises, which is just one of the many kinds of financial service that may be involved. This chapter reports on some detailed studies of the impact of microfinancial services on poverty and on social relations of gender and class. The author reports on the impact which business credit may have had on incomes (its 'promotional' role) and income equality, as well as on the 'protective' role which microfinancial services can have, for example through enabling people to reduce their vulnerability to debt. There is clearly no blueprint for delivering microfinancial services to poor people.

In Chapter 5, Thomas Fisher examines the record of the fledgling providers of microfinancial services in Britain and their potential for expansion. Such schemes are known in Britain as 'community finance initiatives'. They include funds devised to attract investment into areas of multiple disadvantage, as well as to deliver financial services for individuals. Because of their relatively recent origins, there is little evidence of their impact. However, it is possible to use the information available on the impact of microfinancial services on poverty and social exclusion in other countries to draw out inferences about the potential of community finance initiatives to reduce poverty and social exclusion in Britain. Here too, it is important to set the initiatives in their wider context: the chapter outlines microfinancial services provided by institutions whose motives are not explicitly social, including mainstream commercial banks, post offices, and private moneylenders, as well as the services provided by community finance initiatives.

Chapters 4 and 5 work through the actual and potential impacts of the increased availability of microfinancial services to people in various degrees of poverty and exclusion. Protective services — such as savings, insurance, and loans for 'getting by' — are found to make more difference to the poorest people than credit for micro-enterprise. The latter has primarily benefited those who are less poor, though on low incomes, and who are better able to withstand the inevitable degree of business failure. However, community finance initiatives in Britain have also sought to increase employment in particular areas, through loans to small and medium enterprises that are unable to obtain sufficient capital from banks. In Chapter 5, Thomas Fisher also considers the potential for community finance and microfinance to offer an evolutionary way of combining practical action with structural change.

In the concluding chapter, the authors seek to draw out some of the important lessons for Britain from the diversity and the innovations of international experience in providing microfinancial services. The evidence presented in the book suggests that there are important lessons to be learned from these initiatives for agencies that aim to combat poverty and social exclusion in Britain. Many of these lessons concern the critical task of helping people to manage their money and thus cope better with lack of earnings, with insecure and low-paid employment, with changes in family structures and individual circumstances over the life-cycle. Initiatives that provide microfinancial services could potentially contribute to a more transformative approach only if integrated with wider strategies for social change and economic improvement.

Microfinancial services in Britain have the potential to widen poor people's access to financial services in general and to more appropriate services in particular. When successfully integrated with other anti-poverty initiatives, such services can enable people to protect themselves better against the impact of structural change, and so give them more effective control over their lives.

2 Poverty and social exclusion in Britain: where finance fits

BEN ROGALY

INTRODUCTION AND BACKGROUND

THIS chapter places finance and financial exclusion in the context of the broader dimensions of poverty and social exclusion. It concentrates on synthesising some of the currently available evidence about the meanings and dimensions of poverty and social exclusion, and their different causes. This is a process of clarification. If the stated objectives of an intervention are to bring about change, it is essential to be clear about what it is (in this case poverty and social exclusion) that it is sought to change. The discussion of causes serves to focus on the question of what it is possible (and not possible) to achieve at the local level or via the linking of local initiatives.

In the following section of this chapter, meanings of poverty and social exclusion in Britain are discussed, and definitions to be used in this book are set out. The third section explores dimensions of poverty and social exclusion in Britain. The fourth considers some of the ways in which changes in the level and nature of employment have determined current experiences of poverty and social exclusion. Some of the underlying causes of structural change in the labour market and other causes of poverty and social exclusion are considered here. The fifth section examines where finance fits: for example, what are the structural causes of financial exclusion? How do poor and socially excluded people manage their finances? What part do debt, credit, and savings presently play in people's lives? This section identifies important challenges for the provision of microfinance in Britain, as set out in Chapter 5. The findings of this chapter are summarised and conclusions are drawn in the final section.

MEANINGS OF POVERTY AND SOCIAL EXCLUSION IN BRITAIN

While professional commentators have disputed the meaning of poverty and the processes, such as social exclusion, which bring it about, Britain has seen, since the late 1970s, an increase in the geographical concentration of poverty,[1] and a growing inequality between rich and poor people. Many people live in households lacking secure shelter, diets of adequate quantity and good quality, relations with friends and family, or a capacity to influence events in their neighbourhood or more widely. The experience of *relative* poverty is well documented and, as recent research has shown, can lead to a higher incidence of illness and early death.[2] *Absolute* poverty is more contentious, as it is defined differently by poor people themselves, by professionals and by various national statistical exercises. Analysis of data on trends in the real income of the poorest 10 per cent showed that their incomes fell by 8 per cent between 1979 and 1994/95.[3] The present Labour government has made a commitment, through policy statements, to reduce poverty and social exclusion.

As the main task of this book is to examine the ways in which the provision of microfinancial services may enable poor and excluded people themselves, together with others working alongside them, to become less poor and less excluded, it is necessary to be clear about what is meant by the terms 'poverty' and 'social exclusion'. The loose usage of these expressions and the interchanging of them in other writing have been criticised. One problem is that different meanings of social exclusion can carry diametrically opposed implications for public policy. Evans points out, for example, that for some commentators welfare provision itself brings on social exclusion, rather than being a way of tackling it.[4] Terms such as 'poverty' and 'social exclusion' are inevitably loaded with normative or ideological assumptions about the kind of society that the user would like to see.[5] Social exclusion is defined differently at the national policy level in different countries.[6]

Here, the terms 'poverty' and 'social exclusion' will not be used interchangeably. My ideological starting point can be set out on the table at this stage. I am committed to an equality of opportunity that goes beyond non-discrimination, important though that is. This commitment involves working to change the institutions that create and perpetuate inequalities of outcome, including wealth inequality.[7]

Definitions of poverty and social exclusion

Poverty is defined in this book in relative terms as the experience of living in a household with a level of income or wealth which is below that necessary to purchase the range of goods and services considered by the standards of the majority in a particular reference group to be sufficient for living.[8] This definition of poverty encompasses vulnerability to a sudden loss of income and therefore to indebtedness through unexpected shocks or regular strains on finances, in cases where such losses are not underwritten by wealth or job security. **Social exclusion**, much more broadly, is used here to refer to the processes which bring about a lack of citizenship, whether economic, political, or social. **Economic citizenship** refers principally to access to work (whether or not through paid employment) which has the potential to increase an individual's sense of control over his or her life, and his or her capacity to transfer this across generations, partly through increased income, wealth, and spending power and reduced vulnerability, but also in terms of self-esteem. Economic citizenship may also refer to access to financial services; it encompasses financial literacy.[9] **Political citizenship** means being able to take part in and exert influence on processes of decision-making, both formal and informal, that affect one's own daily life. **Social citizenship** refers to a sense of belonging and, in particular, to the capacity to accumulate and maintain social assets in the form of helpful contacts, relations, and networks.[10]

To be poor does not necessarily mean being socially excluded, but it increases the chances of such an outcome. For example, lack of income, together with lack of wealth, reduces one's capacity to partake in social life and may reduce the quantity of one's social relations.[11] In other words, poverty, which is often an aspect of social exclusion in terms of lack of economic citizenship, also makes *social* non-citizenship more likely. Furthermore, the various processes of social exclusion outlined here are interrelated — each one increasing the likelihood of the others.

Exclusion and disadvantage

This book's perspective on social exclusion highlights the disadvantages that such exclusion entails. Unemployed people seeking work, if they live in areas with few jobs, are effectively excluded from the labour market. Women are excluded from certain types of work and employment, from networks, and from political decision-making. Though this does not apply to all women, as a category of people women are disadvantaged in relation to careers in paid employment by socially constructed notions of what women and men should be or do, as well as by the biologically determined 'reproductive tax'.[12] Many black and ethnic-minority people in Britain are excluded through discrimination on grounds of colour, religion, or language.[13]

Among elderly people, there is an increasing gulf between the wealthy who have significant private incomes from lucrative pension deals or stockmarket investments, and those who rely entirely on state pensions.[14] For many elderly people, particularly those with fewer material resources, retirement means a decline in social as well as economic citizenship, because of their increased isolation. Those of the elderly who lack income (and often therefore their own means of transport) suffer most from the closure of local shops and public services. This group are also the least able to defend themselves from violent crime.[15]

Social exclusion as the term is used here refers to processes leading to a decline in economic, political, and social citizenship, and thus to reduced equality of opportunity and access to resources, including social and material wealth. More effective citizenship along economic, social, and political lines means more power to control one's own life, more room for effective action, and the capacity to redefine the rules regarding what it means to be a citizen.

'Deviance' and diversity

This view of social exclusion stands in marked contrast to the assimilationist view, which places the emphasis on inclusion in some kind of culturally defined mainstream. Demanding assimilation of people who are, in some ways at least, self-excluded does not fit with my definition of political citizenship. Identities can be cultivated on the basis of exclusion. A strong sense of self and of belonging may be gained from apparently deviant behaviour. Romani gypsies are Britain's most persecuted minority, according to one commentator.[16] Yet this group affirms its identity in part by 'deviance' from societal 'norms'. Similarly, on the Cruddas estate in the West End of Newcastle-upon-Tyne, where almost all young men are without jobs, many would not consider visiting a Job Centre in the city centre, perhaps placing a higher value on one dimension of citizenship (maintaining relations with friends and neighbours) rather than another (obtaining a job). In the case of women in general, questions have been raised about the extent to which they *want* to be included in 'male' networks, and the degree to which some kinds of 'exclusion' enable them to develop forms of identity and action with which they are more comfortable and which they adopt in preference to conforming to or being included in what they perceive to be a flawed 'male norm'.[17]

Furthermore, it is important to avoid confining ideas of social exclusion to particular categories or groups of people. To represent a particular ethnic group, women, elderly people, or young people as excluded is to deny diversity within that social category and to deny the possibility of change, which is brought about in part by people's own actions. While black and ethnic-minority people are discriminated against as a group, there is much diversity of outcomes among different sub-groups. For example, people of Chinese or Indian origin have been found to be less likely than black Caribbean people and people of Pakistani and Bangladeshi origin to live in areas of extreme poverty. Indeed, a larger proportion of Chinese and those defining themselves in the 1991 Census as 'Other' lived in wards with the highest proportion of highly qualified people and social classes 1 and 2 than any other ethnic group (including whites).[18]

This book attempts to explore the extent to which local financial services initiatives, in partnerships between local people and a combination of the private, statutory, and voluntary sectors, can successfully combat social exclusion in its various forms and can help people to find ways out of income poverty and vulnerability to it, by means including the accumulation of wealth and greater equality in its distribution between women and men, classes, and races. As will become clear in Chapters 4 and 5, microfinance initiatives involve processes and outcomes that are social and political as well as economic.

DIMENSIONS OF POVERTY AND SOCIAL EXCLUSION

As the processes involved in bringing about exclusion from economic, social, and political citizenship suggest, the experiences of poverty and social exclusion are multidimensional.[19] However, the particular dimensions concerned are context-specific.[20] In his comparison of exclusion in the UK with that in southern Italy, Mingione highlights 'family fragmentation' and disadvantages faced by ethnic-minority groups in the UK[21] which are not central factors in the experience of exclusion in southern Italy. There, 'an account of social exclusion must cover the striking connection between, on the one hand, the growth of mass youth unemployment in a fragile economic system, characterised by widespread informal work, and, on the other hand, high levels of poverty, with citizens segregated in parts of the cities and discriminated against institutionally in terms of access to welfare'.[22]

So, what are the dimensions of poverty and social exclusion in Britain?

Income and wealth

Most of the existing evidence on trends in poverty is concerned with income poverty. **Income** has formed the basis of calculations compiled from aggregate statistics to indicate the number of people below a 'poverty line'. In recent decades, the poverty line used by analysts of public policy has been related to the average income of British households. The most common measure of the extent of poverty has been the number of individuals living in households with less than half of the national average income.[23]

However, even if definitions of poverty are limited to a household's financial status, poverty is not measurable by average annual or weekly income alone. Income streams, for example for the self-employed, can vary in size over the course of a year, and for most people net income — after heating and lighting bills and seasonally heavy spending at festivals such as Christmas — is variable. Some income streams are less vulnerable than others and fluctuate less than others. This lower vulnerability should be an additional signal of the relative security of a household's livelihood.

Poverty is more fundamentally a matter of lack of **wealth**. The possession of relatively little or no wealth, in the form of owned assets, increases vulnerability to fluctuations in income. More than this, wealth has long had an important role in structuring opportunity in Britain. Inequality in wealth in Britain hardly changed between 1911 and 1960.[24] Indeed, writing in the late 1970s, Townsend held that the unequal distribution of wealth was the 'single most notable feature of social conditions in the UK'. ... '[A]ccess to occupational class tends to be a function of class origins and family wealth.'[25] More recently, a major study of the underlying structures responsible for Britain's political, economic, and social conditions suggested that there was a direct link between wealth and class, which 'hardens subtly into caste' via the education system. Those born with little wealth could not afford the private education in which an increasing proportion of children were enrolled during the 1980s.[26] Privileged education marked out life opportunities bounded by initial wealth or class.[27] Indeed, wealth distorts access to better-quality state education as well as to the private system, with the location of many of the highest-performing schools corresponding to concentrations of wealthier residents.[28] House-price differentials perpetuate the transmission of uneven life chances across the generations. This indicates one of many links between poverty and exclusion — in the sense of both economic and social citizenship — as experienced by those who are denied access to opportunity (as opposed to those who can choose).

The experience of living on low or insecure incomes with little or no wealth was compounded by the rapid growth during the 1980s and early 1990s of **inequality of incomes**.[29] The experience of income inequality has been found to contribute significantly to social disaffection and ill-health.[30] As the distance between the lowest and highest income deciles increased, the occupational composition of the bottom decile shifted from a preponderance of pensioners in the 1960s to domination by the registered unemployed as the largest single group in the 1980s and 1990s. However, there was also an increase in the number of people in work but with very low incomes,[31] including an independent increase in the proportion classified as self-employed. The proportion of self-employed people in the lowest income decile increased by 23 per cent between 1984 and 1994.[32]

Other researchers looking at income poverty over time have identified a process of 'churning'. Using panel data involving interviews with the same people over several years during the early 1990s, Jarvis and Jenkins found that people move in and out of poverty because of inter-annual fluctuations in income.[33] The implication of their research is that many of those who were in the lowest income group in the early 1980s are in higher income groups now and *vice versa*. The explanation for the growing gap between rich and poor in terms of income is not as simple as it had seemed. Moreover, other evidence suggests that, although the real incomes of the lowest income decile fell by 18 per cent (after housing costs) between 1979 and 1992/93, their expenditure rose.[34] Access to consumer durables, such as televisions, videos, fridges, telephones, and washing machines increased for this decile between the late 1970s and the 1990s.[35]

Jarvis and Jenkins do not imply a trend of upward mobility, but rather reveal the precarious existence of a group of households who move in and out of income poverty, depending on changes in family size and structure as well as employment status. Of those people in households whose incomes declined to below half of average incomes between 1990/91 and 1993/94, in just under one-third of cases it resulted from one household member losing employment, and in about one in seven cases from one adult member departing.[36] The experience of poverty is not fixed. Rather it is dynamic, and there are many different trajectories. However, while it may be true that for a minority 'low incomes are a life-cycle phenomenon', for most people in the lowest income groups, increases in income do not take them far out of income poverty.[37]

A document on poverty and inequality published by HM Treasury in 1999 also examines the dynamics of poverty. One in six families is pushed into poverty (defined here as the bottom fifth of the income distribution) by the birth of a child. The impact of poverty and inequality on children's life chances starts early — with clear class-related differences in the rate of educational development by the time children are 22 months old. And this inequality is passed from generation to generation, with the children of the low paid much more likely to be low-paid adults in their turn.[38]

Many people *are* 'stuck' in income poverty. More than half of those in the bottom twenty per cent of incomes remain there for at least three years. Being stuck is associated with an unstable family background, early pregnancy, past criminal convictions, and illegal drug use. Significantly, it is also connected to a lack of 'the tacit, informal skills of networking, identifying opportunities and using initiative and imagination'.[39] This is, of course, dangerous terrain, because these same skills are used by some people of considerable wealth to distort opportunity in their own direction. I do not take the position that poverty is *caused* by behavioural factors. On the contrary, I believe the explanation to be largely structural (see below). For example, as access to free and subsidised public services, including educational and health facilities, declines, those lacking access for want of money are also more likely than others to remain in income poverty.[40]

For microfinance initiatives aiming to reduce poverty and social exclusion, it is important to take a broad perspective of their different dimensions. Monitoring of the process and outcomes of microfinance initiatives can then use a broad range of indicators, which may well have moved in different directions. This is a serious approach which does not take the impact of such initiatives for granted, but rather seeks to gather information on successes and failures, so that learning and improvements can continue.

The role of unemployment

Unemployment is perhaps the most important aspect of exclusion and the major proximate cause of poverty in contemporary western Europe. Amartya Sen argues that unemployment is at least as significant a cause of inequality as low income, because it is the proximate cause of a number of other dimensions of deprivation.[41] These include loss of confidence, dejection, ill-health, and increased tensions inside households. Women and men experience unemployment differently. At the societal level, widespread unemployment can increase tensions between indigenous and immigrant groups; it is also a waste of productive potential.[42] Many people gain a 'sense of worth' and pride through earning a living,[43] which can be destroyed by long-term unemployment. Yet it is also important to note that degrading employment on insecure terms at very low wages can have a similarly damaging effect. The rising number of individuals in the UK experiencing poverty in work has already been noted; this theme will be considered again below, in a discussion of how the changing nature of the labour market causes exclusion from economic citizenship in ways other than unemployment.

Being unemployed affects people's access to personal financial services, such as current accounts, deposit facilities, and insurance, and the ways in which these are used (see below: 'Where finance fits'). The chapters that follow also discuss the potential for credit for self-employment to enable unemployed people to move out of poverty.

Intra-household dynamics

Despite changing ideas about men and women, in Britain women remain the major carers (for example of elderly relations) and rearers of young children. These 'roles' create strain and tension and necessitate juggling, whether or not women are in paid employment. The process of juggling is further challenged by lingering societal notions of women as dependent on men. For example, married women not in employment can lose access to current-account banking on divorce.[44] Women were assumed to be economically dependent on men in the Beveridge model of social insurance, much of which remains intact at the time of writing, as will be seen in Chapter 3. Elaine Kempson's synthesis of more than thirty qualitative studies of 'Life on a Low Income' shows the complexity of women's and men's differential experiences of poverty. Despite tensions associated with living in restricted spaces with no family member in employment, '[t]hose who coped best with living in poverty tended to be couples who had very strong relationships to start with'.[45] It was harder to cope alone, although men's 'struggle to come to terms with failing to succeed as breadwinner' would create problems for women too. Women out of (or in and out of) employment tended to continue to be less cut off than men from others of their own sex.[46] It may be that the networking and social skills involved in managing tight family budgets and in finding child-care arrangements, both of which were often found to be the role of women rather than men, meant that unemployed men, even those in households with two or more adults, could be more isolated than unemployed women.

Large numbers of children live in households experiencing poverty (not surprisingly, given the over-representation of lone parents and two-parent households in the lowest income decile, compared with the proportions of both in the population).[47] Nevertheless, parents out of work and on low incomes continue to attempt to protect their children from deprivation. For example, parents on benefits spend almost the same amount as other parents on their under-elevens at Christmas.[48] In seeking to explain the relatively small differences between what different parents spend on their children, Goodman *et al.* examined a number of possible associations, including living in a one-parent family, having a parent who smokes, being on income support, having siblings, or having parents who are not working. The last factor was found to matter most. However, much of the additional amount spent by working parents is spent on child care.[49]

It has already been noted that many of those who rely on state pensions experience income poverty, and that parents with children are over-represented in the lowest income decile. Yet intra-household relations are not static: they change over a household's life-cycle. Changes in household structure explain some of the dynamics of income poverty already described above. A household not classed as income-poor at one stage could fall into that category later, for example after a birth involving loss of employment income (see discussion of HM Treasury report above), and move out of it again later, when and if employment income rose. Household dissolution involving the loss of an earner is also a major cause of sudden declines in income.[50] However, as noted above, people experiencing income poverty face adverse structures of opportunity and access to resources, including wealth, which means that movements out of, say, the lowest income decile tend not to be long lived or far removed.

Intra-household relations affect the way in which money is managed and who manages it. Life-cycle changes create particular demands for financial services such as insurance and pensions. All these have implications for microfinance initiatives, in terms of the way they are organised and the services they offer. These issues are discussed in more detail towards the end of this chapter ('Where finance fits').

Spatial dimensions

Material poverty and the multiple processes of social exclusion are concentrated in particular geographic areas.[51] The most acute experiences of deprivation are in urban areas such as Newcastle-upon-Tyne and Liverpool, where unemployment has hit hardest with the decline of heavy manufacturing industry. Analysis of census data indicates a 'greater spatial concentration of poverty and wealth over the decade to 1991'.[52] But there is diversity in spatial patterns and hence in the experiences of deprivation. For example, certain housing estates on the outskirts of Newcastle became the focus of very high levels of unemployment, while the city centre remains prosperous and flourishing. Part of the experience of poverty in Newcastle is the sense of social as well as spatial distance between these two worlds.[53] In Birmingham, by contrast, the most severe deprivation is located in the inner city.[54] Green's detailed study, which uses a variety of indicators of poverty and wealth, also shows up the situation in London, where many of Britain's poorest and wealthiest people live in close proximity.

Spatial dimensions are experienced differently in these three examples and elsewhere. A sense of economic non-citizenship may be collectively shared on an isolated outer housing estate. Exclusion from social networks may be felt more acutely by people living in poverty in inner London. In all these locations, deprivation is multidimensional, characterised by low-quality and crowded housing conditions, food poverty,[55] ill health, and low-achieving schools. Groups of people whose choices are limited, particularly unemployed people and lone parents, end up being clustered together on particular estates.[56]

Others emphasise that the co-existence of rich and poor people in the same space prevails across different parts of Britain. 'In Britain the big divisions are no longer between north and south. They are between often quite small areas of the same towns, the same cities and same regions.'[57] Indeed, there remains widespread *rural* poverty in Britain. The rural population of England alone was 13.5 million in 1996, an increase of 2.5 million since 1971. It has been estimated that one-quarter of those living in the countryside are 'in or near the margins of poverty'.[58] The experience of social non-citizenship in the countryside involves the strain of suppressing and hiding material poverty from public view — a strain brought on by 'living in a "goldfish bowl"', which can lead to severe mental-health problems.[59] Inequality of pay and job insecurity for those in farm work are especially marked, as jobs are regularly threatened by the use of outsiders bussed in, sometimes from inner-city areas.[60]

An understanding of the spatial dimensions of poverty and social exclusion is required for the design of policies and programmes aimed at tackling them. These include microfinance schemes. For example, the concentration of people and the extent to which people interact socially and economically, as well as the nature of that interaction, all affect the degree to which group-based microfinancial services can make a positive impact on social exclusion. Furthermore, as will be seen in Chapter 3, it is important to match an awareness of the mutually reinforcing multiple dimensions of exclusion in particular places with the need to work simultaneously on multiple levels, national as well as local. Singling out particular neighbour hoods as 'problem areas' can itself perpetuate exclusion and distract attention away from the causes of poverty and exclusion, which are the subject of the next section. The section begins with an assessment of how the ways in which the labour market operates (and how this is changing) have *caused* poverty and exclusion. It goes on to examine some of the underlying causes of recent structural changes in the labour market and to review some of the other major causes of deprivation in Britain.

THE CAUSES OF POVERTY AND SOCIAL EXCLUSION

Because the provision of microfinancial services is advocated as a means of tackling poverty and social exclusion, and not merely financial exclusion, it is necessary in this book to consider the major causes of poverty and social exclusion in Britain. In Chapters 4 and 5, which focus on microfinance, it will then be possible to comment on the potential for microfinancial services to tackle those causes.

The changing structure of the labour market and work-related exclusion

In Britain, the most widely cited proximate cause of both poverty and the economic process of social exclusion associated with work is the changing structure of the labour market. Two major trends stand out: a rise in the scale of registered unemployment from the 1970s, and a 'casualised' and more 'flexible' workforce, with higher proportions of both short-term and part-time contracts.[61]

As manufacturing industries and coal mines closed down, there were major changes in the kinds of worker sought by employers. On the one hand, there were jobs requiring relatively little skill but also paying very little, such as work in residential care, catering, and cleaning. On the other hand, employers increasingly began to seek workers with skills suitable to high technology, including information technology.

At the same time, the demographic structure of the labour force changed. There was a big rise in lone parenthood between the early 1970s and the early 1990s. Some studies have suggested that unemployment is the main cause of the increase in lone parenthood.[62] Over the same period, the proportion of women in part-time work rose from one-fifth to one-third, while the proportion of women in full-time employment hardly altered. The 'proportion of working-age men in full-time employment fell by almost a fifth'.[63]

Some men experience stigma unacceptable to them if they enter certain types of work and receive very low remuneration, because of sets of ideas about gender and work that are prevalent in society. This may have been part of the reason for the increasing ratio of women to men in employment. Part-time workers in Britain can still be paid less per hour than full-timers in equivalent jobs. Moreover, many women were employed in occupations, whether full-time or part-time, paid at rates lower than had been the practice in manufacturing industry. Women in full-time employment earn on average only three-quarters of men's pay for each hour worked.[64] Disturbingly, 1997–98 was the first year since 1986 when the hourly pay differential between women and men (taking full and part-time workers together) actually *widened*. [65]

A further cause of 'casualisation' and 'flexibilisation' was the weakening of workers' rights through employment legislation enacted through the 1980s. The overall result was the segmentation of the labour market, which 'sculpt[ed] the new and ugly shape of British society'.[66] The country was divided between those on the edge of or outside the labour market, those inside but in insecure jobs, and the group at the top with both high incomes and economic security. The changing labour market was a major cause of income inequality. Those whose earnings consisted partly of returns on investments and private pensions saw their income increase rapidly. Inequality of incomes increases the sense of relative deprivation — and thus poverty — and also the experience of exclusion from economic citizenship. Unemployment is perpetuated by the spatial concentration of workers, because this reduces the chances of using networks and contacts to find out about and be informally recommended for job opportunities.

Moreover, 'the impact of economic restructuring on social life in neighbourhoods where place, [people] and work were once closely intertwined has been devastating'.[67] This decline in local social interaction is not confined to areas of high unemployment. Among employed people, the increase in hours worked has made for less associational life. British society is 'divided between a well-connected and active group of citizens with generally prosperous lives and another set whose associational life and involvement with politics is very limited'.[68] Thus, for many people political citizenship has declined.

Identifying processes of social exclusion in this way does not mean stigmatising *self-exclusion*. Indeed, self-exclusion from certain forms of employment may increase an individual's capacity to participate in social and political citizenship. For example, some types of paid work can be boring and exhausting and lead to deteriorating health. Morris suggests that some unskilled manual workers withdrew from the employed workforce in Britain because of the impact of 'inclusion' on their health.[69]

Many workers who have left or been pushed out of employment have turned to self-employment, often helped by government schemes. However, this is an economic status increasingly represented in the bottom income decile. Whereas in 1961–63, just 8 per cent of the lowest income decile were self-employed, by 1991–93 this proportion had risen to 15 per cent.[70] Credit for self-employment is one kind of microfinancial service. Self-employment is discussed at greater length in Chapter 3; Chapters 4 and 5 analyse the impact and potential impact of credit for self-employment on poverty and social exclusion.

Underlying causes of changes in the labour market

As will be seen below, poverty and social exclusion in Britain are not caused by labour-market exclusion and restructuring alone. However, in as much as they *are* caused by these processes, it is important in a book such as this, which purports to reflect on the possibilities for microfinance to counter poverty and social exclusion, to review some of the underlying structural causes of changes in the labour market.

The types of worker sought by employers and the terms of employment offered are rooted in calculations about costs and about product markets.[71] Capital flows, including productive investment, have increased as barriers to inward investment have been lowered and a trend towards deregulation has become more marked. Investment and divestment may be expected to occur more frequently, as producers and providers of services seek to reduce their costs. Because of the trend towards 'slicing up the value chain ... employment [has become] more vulnerable to wage changes'... and the 'threat of relocation [of production] more credible'.[72]

Economic choices are emphasised in accounts of 'globalisation' which interpret the decisions of international corporations as being about moving production to lowest-cost sites of production or finance, to reap the highest available returns on capital. Such analyses emphasise the trend away from national-level autonomy in economic management and an increase in the relative power of globally mobile capital.[73] Yet national policy choices are influenced by political economics as much as by market economics.

In the view of one influential commentator, Will Hutton, British government policy is strongly influenced by nationally privileged groups, including owners of large-scale capital. Hutton suggests that the argument continually invoked by Britain's governments since 1979 — that the nation needed to play its part in 'freeing' international trade and financial flows, and that this included legislation to curb union power and 'flexibilise' employment — was not about technical economics, as it was presented. Rather these arguments were part of the 'enlist[ment]' of 'the authoritarian capabilities of the state to serve ...[the principle of loyalty to the market], which neatly chimes with longstanding British values and institutional structures'.[74]

There is evidence from other European countries that employment and relative wage equality can increase together. National policy matters, because divergent policies produce very different outcomes. While unemployment in the UK remained high in the 1980s and 1990s, wage inequality, as already noted, also grew — because of anti-union government action and the lack of a minimum wage. Yet, at the same time in the Netherlands both employment and wage equality grew.[75] There are three competing explanations for the fall in demand for unskilled workers in rich countries in general. One holds that changes in the technology of production have required a higher average level of skill per worker. Another suggests that increasingly 'free' trade has led to the relocation of relatively unskilled jobs to the lowest-wage economies. Both of these explanations are true to a degree; but because there have been such major differences between countries such as the Netherlands and Britain or the United States and Canada, in terms of distribution of employment and income, the third explanation — the different policy conditions in those countries — is especially convincing. Policy differences were found to be the greatest in relation to labour-market 'institutions', in particular unions and the minimum wage. In other words, the deliberate weakening of organised labour in Britain and the previous lack of a minimum wage have been major causes of the split in the labour market between relatively highly paid skilled workers and very low-paid unskilled workers.

Other causes of poverty and social exclusion

Unemployment is clearly not the sole cause of poverty or social exclusion in Britain. Indeed, in 1950s Britain poverty co-existed with full employment.[76] And as has been noted, one of the most dramatic trends in recent years has been inequality of reward, job security, and other conditions of work *among* those in employment.

Many low-paid workers and most 'workless'[77] households rely to a greater or lesser extent on state benefits.[78] These will be discussed further in Chapter 3. However, it is important to note here that the level of benefits — the cash-in-hand received — directly affects poverty, and the capacity to participate in citizenship. It has been shown that a major part of income inequality is due to differences in incomes between benefit recipients and people with incomes from other sources. Earlier cuts in benefits in 1988 had the effect of increasing the income poverty of many claimants.[79] Recent reductions in entitlement to housing benefit have also meant that recipients have had to draw more and more on income intended for day-to-day needs to cover their housing costs. Between 1983 and 1995, the value of the state pension declined from 47 per cent of average income to 36 per cent, and unemployment benefit fell from 36 to 28 per cent.[80]

While the current Labour government is right to be restructuring the benefits system to make work pay for those who want to work and can find jobs, it should not neglect the level of benefits for those who remain 'workless'. For some 'workless' individuals and households, there is no choice: in many areas there are no jobs. For others, particularly disabled people and the carers (mostly women) of young children, elderly, or sick people, it is the level of benefits that is likely to make the most difference to their standard of living, rather than schemes to entice them into employment.[81] The government has recognised this by raising benefits available to some of these groups. The increase in accessibility of child care and help to pay for it is welcome for parents who otherwise would be unable to work. However, it should also be recognised that some parents would like to have the choice of caring for their children themselves, that some have seemingly unavoidable full-time caring workloads, and that in both these cases the unpaid work of parents is an important contribution to social stability. Moreover, increasing the gap in income between those living on benefits and those with access to higher employment incomes has other effects, which can increase social exclusion. These may include the tendency of people with more money to go shopping by car, and the decline of local shopping facilities for those with less money and less transport.[82] Of course, the distribution of wealth is directly influenced by the types and levels of taxation, as well as by the benefit system. Taxation of wealth as well as income is another way in which governments can influence trends in poverty and inequality.

A further important cause of poverty is lack of access to education, health care, and other services.[83] Unequal access to education and health services excludes poor people from a 'reasonable share in the wealth of their own society' as well as from full political citizenship.[84] Changes in the value of public services — after allowing for the rising relative cost of services, the effects of demographic change, and potential public-sector productivity growth — mirror the trend in cash incomes for the poorest between 1979 and 1993.[85] Lack of services is part of the multi-dimensional experience of poverty and social exclusion. It is also a major cause of it. Inadequate or inaccessible services can perpetuate or increase ill-health and illiteracy, which are barriers to social, economic, and political citizenship as well as to increased income and accumulation of wealth. Health and education are of course not the only services on which people rely. Financial services are also crucial, because they can, among other things, strengthen people's capacity to manage their finances to avoid periods of extreme financial stress. The section that follows examines where finance fits into the experience of poverty and social exclusion, and the contribution that growing exclusion from financial services has made to that experience.

WHERE FINANCE FITS

The main aim of this book is to analyse the potential of microfinancial services for tackling poverty and processes of social exclusion. It is now necessary, therefore, to look at where finance fits into experiences of poverty and into the analysis of its causes. The section is divided into three parts. The first focuses on the ways in which poor people manage money, and shows how lack of money causes social exclusion. The second part describes the exclusion of poor people and people living in areas of multiple deprivation from access to financial services. Finally, the third part considers some of the structural causes of financial exclusion.

Money management, poverty, and social exclusion

Income poverty is, by definition, associated with financial hardship. Detailed studies of how people on low incomes manage their finances in Britain also shed light on the interaction between financial constraints and processes of social exclusion.[86] These studies suggest some general patterns, in addition to indicating much diversity.

Demands on money come at different times, some of them predictable. For example, fuel bills and clothing bills increase in the winter, school holidays are more expensive for parents than term times, and festivals such as Christmas are often the greatest single strain on the budget during the year.[87] Weddings and the births of children are also times of high expenditure, as are funerals.

Faced with intermittent demands for single expensive items and the continual need to keep up payments on utilities (despite seasonal variations in some bills), low-income households with savings may be able to draw down on these in times of financial stress. But for most low-income households, this is not an option, and the money-management choice — which does not come without a price in terms of social relations, as will be seen — is one between 'juggling' bills, often using multiple sources of credit to keep various creditors at bay, and 'going without': cutting spending down to levels which the budget can manage.[88] As is shown in the Policy Studies Institute study, *Hard Times?*, people change their approaches to money management, depending on whether or not they have a job. When a household moves to full dependence on social security, money management can become 'a full-time occupation'.[89]

Money management is required from day to day and week to week, and in between receipt of payments it may still mean going without. But efforts to 'smooth consumption' and avoid scarcity in times of hardship are one thing; access to earnings is more or less cut off at retirement age, and thus the inability to smooth consumption *across the life cycle* through pension provision (because of low pay, unemployment, or having spent many years in unpaid caring work) is another important financial dimension of poverty.

Interestingly the studies are not consistent in distinguishing between men and women as managers and controllers of money. While, according to one study, 'men generally control and allocate the resources and women undertake the day-to-day management',[90] another suggests that, for low-income families with children, women are as likely as men to *control* household budgets.[91] The studies agree that *management* tends to be women's responsibility.[92]

While the ways in which people manage money depend in part on their attitude to credit and debt,[93] they also vary according to a person's resources in terms of financial literacy. Financial literacy includes a knowledge of sources of credit and rights in relation to specific creditors, budgeting skills, and an understanding of basic financial terminology, such as annual percentage rates for comparison of borrowing costs.[94] It is also about knowledge of entitlements to state support. Indeed, adequate knowledge of benefits was considered of more importance than access to savings in a study of mortgage debt among low-income borrowers in the late 1980s.[95]

For those reliant on state benefits, the timing of payments is also a critical determinant of deprivation. Some families living on benefit actually prefer to have payments on utility bills, Social Fund loans,[96] and housing deducted at source. And the periodicity of earnings as well as benefits has direct effects on diets in this context too. For example, low-paid, intermittently employed agricultural wage workers varied their own and children's diets in periods between receipt of payments. At times 'the family live[d] on baked beans on toast for the second half of the month ... mothers [came] to ask [social workers] for spare nappies because they could not afford to buy any more'.[97]

It is especially important to note the exclusionary processes associated with debt. 'Debt' is used here to refer to default or arrears rather than all credit.[98] Indeed, debt can arise through unpaid bills and need not have involved credit in the first place. Debt has major personal and social implications, leading to tense and deteriorating intra-household relations, and reducing or curtailing wider social relationships. 'In some respects, the experience of debt magnifies and reinforces the experience of poverty — the watchfulness and anxiety over money, the calculation and moving around of limited funds.' There is a statistically significant association between level of indebtedness and female stress. It can also mean a greater threat of exclusion, as legal processes can be invoked and might even lead to homelessness.[99]

Earlier it was suggested that there is significant churning, with people moving in and out of income poverty. The loss of a job or the end of a relationship with a partner, for example, may push people into debt when they cannot (often temporarily) manage their finances. The commercial banks have been criticised by the National Consumer Council for failing to deal appropriately with those of their customers who fall on hard times. The Council concludes that 'local branches have neither the authority, nor the expertise, to deal sympathetically and positively with people in financial difficulty. ... In fact the banks' approach ... often seems to be counter-productive, resulting in bigger charges from a variety of different sources falling on the customer, and an ever-increasing spiral of debt.' 'The vast majority of advice agencies[100] said ... banks give priority to meeting any debts due to themselves. A result of this is that customers' housing can be put in jeopardy by delays in mortgage or rent payments, or that they can incur other penalties as a result of late payment of tax due. It is difficult to see how banks can consider this practice to be consistent with the best interest of their customers when it means housing and utility bills are not paid, and the customer has no income left for day-to-day living expenses.'[101]

Financial exclusion

There has been a rapid withdrawal of private commercial bank branches from areas of multiple deprivation.[102] Estimates of the proportion of adults without a current account vary from 14 to 23 per cent of the population. Between 6 and 9 per cent of adults have neither a current nor a savings account. Most are among the poor and socially excluded: the unemployed, the sick, disabled people, pensioners, and lone parents, usually living in rented accommodation, on very low incomes and reliant on benefits, are all over-represented among people without an account. Many of these people had not applied for an account because of personal and financial circumstances which would have made it difficult to get an account. Only a minority had actually been refused one. Many of the 'self-excluded' could in fact be said to have been excluded by the kinds of product offered by banks, which did not match their needs.[103]

Lack of suitable services is also a major reason why one-fifth of households do not have insurance cover on the contents of their homes. Insurance companies' standard products involve very high premiums in areas identified as having a high risk of burglary.[104] Such areas coincide with areas of multiple deprivation.[105] Often the poorest people face the highest charges for this financial service. Poor people wishing to start up micro-enterprises with relatively small amounts of credit also face higher interest rates and higher arrangement fees and other charges than existing businesses and larger-scale start-up enterprises.[106] In both these cases, exclusion is brought about by commercial providers of financial services, who have had to cover the costs of exposure to higher risks and, in the case of loans, the higher relative costs of providing small loans. As has been shown in the case of home-contents insurance, however, products such as 'insure with rent' have been found viable in partnerships between some insurance companies and local authorities (and housing associations), because of limited competition and high levels of customer loyalty.[107]

The extent to which people in income poverty have savings or other assets or wealth influences the degree to which they can choose between different types of credit. Savings and credit form important parts of the experiences of income poverty and social exclusion in Britain. However, the '[a]bility to save was clearly linked to having a job'.[108] The *Hard Times?* study involved 74 low-income families in England. Most people surveyed in it who had previously been regular savers were now running down their savings. And for those who were still saving, it was irregular — a matter of 'an extra jar or piggy bank into which any spare cash was put at the end of the week'.[109]

Before going on to discuss the types of credit used by poor families, it is important to mention that the preferred form of credit for families involved in the *Hard Times?* study was borrowing from friends, neighbours, and relatives. One-third of the households in the study took this form of credit. Credit is thus directly tied up with kinship and other social relations — but not just any relations. 'The most common single source of informal help was from mothers to daughters.'[110]

Financial help from kin and via other social relations is double-edged. On the one hand, low-income households benefit from a flexible source of credit, which normally comes without money interest and is often reciprocal, rather than one-way. On the other hand, help may be given only grudgingly, and this, together with failure to repay, can involve conflict with family or friends and thus diminished relational capital as well as reduced self-esteem. Furthermore, there is a hierarchy of kinds of help, in terms of its acceptability to those receiving it, beginning with exchange of goods, followed by cash loans, with cash gifts coming last. 'The rationale behind this hierarchy [is] the need both to save face and to maintain independence'.[111] Even informing relatives of the problem is avoided by many low-income households. Debt, more than income poverty *per se*, is seen by many as a major source of shame.

Comparing households with weekly incomes of over £400 with those with weekly incomes under £100, Berthoud and Kempson found that a negligible proportion of richer households had debts, as against one-third of poor households.[112] The same study found that younger families and those with children, as well as those on low incomes, were more likely than others to be indebted. Such households use credit (and become indebted) in different ways. A dual credit market was identified by the *Hard Times?* study, which distinguished between 'upmarket' and 'downmarket' sources of credit. The first was dominated by credit cards and overdrafts, the latter by doorstep lenders (including those lending shopping vouchers as well as cash) and pawnbrokers. The 74 households interviewed fell into two groups, largely on the basis of whether or not the household was dependent entirely on benefits or had some employment income. The only source of credit that was used by both groups was the most popular of all sources of commercial credit: mail-order catalogues.

There are further differences according to ethnic group. For example a relatively low proportion of African-Caribbean people take loans from High Street banks.[113] This is due as much to structural discrimination which 'means that [African-Caribbean people] are much more likely to have social and economic circumstances that would fail credit screening by high-street creditors' as to racism and the small number of African-Caribbean staff employed in these institutions.[114]

Financial exclusion in terms of exclusion from particular sources of credit and other financial services (including insurance, bill-payment services, and accessible deposit accounts) is a major theme of this book. As the studies cited in this section make clear, financial exclusion is not as straightforward as many conventional assumptions suggest. Many of the low-income people who do not use a bank account either keep one dormant or *choose* to close down an account which they had used while in employment, and they now use cash instead. 'Loan sharks' are the exception rather than the norm, and many low-income families without employment make use of registered doorstep lenders, who may lend in kind or cash, as part of a portfolio of credit sources.[115] Indeed, the whole idea of 'loan sharks' is ambiguous: on the one hand, the term suggests that all private money-lending for profit is highly exploitative; on the other, 'poor borrowers are reluctant to see any avenue of credit closed to them, however costly'.[116] Interventions in microfinance, discussed in detail in later chapters, need to take account of the actual rather than imagined nature of financial exclusion in Britain.

Trends in the structure of the financial-services industry

The causes of financial exclusion lie in the changing structure of the financial services industry. This is particularly evidenced by the withdrawal of bank branches from areas of multiple deprivation, and many people's reduced access to personal financial services. The market is highly competitive and changes rapidly, driven by deregulation, new technology, and financial globalisation, which have led to extensive rationalisation, mergers, new entrants, and branch closures.

New competitors, ranging from telephone banks and insurance providers to supermarkets, utilities, and other service companies like British Airways, often use the extensive growth of customer databases to target the lucrative parts of financial services markets.[117] To retain their profits, the large retail banks have also sought to change the profile of their customers, focusing on more profitable customers to whom they can cross-sell other financial products, and reducing, or charging more heavily for, their exposure to less profitable customers.[118] This has meant, for example, a shift from overdrafts and other 'debt-related products to the selling of investment services'.[119] The traditional cross-subsidisation of less profitable customers is no longer considered feasible within these competitive markets. In 1998, bank share-prices fell sharply, following the global financial crisis. This is likely to have prompted further action to protect profits.

Technological advances are also making branches increasingly redundant as providers of traditional money-transmission services for household and business customers. In response to increasing competition, banks have reduced costs through branch closures, while exploiting new technology to raise their productivity. Since 1987 the number of bank branches of the four main High Street banks has declined by one-third.[120] This has contributed to the decline of High Streets, creating cash-handling problems for retail businesses and making customers with access to adequate transport go elsewhere for their banking, taking their retail spending with them. Branch closures are also distancing banks from potential borrowers of small amounts. In guiding decisions about loans, there is a limit to which centralised data can compensate for the decline of relationship banking[121] and the loss of detailed local knowledge of economic opportunities.

It is therefore not surprising that at least three million people borrow money from licensed money-lenders.[122] As the Chief Executive of one of the largest money-lending companies puts it: 'The banks are all leaving this market. Every time they close a branch, every time they cut staff, there are more people dropping into my market.'[123]

Especially in disadvantaged areas, access to affordable financial services is becoming increasingly difficult. Disadvantaged neighbourhoods are most likely to face credit rationing: they are suffering more from bank-branch closures; and the size of loans and other financial services requested is generally well below the average, while perceived risks may be above the average. In the insurance industry, risk is now assessed by the full postcode, right down to individual streets. In 1995 Newburgh Road in Aberdeen was the street with the lowest risk, while Cuthbert Road in Birmingham and Villiers Close and Myddleton Road in London were those with the highest risks.[124]

This exclusion in turn accelerates the growth of underlying patterns of multidimensional disadvantage, including poor housing, low income, inadequate services, and limited amenities. In such situations, even the *perception* of high risk can easily become a self-fulfilling prophecy, with at first the retreat and then the complete withdrawal of financial services. As credit-scoring screens against indices of social and economic disadvantage (such as rented accommodation, lack of credit-card ownership, lone parenthood), its increasing use by banks is further excluding individuals in disadvantaged neighbourhoods.

Patterns of disinvestment are leading to no-go investment localities. This poses a massive threat to those with long-term investments in such potentially blighted markets, including local homeowners, business owners, landlords, housing associations, and local investors generally. Already, in most major cities, there are areas where properties are being abandoned on a large scale.

At the time of writing, the UK government is preparing legislation for a new Financial Services Authority (FSA). As has been shown by the US Community Reinvestment Act, government regulation can be effective in creating incentives for commercial banks to adopt social roles.[125] Researchers Andrew Leyshon and Nigel Thrift argue that a two-pronged approach to countering financial exclusion is required: resisting the banks' 'flight to quality' on the one hand, and creating an 'alternative financial infrastructure' on the other.[126] The latter might include intermediate financial infrastructure, such as home insurance provided through social landlords, and greater use of the Post Office.[127] Equally important are changes in the demand from customers for financial services. For the better-off, the range of financial products, and competition among their providers, has led to far greater choice, which they can assess through an expanding range of information sources, in the media and from financial advisers.

> ... [T]he more affluent groups are experiencing a process of 'superinclusion'. Their money power results in them being offered higher levels of information and more service provision, which in turn provides them with the opportunities to make more money. However, the corollary of this process of inclusion is that poorer people are increasingly subject to financial exclusion ... [They] are doubly handicapped, as they live in both a financial and an information shadow. Such individuals are likely to pay an increasingly heavy price for their exclusion, particularly given the collapse of universal welfare provision and the allied growth of private welfare-related financial products.

An important part of any policy response must be much greater emphasis on financial literacy, at school and elsewhere, as an important element of citizenship, although greater financial literacy would also help financial-service providers to argue against their responsibility for mis-selling financial products, and the government to legitimise the reduction in welfare provisioning.[128]

Leyshon and Thrift point out, with regard to adapting lessons from US legislation,[129] that the British context is distinct, and any alternative infrastructure needs to reflect this. For this reason, Chapter 3 sets out the range of recent actions to tackle poverty and social exclusion in Britain. Chapters 4 and 5 then take up the question of whether and how microfinance might be able to play a part.

SUMMARY AND CONCLUSIONS

This chapter has attempted to ground the analysis of the remainder of the book by reviewing the dimensions and causes of poverty and social exclusion in Britain, and then examining where finance fits into the picture. Poverty and social exclusion are both multi-dimensional and are defined here in relative terms. They overlap and contribute to each other, but they are also distinct. Both are dynamic: some people are stuck with low incomes, but many move into and out of income poverty. Inequality of income increased dramatically from 1979 to the mid-1990s. Inequality of wealth leaves those with the least assets with little to pass down to succeeding generations. Income and wealth give access to networks which can enable people to combat social exclusion and poverty. Combating social exclusion is about increasing control over one's life through greater social, economic, and political citizenship.

Women and men, the young, and the elderly experience poverty and social exclusion differently. So do different races, nationalities, and religions. These differences in turn vary across space: between rural and urban areas, for example, and between particular towns and cities. However, the aim of understanding poverty and social exclusion is not to define a static notion of national citizenship into which everyone should fit. This would be to take an assimilationist perspective, akin to the French notion of social exclusion: one which risks, through misrepresentation and stigmatising difference and 'deviance', increasing the very exclusion it attempts to analyse. Political citizenship does not mean 'inclusion', but rather the capacity and power to change the rules.

Unemployment causes much income poverty and is also the proximate cause of the exclusion of many from social citizenship. This is self-perpetuating, because chances of returning to employment are greatly enhanced by networks and contacts.

As the labour market has become increasingly polarised between skilled and unskilled sectors, so the experience of poverty *in work* has become more prevalent. The inequality associated with this dual labour market is a major contributor to social exclusion. The causes of structural change in the labour market lie at the national as well as global level and are political as well as economic. Poverty and social exclusion are also caused by government action and inaction in spheres other than the labour market. These include the levels of benefits, taxation, and the quality, accessibility, and pricing of health care and education.

This chapter has shown how part of the experience of poverty in Britain is lack of control over one's finances — running into continual debt — or (for others who go to any length to avoid debt) going without food and other basic goods. Moreover, increasing numbers of people are excluded from financial services by the changing structure of that industry. Extending access to savings, money advice, bill-payment facilities, and financial literacy may thus be critically important. Doing this in ways relevant to intended users involves understanding the existing ways in which people make ends meet, including their use of relational capital (such as networks of neighbours and kin).

Part of the experience of social exclusion is not being able to participate in economic citizenship. Access to micro-enterprise loans and training may enable some people to regain their economic citizenship through self-employment, which may serve as a route back to more secure employment. Over-zealous promotion of self-employment credit could, however, be counterproductive, because it could cause increased indebtedness. Different kinds of microfinance intervention will be discussed in detail in Chapters 4 and 5. Chapter 3, which follows, examines a wide range of policies and initiatives to combat poverty and social exclusion at the national and local levels, including efforts by poor people themselves, in order to place microfinance initiatives in their proper context.

3 Responses to poverty and exclusion: the social policy context for microfinance interventions

BEN ROGALY

INTRODUCTION

Background

THE purpose of this book is to explore the potential for microfinance to combat poverty and social exclusion in Britain. Microfinance has been defined as the local provision of financial services to people with limited access to conventional services. Chapters 4 and 5 discuss in detail the various ways in which microfinancial services can make a difference, and examine the evidence for their international impact. The present chapter analyses the wider policy and practice environments in which poverty and social exclusion are being tackled in Britain.

The aims of providing a critical analysis of the specific policy context in which microfinance is practised are two-fold.

- Firstly, it is intended that reflections on other work aimed at reducing poverty and social exclusion in Britain reveal the extent to which these goals are already being achieved by other means. For example, Britain's state-provided social-security benefits constitute an effective minimum income that is not available in countries such as Bangladesh and Indonesia, where microfinance is more widespread. This book seeks ways in which microfinance might complement rather than replace existing policies and practices.

- Secondly, putting microfinance in its place enables an attempt to give a balanced view — neither understating nor overstating its potential — when, later in the book, microfinancial services are specifically considered.

Approach

This chapter will consider policies and practices that have the actual and/or stated intention of reducing poverty or combating social exclusion. Policies and practices will be assessed according to their potential for reducing poverty and inequality (in terms of income or of wealth) and combating social exclusion (in terms of social, economic, or political non-citizenship). It is important for several reasons to be clear from the outset that these should not be seen as technical solutions. First, actions motivated by the desire to reduce poverty or combat social exclusion have not necessarily succeeded in doing so. In some cases and for certain groups of people, they may have made matters worse. Secondly, actions that are not explicitly designed to address poverty and social exclusion may still have an effect on them. Thirdly, 'policy is as policy does': the politics of policy announcement, design, and implementation require us to probe behind the rhetoric. Are policies which announce themselves as being concerned with poverty reduction and combating social exclusion actually designed for that purpose? Clearly politics, formal and informal, will determine, in part at least, what is intended and what is achieved. For this reason, the struggles over the language of policy are not redundant. Policies and practices reflect ideologies, and in places the analysis in this book seeks to make unstated agendas more visible. The perspective developed in Chapter 2 is that poverty has largely structural causes, located in the labour market, in the finance market, and to some extent in government policies that are ostensibly designed to protect people from poverty (for example, through low levels of benefits). On the other hand, to label poor people as victims is also to stigmatise them and to deny that they have the potential to move out of poverty and cope better with adverse structures. In other words, in this book I do not subscribe to the view that poverty is due to the inherent characteristics of individuals, nor to the implication in some policy rhetoric that there are 'deserving' and 'undeserving' poor people.

The chapter is structured as follows. In the next section national policies and practices will be assessed, including social security and its connection to the current British government's 'active labour market' policies. Types of local response to poverty and to social exclusion are described in the third section. Just as national-level action increasingly involves a mix of sectors in so-called 'partnerships', the same is true of much local action. It is at the local level that fledgling microfinance institutions already exist in Britain, and the focus of new ideas for microfinance as an intervention capable of tackling poverty and social exclusion has been at this level, though not exclusively so (see Chapter 5).

The fourth part of the chapter examines the experience of self-help, whether mutual or otherwise, by poor and/or excluded people themselves. Again, this level of action includes people's efforts to establish credit unions (discussed in detail in Chapter 5) in a small neighbourhood, as well as the much more common practice of support by kin and by friends. Tentative conclusions are drawn in the final section.

NATIONAL POLICIES AND PRACTICES

Social security

Through social security the state has, since the 1940s, aimed (not always successfully) to insure people against material deprivation during periods of unemployment and old age, and to provide means-tested social assistance to those who could not make sufficient contributions. In other countries with less extensive social-security arrangements, microfinance has sometimes been seen as a potential means for establishing insurance against similar life-cycle events and for protection against vulnerability to regular down-swings as well as unexpected shocks. Chapter 4 offers illustrations of such initiatives involving savings and consumption and emergency loans. In Chapter 5 it is argued that similar microfinancial services could reduce vulnerability in Britain — not as an alternative to social security, but as a complement to it.

Social policy in a changing Britain

Much has changed in Britain since Beveridge wrote the report on which the original design of the social-security system was based. Especially important — in terms of the relevance of the model — have been changes in labour-market structure and in family structures. The Beveridge model was based on the then prevailing 'norm' of male full-time earner and female home-maker and carer, living together with the children of their marriage. By the 1990s, the central assumptions of Beveridge had been rendered seriously out of date by increases in the proportion of women earners, the number of lone-parent families, the incidence of male unemployment, and the continuing growth in the proportion of elderly people in the population, among other changes.

The effects of these changes, combined with successive governments' policies towards the social-security system, were, firstly, that the cost of social security, in absolute terms as well as relative to other government spending, had continued to grow;[1] and, secondly, that there was a rise in the proportion of means-tested benefits in the total social-security budget, including support to many people receiving insurance benefits but who nevertheless remained below what was considered the safety-net level.[2]

Social-security design: impacts on poverty and social exclusion

The way in which the social-security system is designed and changes in that design have direct impacts on poverty and social exclusion. For those in employment, the system provides limited insurance against being made jobless. For many elderly people, the state pension, despite substantial falls in relative value since it was delinked from trends in earnings by the

Conservative government of the early 1980s, remains the key source of subsistence. For most people of working age in households with no earner, means-tested income support/Jobseeker's Allowance, housing benefit, and council-tax benefit provide an essential subsistence income and means of access to shelter.[3] It thus *alleviates* material poverty.

State pensions are not the only benefits that were allowed to fall relative to earnings during the 1990s. Being on benefits and living in relative poverty thus go hand-in-hand as inequality widens. However, as was seen in Chapter 2, although some people are 'stuck' on low incomes and with little or no wealth, many others move into and out of poverty as household members enter or leave the labour market, and as families experience separation or divorce of partners, births, sickness, and death through the life-cycle.[4] Reliance on social-security benefits varies over time for many households. With the growing insecurity of employment for all, a high-quality universal social insurance system is likely to be more appropriate than the increased targeting involved in means-testing.

The social-security system may hold back mass deprivation but, depending on the form it takes, it may also cause social division and an experience of social and economic non-citizenship. For example, the stigma involved in receiving certain types of benefits can be a *cause* of social non-citizenship. Receiving benefits that are means-tested is often constructed by society as worthy of stigma. The means test so widely used in the 1930s left 'an indelible mark on popular culture. The ... test ... was a family one which involved a household assessment ... Its inquisitorial tone produced resentment and frustration among applicants and heightened family tension....'[5]

Low levels of benefit for people looking for jobs, who are living on only the basic means-tested allowance, can prevent the kind of social interaction that is necessary to remain informed of available jobs and the contacts necessary to access them.[6] As the relative value of such benefits declines, economic non-citizenship increases: exclusion from the labour market grows because long-term unemployment is associated with decreasing employment prospects. At the same time, such people lack access to the (rising) minimum consumption standards of wider society.

The design of the social-security system works in particular against women's citizenship. Even in the period immediately following the release of the Beveridge report in 1942, it was argued by some that the plan was flawed because of its 'failure to treat women as full and independent fellow citizens with men'.[7] Women's citizenship in terms of the social-security system was designed to be contingent on that of their husbands. 'As long as retirement income [was] earnings related, something [was] required in the policy package to help restore the earning power and pension-earning power ... of those whose pension rights have taken second place to caring responsibility'.[8] Current government proposals for pensions reform herald progressive changes, which include counting carers' unpaid work as a contribution towards a state pension.[9] However, the dilemma remains that in recognising the contribution made by unpaid care, women might be entrenched 'into a caring role which excludes them from power and influence'.[10] According to Lister, full citizenship for women depends on their political participation in representing their own needs and working to improve their situation.

Social security and microfinance interventions

The state social-security system in Britain is a central part of the policy context in which microfinance interventions have to operate. It works to prevent widespread material poverty and economic non-citizenship. However, partly because it has not fully adapted to changing labour-market and family structures, and partly because of the rise of means-testing, it may have contributed to social exclusion. Microfinance, as suggested later in the book, is not considered by us to be an alternative to state-provided social security. Without the latter, poverty and social exclusion in Britain would be many times worse than at present. However, microfinance interventions need to build on the achievements of the social-security system in seeking further to enable people to reduce vulnerability, for example via more widespread access to personal financial services. When training and other support is provided for people on benefits seeking to start their own businesses, microfinance may be a valuable source of credit. Discussions are underway with the government on possible benefit waivers which would mean that initial involvement in such a business would not be conditional on an immediate cessation of benefit payments.[11] Microfinancial services may also be able to help people to cope with poverty and social exclusion caused by the social-security system through the ways in which it operates and the declining level of benefits in relation to earnings. However, the ways in which social security is delivered are not based entirely on technical formulas, and debates about them reflect differing political philosophies, which (see below) have implications for microfinance interventions as well.

Differences of political philosophy: liberalism, social democracy, and communitarianism

Arguments over the role of social security took place among members of the Conservative governments between 1990 and 1997. While some emphasised the need either for a hugely increased role for private provision of welfare or for greater targeting (i.e. means-testing) of benefits for the poorest,[12] others were strongly in favour of the continuation of insurance-based contributions, particularly basic state pensions.[13] Parallel disagreements have taken place within the current Labour government. There is thus no simple polarisation between the main parties on the issue, but rather a debate within both. On the one hand, neo-liberals see an individual's responsibility for his or her own life as paramount, with echoes of the Victorian notion of the 'deserving' and 'undeserving' poor; on the other hand, social democrats, who are motivated by the need to address structures of inequality, argue for more generous benefits and a universal social insurance system.

The approach developed in Chapter 2 would suggest an affinity with the second of these perspectives. At the same time, it is important to recognise that the debate cannot and should not be reduced to 'market' versus 'state' provision. There are other visions of social security, not least that of communitarians, who, like liberals, place emphasis on responsibilities as well as rights, but advocate that responsibility be exercised at the level of the 'family' and the 'community', and that welfare policy should be built around strengthening such institutions. While there is much to be learned from this approach — as we have seen, supportive social networks, where they exist, increase people's ability to take control over their lives — it too has problems. In particular, as will be seen later in this chapter, family and 'community' have darker sides: some of the social relations involved are laden with power, and they are thus not necessarily conducive to a sense of individual citizenship.

Just as differing ideologies lie behind particular positions taken on the social-security debates regarding the interrelation between certain types of benefits (or tax credits) and poverty and, separately, social exclusion, the same has been true of microfinance.[14] Much of the international promotion of microfinance as a poverty-reduction tool has emphasised neo-liberal ideas of the role of individuals and markets — sometimes portraying poor people as little more than 'budding entrepreneurs', with only lack of access to business credit standing between them and the poverty line.[15] At the same time, others have argued from a social democratic perspective for more equality of access to basic financial services. They argue further that, with apparently declining willingness to spend public money to tackle poverty and social exclusion, if microfinance can steer more resources in that direction, then it is to be welcomed. Because of the local manifestation of much microfinance, often involving users in working in close connection with staff and with each other, microfinance has also been portrayed as a way of building stronger supportive networks, along communitarian lines. The point is that the way in which microfinance is discussed has an impact on policy decisions and therefore on poverty and social exclusion. Indeed, as noted already, public discourses themselves can potentially contribute to or reduce social exclusion.

Active labour markets

In British social-policy discourse under the current Labour administration, the labour market is being portrayed as the main route out of poverty, as well as the means of 'social inclusion'. There is a strong link here to the social-security system, as attention is focused on ways in which reforms to that system can provide incentives for people not currently in jobs to (re)enter paid work. Closely connected in turn are reforms to workplace rights, floated in the May 1998 White Paper *Fairness at Work*.[16] This sub-section first outlines some of the key aspects of current and proposed 'active labour market' policy before examining their implications, including the implications of the language in which they are framed, for poverty and social exclusion and for microfinance.

Encouraging people (back) into employment

The government has begun to provide more flexible support to paid work through the Working Families Tax Credit, announced in the budget of March 1998, and through plans for a massive expansion in the provision of child care for under-fives and an increase in the level of earnings subject to a child-care waiver. This is encouraging, in as much as it recognises the diversity of household structures in Britain today. Moreover, a minimum wage has now been implemented, albeit at a figure considered by many to be too low (£3.60 per hour, and less for the youngest employees).

Other high-profile government proposals concerned directly with the labour market suggest a recognition of the importance of part-time working and of the need for workers to be flexible in adapting their skills and not expecting jobs to be life-long.[17] The New Deals are the centrepiece of the government's active labour-market policies. They involve a subsidy to employers for taking on a new employee, and a grant towards providing training on a one-day-per-week basis. People aged 18 to 24 who receive Jobseeker's Allowance for longer than six months and those over 25 who have been unemployed for over two years are the New Deal's targets, as well as lone parents and disabled people. The New Deal for each specified group has different provisions and rules. As it is expected that the schemes will lead to large numbers of parents, especially women, rejoining the labour market, the New Deals are also being used to train a new cadre of child-care workers.

The language of government policy on unemployment now involves talk of partnerships between private, voluntary, and statutory sectors, and it attempts to conjure up win–win situations:

> 'New Deal is … a genuine deal because everyone gives something
> *   *Employers offer people a chance to show what they can do*
> *   *People provide abilities and potential*
> *   *The Government is committing up to £3.5 billion over four years*
>
> 'And everyone gets something in return
> *   *Employers get new talent for their business*
> *   *People get new skills, new opportunities and a new start*
> *   *We all benefit from a more successful economy and a vibrant community'*
>
> (New Deal Website, August 1998,
> http://www.newdeal.gov.uk/homesub1.asp)

Implications for poverty and social exclusion

The present Labour government may be expecting to cut the benefits bill by reducing the number of people out of work and at the same time tackling social exclusion, which they see as primarily located in the labour market. However, although there is some special help for some people seeking to start up their own businesses (18–24 years olds who have been on Jobseeker's Allowance for six months or more), there is still no official recognition of the important role which informal work experience in the 'shadow economy' can play in bridging the gap between benefits and employment.[18] The benefits system still punishes those considered to be cheating it by earning in the shadow economy, so there is an incentive not to declare earnings. One local attempt to counter this in Speke-Garston in Liverpool involved a 'skillseekers' amnesty', encouraging unemployed residents to register any skills, no matter where they had learned them.[19]

The announcement in the *Fairness at Work* White Paper of the belated implementation of European Union legislation with respect to the labour market should be welcomed. Key reforms enacted by the preceding Conservative governments have not been reversed — particularly in respect of the ways in which trade unions function and the legality of certain types of industrial action; but the right of a union to be recognised for the purposes of collective bargaining if a majority of the workforce votes for it, and the introduction of a minimum wage, are likely to improve the quality of employment for many of those who, despite being in employment, still experience economic non-citizenship. Contrary to the opinions of those who regard strong unions and minimum-wage policies as likely to increase unemployment, recent reviews of international evidence suggest that this is not the case.[20]

However, important questions of detail remain. The lower minimum wage for young people may lead to divisions in the workforce, with younger people particularly vulnerable to structural unemployment.[21] Further, it could be argued that the Working Families Tax Credit is likely to be retained by male partners as 'it will normally be paid through [their] pay packet[s]'.[22]

More disturbingly, the emphasis, at least until the time of writing, on labour-market oriented social policy leaves unanswered questions regarding the large numbers of people who *cannot* work.[23] Recipients of out-of-work benefits risk being further stigmatised by the creation of two types of citizen: those in employment and those out of it. Many people, particularly disabled people and women with caring responsibilities and other unpaid work, remain outside the labour market. Questions about their 'citizenship' remain, both in economic terms related to social insurance and rights to a state pension, and in terms of being stigmatised by a new exclusionary language, which implies that having a job is the ticket to being a full member of society. For example, the New Deal does not explicitly value parents who would *prefer* to care for their children themselves in the early years.[24]

Implications for microfinance interventions

As mentioned above, one microfinance programme — the Full Circle Fund run by the Women's Employment, Enterprise and Training Unit (WEETU) in Norwich — has been active in lobbying the government for a 'welfare waiver'. Full Circle specialises in credit for self-employment for women on low incomes, many of whom are dependent on benefits. It is concerned that women who want to follow the self-employment path to economic autonomy need a transitional period, supported by benefits, until their business can support their family needs.[25]

Microfinance interventions could play a role in enabling people to manage money across periods of unpaid parental leave and part-time and short-term contracts. Unpaid parental leave is one of the new provisions of the Employment Relations Act.

Although the government's focus on employment as the main way of tackling social exclusion is understandable, there are risks involved in the language of the policy, which may be interpreted as exclusionary by those who cannot work or who live in areas where almost no jobs are available. Microfinance interventions would do well to avoid such exclusionary language. They should place emphasis on widening access to financial services, rather than pushing particular models. International practice in microfinance has been characterised by its diversity, which is one of its strengths (see Chapter 4).

The Social Exclusion Unit

Microfinancial services are part of the rapid policy-development programme of the government's Social Exclusion Unit. The Unit, which was set up soon after the present Labour government came to power in 1997, explicitly recognises the multidimensional character of social exclusion and the need to devise 'joined-up solutions to joined-up problems'.[26]

Despite the government's identification of the New Deals and other aspects of its labour-market policies with the aim of tackling exclusion, the Social Exclusion Unit (SEU) did not initially focus on employment. It began by targeting specific groups and issues: rough sleepers, exclusions from schools, and deprived neighbourhoods.[27] It has now developed a much broader agenda. The policy-development programme set out in the Unit's report, *Bringing Britain Together: A National Strategy for Neighbourhood Renewal,* involves 18 cross-cutting 'action teams'. Microfinancial services are the remit of the action teams on business and shops, and also of the dedicated financial-services team. The latter team has been set up to investigate 'the scope for widening access to financial services'. The SEU report makes reference to 'red-lining' of specific areas by insurance companies, the withdrawal of retail banks, and the regulatory constraints on credit unions.[28]

The setting up of the SEU — dedicated to combating social exclusion — is to be welcomed. Such high-level government action to tackle poverty and social exclusion is a major advance over the previous government's denial of the very existence of poverty (and indeed of society). The initial work on truancy and exclusion from schools should tackle some of the underlying causes of the lack of political and social citizenship. However, in the main, the unit began life with attention to some of the symptoms rather than the causes of social exclusion. Its work on homelessness, for example, concentrated on the 2,000 people sleeping rough, rather than the quarter of a million young people and others who became homeless in the United Kingdom as a whole in 1995.[29] One of the major proximate causes of homelessness among unemployed young people was the reduction in their entitlement to housing benefit — an issue beyond the scope of the SEU.

The Social Exclusion Unit's work on rough sleeping is not sufficient to tackle some of the underlying causes of homelessness in Britain either.

These causes include the sale of one million units of council housing from the mid-1980s,[30] and the subsequent large-scale repossession of owner-occupied housing following defaults on mortgage payments when interest rates rose in the late 1980s. The massive scale of repossessions provides sobering lessons for those microfinance interventions based on the premise of extending debt.

In contrast to the Social Exclusion Unit's earlier work, the programme identified in the *Neighbourhood Renewal* report is set within the context of an analysis of the causes of area-based poverty. There is good reason for the continued focus on specific poor neighbourhoods. As seen in Chapter 2, social exclusion and poverty have increasingly become mutually reinforcing in particular areas. Deprivation is multi-dimensional: there are links between debt, unemployment, lack of access to basic services, fear of crime, low self-esteem, minimal networks, and low levels of political influence. Many — though by no means all — poor neighbourhoods are characterised by a preponderance of social housing. When council properties were first built, households with employment income lived side by side with jobless households. Yet between 1979 and 1991, the proportion of household heads who were tenants of councils and housing associations, earning income from employment, declined from 59 to 41 per cent; the parallel decline for heads of other households was from 75 to 69 per cent.[31] With a much higher percentage of people than before receiving benefits and thus living on low incomes, effective demand for local services, such as shops, disappeared.[32] The reduction in local shops and post offices has direct links to microfinancial services — whether because of the availability of shop credit or because of the essential cheque-cashing and other services provided by post offices (see Chapter 5). The links have been explicitly recognised in the work of the 'shops' action team of the SEU.

However, at least three major difficulties have been identified with the focus on specific places. Firstly, focusing on and therefore labelling areas as having concentrated problems may perpetuate deprivation in those areas. If investors were considering such an area for a new plant, for example, they might well be deterred.[33] Secondly, the need for poor neighbourhoods to get together to prepare bids to join the 17 areas earmarked as 'pathfinders' could encourage neighbourhoods to compete to paint an exaggerated picture of deprivation in order to win funding. Thirdly, the labelling of particularly deprived areas as 'worst estates', like the use of the term 'underclass', could inadvertently — because this

is certainly not the intention of the Social Exclusion Unit — cause a
resurgence of behaviour-dominated understandings of poverty and
exclusion: an assumption that the causes lie in the actions of poor and
excluded people themselves, rather than in the dynamics of wider
structural forces.[34] Damer's study of Moorepark housing scheme in
Govan, Glasgow, documents the continuity of such 'offensive' positions
adopted by officialdom, by sociological researchers, and by residents of
adjacent areas towards that scheme from the 1930s to the 1970s.[35]
Problems caused by prejudicial labelling and discourse, and by the
process of becoming identified as a 'poor neighbourhood', need to be
addressed if neighbourhood renewal is not to perpetuate unintentionally
the multi-dimensional poverty and exclusion of particular areas.[36]

The present Labour government aims to tackle both poverty and
social exclusion in many different ways, and its record on social
exclusion is by no means limited to the results achieved by the Social
Exclusion Unit.[37] The indications from the government's first two years
in office are that the emphasis in national policy on perceived problems
with the supply of labour (an assumption that people need to be helped
back to work through reorienting incentives and providing advice and
training) has neglected the necessary counterpoint to address the
demand side. There are exceptions, such as the 'business' action team's
mandate to improve the access to capital of unemployed people seeking
to start their own businesses, which is directly concerned with one kind
of microfinancial service. However, in the main, neither the Social
Exclusion Unit's work, nor the 'active labour market' and social-
security policies directly address the need to attract job-rich investment
to areas where there are few opportunities for employment. One
commentator puts it simply: there are 'not enough jobs in the places
that they are needed'.[38] The analysis in Chapter 2 suggested that
national government had an important role to play in this: that
countries, particularly relatively wealthy ones such as Britain, were not
simply at the mercy of under-regulated global capital flows. Indeed the
British government has been at the forefront of international attempts
to bring in new regulation for short-term capital movements. And it has
recognised the need for regions and countries within the United
Kingdom to be able to attract investment, for example through the
setting up of Regional Development Agencies. As will be seen in
Chapter 5, there is a potential role here for one kind of community
finance initiative — social investment — to help to draw money into
poor neighbourhoods.

National action by non-government actors

In the age of 'partnership' across statutory, voluntary, and private sectors, government policy initiatives to combat poverty and social exclusion rarely involve the government acting on its own. For example, recent announcements of special zones to improve schools in areas of disadvantage have envisaged a potential role for the private sector in management.

There are many other important national actors outside government explicitly or implicitly engaged in responding to poverty and social exclusion. These include religious and cultural organisations, trade unions, and national voluntary organisations. Non-governmental scrutiny of government policies and practices is especially important when the government itself controls information tightly. Governments will always have electoral reasons for wanting to put a gloss on the results of their policy initiatives. This applies to the Labour administration as much as to any other government, despite the aspiration of some of its advisers to evidence-based policy change.[39]

Religious organisations and trade unions

National non-government organisations have long played an important role in campaigning for changes in government policies and practices at the national and local levels. The changes advocated have often included measures to reduce poverty. Religious organisations have been particularly vocal. The Anglican Church, for example, took a consistently critical line on policies that it saw as promoting poverty and inequality in the 1980s and 1990s. Like other faith-based organisations, churches have also been active at the local level. Jewish and Islamic religious organisations, as well as some of the black evangelical churches, have national networks linking local initiatives often focused on their particular constituencies.

Trade unions are much weakened players in anti-poverty work. As unemployment grew and trade-union membership, for that and other reasons, shrank from the late 1970s, the role of unions in anti-poverty work diminished. The network of centres for unemployed people has had strong links with trade unions, and they were key campaigners for the minimum wage. But there has been a growing concern with negotiating deals on services for members. Moreover, the role of unions in areas of their traditional strength, such as former mining villages and towns, where they played an important role in the provision of mutually based social security, has changed beyond recognition.

Voluntary-sector organisations

National voluntary-sector organisations have also increased their emphasis on service provision. They have a crucial role to play in the context of a rolled-back state, to protect people from the worst consequences of structural change. Moreover, advice centres and welfare-rights organisations have been essential to enabling people to access benefits. The national-level voluntary sector continued to swell in size and to take on diversified roles in the 1990s.[40] This very diversity demands that the sector should no longer be seen as a single entity.[41] The 1998 'compact' between voluntary organisations and the government recognises the importance of the former.

Increased service provision by the voluntary sector, while crucial, also carries dangers. The first of these is that more service provision and less campaigning means that there is less scrutiny of the government's work by organisations specifically dedicated to developing means of reducing poverty and social exclusion. Secondly, the reduction in statutory provision could also see a creeping shift in government expenditure, whereby funds dedicated to charity are siphoned off for services previously provided for from central resources held by the Treasury — as allegedly happened with monies moved from the control of the National Lottery Charities Board to the National Lottery New Opportunities Fund. Thirdly, the increased practice of contracting services to voluntary-sector organisations may have blunted their critical edge in keeping a watch on government policy on behalf of disadvantaged constituencies. Indeed, in the 'contract culture', raising funds requires some compliance with the views and ways of working of the contractor.

Implications for microfinance

There are some very important lessons here for providers of microfinancial services. Clearly, microfinance is at least in part about service provision, and the community finance institutions discussed in Chapter 5 are, with notable exceptions, not campaigning organisations. Yet, where reducing poverty and social exclusion is the goal, it is vital for such organisations to retain a primary connection to the changing requirements of their users, and awareness of the overall distribution of resources. In the contract culture, organisations may risk slipping into the mode of self-preservation; indeed, it is necessary for survival to talk up the significance of one's own work. Yet microfinance provision, which is often located in the voluntary sector, may be competing for funds with others also tackling poverty and social exclusion. It should be remembered that these are the goals, and microfinance one of several possible tools as part of an integrated and multi-sectoral approach.

LOCAL ANTI-POVERTY INITIATIVES AND
LOCAL GOVERNMENT

The changing roles of local authorities

The role of local government in attracting jobs is crucial, because local governments understand (potentially at least), the specific conditions of their own areas and the characteristics and location of their workforces.[42] Yet local authorities have faced two major obstacles in the last twenty years. The first, lack of money, was brought about in part by a long period during which councils were not permitted to spend the receipts from the sale of social housing. They had been 'neglected and disempowered' during the 1980s[43] by an actively hostile central government. The second obstacle was created by the authorities themselves. Several authorities began to reveal the results of entrenched power. Allegations against both Labour and Conservative administrators ranged in seriousness from the linking of council jobs to political party membership and support of certain factions in that party to developing special relations with particular contractors/recipients of council money in return for favours. Several local authorities have supported the development of microfinance through credit unions, though available evidence suggests that many credit unions have not been widely used by the poorest people (see Chapter 5).

One of the potential advantages of local authorities is that they can claim a mandate from the electorate. Perhaps because of both the above difficulties, however, turnouts at local elections have been very low. At the same time, the role of local government had already begun to change during the 1990s from a 'narrow service provider role' to a more 'strategic responsibility' for bringing together businesses, the voluntary sector, and statutory bodies for economic and social regeneration at the local level.[44] Such strategies, adopted by local and regional governments across Europe, became important buffers against the uncertainty caused by inflows and outflows of capital.[45] In Britain, central government support for local development came through City Challenge and Single Regeneration Budget funds, subject to the condition that use of the funds should be part of a co-ordinated strategy for social and economic regeneration involving local government and the voluntary and private sectors.[46]

Local authorities, regeneration, and microfinance

In their co-ordinating role, local authorities are a key part of the policy context for microfinance interventions. Especially where start-up funds are required, local authorities may be appropriate conduits between larger corporate funders, such as central government or the European Union, and institutions intending to establish microfinancial services. Loans for self-employment, which are one kind of microfinancial service, have been provided through the Single Regeneration Budget (see Chapter 5). Advocates of neighbourhood-level 'empowerment' — of coalitions of local groups taking the initiative in their own regeneration — also see important city-level and county-level roles for local authorities.[47] According to these authors, such a role ranges from taking the lead on developing a city-wide or county-wide strategic vision to attracting inward investment. In processes of economic regeneration, local authorities also have responsibility to establish a 'framework for equality, accountability and transparency that it expects of all participants in the process, including itself'.[48] In this vision, local microfinance initiatives, such as community credit unions, would be part of wider coalitions of neighbourhood organisations in a 'new democratic settlement' with local authorities.[49]

Local anti-poverty strategies

Apart from their actual and potential role in attracting investment and promoting economic and social regeneration, increasing numbers of local authorities have drawn up specific anti-poverty strategies. Whereas in 1994 only 55 authorities in England and Wales had them, by 1998 there were 117 with formal anti-poverty strategies and another 99 engaged in developing strategies.[50] Initially, welfare rights were a major component of local government anti-poverty strategies. They had become widespread in the 1970s and 1980s with the increased role played by means-tested benefits as opposed to contributory benefits and the associated low take-up.[51]

Of course, local government anti-poverty work cannot by itself achieve a turnaround in areas that have been deserted by jobs. Hence the need for a more integrated approach, as has become increasingly widespread practice. As Thomas Fisher argues in Chapter 5, microfinancial services have a potential role to play in such an integrated approach. As implied in the section on the Social Exclusion Unit above, when done well, area-based work to tackle poverty and social exclusion that is led by local authorities can make a significant difference to people whose lives have been negatively affected by structural change.[52]

The Priorities Estates Project

Moreover, through involving poor or otherwise excluded people in the process, area-based work can improve their political and social citizenship and sense of control over their lives. For example, Anne Power's research on the 'Priority Estates Project' of the 1980s found that significant improvements in residents' lives could be and had been made through the four-pronged approach of the project:

- locally based management office and other services;
- the involvement of tenants and residents through detailed consultation at all stages;
- co-operation between local and central government, and high-level political commitment;
- a supportive outsider to catalyse and facilitate the process.[53]

The kinds of change experienced on one of the sampled estates in the study included, over time, clearing the backlog of repairs, formation of resident self-help groups, reduction in crime, creation of about 100 local jobs, and linking of tenants to people living outside the estate through an interdenominational church project.[54] Power found that conditions on this estate improved considerably *despite* a worsening of income poverty. However, her general conclusions suggest that 'marginal, segregated areas do not become integrated, prosperous and stable through the changes outlined ... Estates can be brought back from disintegration', but the 'rescues' that have occurred on estates in a number of different countries in Europe were 'never mechanism[s] for the clear transformation of the areas from marginalisation to prosperity ... Area decline and stigma are endemic to urban growth and change and therefore disadvantaged areas tend to remain disadvantaged or to recreate themselves.'[55]

Poverty, exclusion, and political citizenship: voice and representation

Power's work stresses the importance of facilitating popular involvement in local change. Yet ideas for activating political citizenship tend to focus on designing mechanisms for consultation, rather than highlighting the ways in which poverty and existing exclusion can militate against involvement. While locally based initiatives are to be welcomed, there is often a gap between 'good ideas' and daily political and economic realities. Take involvement in action to improve the environment, for example. As a recent study of social exclusion, poverty, and environmental action points out, '[I]f environmental action is to be more than just a cause for the worthy and wealthy, it needs to address one of its most fundamental limiting factors — poverty'.[56] The report states further that '[s]o far [Agenda 21][57] has had a minimal impact on deprived communities. There has been a lot of talking, but there is little evidence of change.'[58] Microfinance initiatives aiming to combat poverty or social exclusion need to remain closely engaged with the everyday lives of their users to avoid similar pitfalls.

People living in poverty or who are socially excluded do not often get a chance to represent themselves in policy discussions about their problems and what to do about them. Indeed, much of the discussion takes place far removed from the action. Moraene Roberts of ATD 4th World, the international human-rights and anti-poverty movement, has called for poor people — women and men — to be fully involved as citizens in making proposals for societal change. After all, it is poor and excluded people who have experienced at the sharp end the strengths and weaknesses of earlier social policy initiatives. That first-hand experience is ignored at a price: the continuation of social exclusion and poverty.[59]

Bob Holman's book *Faith in the Poor* exemplifies one kind of antidote: allowing marginalised people, who are usually the object of discussion, to write for themselves.[60] Six of his eight contributors are women — women without employment but for whom, as Holman elaborates at the end, the level of income-support benefits is a much more salient issue than the provision of advice and training to job-seekers. The life histories and daily diaries show the indispensable nature of unpaid caring work, mostly carried out by women, yet not qualifying them for social insurance. Here, poor people reveal the limitation of an approach to social exclusion based on welfare-to-work. Holman concludes that well-supported self-help neighbourhood projects are highly valued by residents of the Easterhouse estate in Glasgow, where he lives. Self-help by poor and excluded people themselves is the subject of the following section.

SELF-HELP: HOW POOR AND EXCLUDED PEOPLE TACKLE POVERTY AND EXCLUSION

To establish the social policy context for microfinance interventions, the previous sections have focused mainly on what governments and other 'outsider' agencies, whether local, regional, or national, can do *for* poor and excluded people. Only in the discussion of the Priority Estates Project, which involved residents themselves as well as local authorities, and what followed, did the emphasis switch to discussing the potentially progressive impacts of involving poor and excluded people themselves in making decisions about resources spent by intervention agencies. This section examines the effectiveness of the means that people design and implement for themselves to cope with poverty and to counter social exclusion. These are referred to as 'self-help initiatives'.

Microfinance is often seen as a self-help initiative, especially when microfinance institutions take the form of co-operatives, as for example credit unions do.[61] In fact, as Chapters 4 and 5 will make clear, this is just one organisational form for the provision of financial services to those experiencing barriers to access. Nevertheless, the literature on microfinance and empowerment lays stress on the *process*, the act of setting up a credit union.[62] Positive stories emerge of people, particularly women, whose lives have been changed by the sense of power and confidence that involvement in a self-help savings and credit group has given them. They have been enabled thereby to increase their sense of control over non-financial areas of their lives.[63] Credit unions are a classic example of microfinance, and their potential in Britain will be examined in depth in Chapter 5.

Self-employment as self-help

Self-employment has become increasingly common in Britain since the reappearance of large-scale unemployment in the 1970s. Although there was a dip during the recession of the early 1990s, the number of self-employed people (also approximately equivalent to the number of micro-businesses with four or fewer employees) was approximately 3.3 million in Spring 1997.[64] There is much movement into and out of these sectors, however, with an estimated 508,000 micro-businesses being set up in 1997, against 489,000 ceasing to trade.[65] Self-employment as a category of occupation is disproportionately common at both extremes of the income distribution. Self-employment is thus characterised by both great wealth and extreme poverty. Research in the early 1990s showed that within the lowest income decile the incomes of self-employed people were on average one third lower than the incomes of employees. The reverse was the case in the highest income decile, where self-employed people were better off than employees in that decile.[66]

Women and men

The same study found big differences between self-employed people of different sexes. While fewer than four per cent of self-employed men earned less than £100 per month, the proportion of self-employed women in this category was 20 per cent. This difference is explained both by the far greater numbers of self-employed women working part-time and by the lower hourly equivalent rates earned by those women, compared with men. Among poor self-employed women, almost half are involved in household and personal services such as hairdressing and cleaning.[67] The great majority of micro-enterprises are sole traders and thus hardly distinguishable from self-employment. The largest single type of business with no employees in 1996 was in the construction industry.[68]

Self-employment and financial exclusion

Microfinance is often narrowly defined as being about finance for micro-business and self-employment. The definition used in this book is very different: it stresses the wide range of financial services, to which many poor people lack access, including appropriate savings, insurance, pensions, and loans for consumption and emergencies. Loans for micro-business/self-employment and accompanying advice and training are, however, important concerns within microfinance. Recent studies have found limited access to finance to be an obstacle to starting up in a micro-business.[69] More than 16 per cent of new firms seeking bank finance were refused in 1994-95. Many more may have just not tried.[70] Banks are not the only sources of finance; for example, 'business angels' are informal providers, aiming to invest where banks do not, to recirculate wealth created locally within a certain radius, and to provide commercial expertise and contacts. One study found that banks provided only one-third to one-half of start-up loans.[71] However, there is evidence of financial exclusion among women, young people, and African Caribbean people, who have difficulty in obtaining bank loans. Asians as a whole have also found it harder to get a bank loan than whites, but the proportion of Indian people experiencing obstacles to obtaining finance was half that of Pakistani people.[72]

Self-employment, poverty, and social exclusion

There clearly are major obstacles to accessing finance for self-employment and micro-business. However, another important question is what difference these forms of economic activity can make to the reduction of poverty or social exclusion. For many unemployed people or people in part-time employment, self-employment may be a coping strategy — a way of getting by. Some argue that this alone is enough reason to prepare people for self-employment: more of us are going to have to do it at some time in our lives, because of the changed structures of the labour market, so it is better to be suitably equipped.[73] Indeed for some people, perhaps a significant minority, self-employment may lead to higher incomes and greater security.[74] For some people from ethnic minorities, self-employment may be a refuge from discrimination in the workplace.[75] Part-time self-employment may also be suited to women's greater needs for flexibility in employment.

However, self-employment and micro-enterprise do not tackle the underlying structural causes of poverty and social exclusion. They should not be presented as solutions, but rather as means, for a minority, of managing some of the symptoms. Start-up businesses run by unemployed people in Britain have been less successful than elsewhere in the European Union.[76] Moreover, self-employment can make such people worse off than they might otherwise have been: '[I]t seems that many of the low income self-employed may also end up with low incomes and financial asset levels in later life, missing out on personal and occupational pensions, and ending up dependent on state benefits.'[77] The chances of having to abandon self-employment are much higher for people without previous experience of self-employment and for people who have experienced long spells of unemployment. Furthermore, poor women's vulnerability to business debt is more acute than poor men's.[78]

Experience shows that micro-enterprise has unpredictable consequences for many people. It is often a last resort, and there are no grounds for advocating it as a nationwide alternative to employment: only a minority of poor people who take up self-employment graduate to running sustainable businesses. The New Deal's earmarked package for 18–24 year-olds wishing to set up in business should be welcomed not because self-employment is the answer to poverty and social exclusion, but rather because self-employment, subject to the above limitations, can enable some people to become more employable and move into the labour market.[79]

Mutual help — 'family', 'community', and supportive social networks

Social citizenship as defined in the last chapter involves the possession of enabling social networks and other social resources, and a sense of belonging. Prime among these for most people are family, friends, and, for some, neighbours and colleagues. According to one study, 30 per cent of those leaving unemployment find jobs through friends and relatives.[80] Clearly, therefore, supportive social networks (social citizenship) are crucial resources for people struggling to quit or remain out of material poverty. International literature on microfinance often stresses the potential for involvement with microfinance — particularly through groups (see Chapter 4) — to lead to the accumulation of this kind of social capital.

At the same time, people without access to High Street banks rely particularly heavily on friends and relatives as sources of loans. Debt avoidance takes on an additional meaning, beyond its stigmatic and immediate material consequences. Credit-worthiness has to be worked at and maintained, because it is a valued resource in itself and because it enables people to draw on important emergency sources of credit. Microfinance institutions can improve credit-worthiness vis-à-vis the informal sector. The importance of the latter is emphasised by Damer, who sees the 'all-important' credit-worthiness maintained by women 'in the neighbourhood' as largely unrecognised in official approaches to tackling poverty.[81] At the same time, if women find a way of reducing their dependence on such sources, they welcome it. This is one of the main reasons why income from employment was found to improve the well-being of lone-parent households more than equivalent increases in other income: it enabled lone parents to get access to formal consumer credit.[82]

Understanding local social relations

It is important for those involved in the provision of microfinancial services to understand the actual rather than the ideal social relations involved in informal financial transactions between relatives, friends, and neighbours. The point is not just that poverty and citizenship are related, but that interventions have social and political as well as economic impacts, through their processes as well as their outputs, and that these have a bearing on social exclusion.

The discourse concerning the future of welfare in turn-of-the-century Britain suggests an increased role for individual responsibility,[83] but also a greater role for 'family' and 'community'.[84] Yet anthropological work among recipients of welfare benefits indicates that, if policy is to rely on self-help via the family and the community, both of these need to be better understood. Self-help to manage the stigma of living on particular housing estates may involve the construction, through language and identification with one group or area on an estate, of an image of an 'other' group, who are portrayed as particularly 'rough' or 'undesirable'.[85] To avoid feeling the stigma of living in a particular place, people may form themselves into a 'community', united by their imagined difference from others in that place. In a similar way, forming a credit union on the basis of neighbourhood common bonds can exclude those who live in streets not included in that bond.[86]

In rural areas, while the 'particular nature of family life' brings a 'strong sense of belonging',[87] the notion of who constitutes family shifts. It matters very much, for example, that many women marry into a 'community' from outside, because they may be seen as a 'threat' to that 'community'. To be relevant and effective, welfare professionals and other outsiders, including microfinance practitioners, need to understand how boundaries around 'family' and 'community' shift, as well as men's and women's very different roles in creating and reproducing those boundaries. The tightness of rural 'communities' may be supportive, but it may also create a sense that one is under surveillance — with the risk of severe mental-health problems as a consequence. In these circumstances, the social implications of debt, for example, may be especially hard to bear.

The importance of language and labels

Others maintain that because 'community' is a two-edged sword and because those most in need of support are often the most peripheral to how 'community' is constructed, it is more useful to talk in terms of supportive personal networks.[88] At best, the loose usage of the word 'community' to describe people living in a particular place is making very bold assumptions about the strength of the common interests of these people, and it ignores their conflicting interests. At worst, the label is used deliberately as a linguistic tool to persuade users that an intervention is benign and in everyone's interest.[89]

'Family' can be more than a supportive social network. It can provide important social bonds, as can a feeling of belonging to a neighbourhood or area. 'Community' is sometimes used to refer to the shifting of power to the local level. This can make welfare provision and other interventions more relevant to particular conditions. However, it does not necessarily mean that poor and socially excluded people within an area will have a voice. The danger of the terms is that this is exactly the impression they often give. Providers of microfinancial services interested in combating social exclusion need to be clear about the real nature of social relations in their area of work and to research the likely impacts on them of encouraging mutual help through 'family' and 'community'.

Mutual help and groups: possibilities and limitations

Historically, situations of adversity have motivated poor or excluded people with common interests to form groups. In nineteenth-century England, these included mutual financial arrangements such as those of the pioneering weaver co-operators of Rochdale, in response to new tariffs on imports of woollens to the United States, and associated deterioration in wages and conditions of work.[90] Self-help groups are run by and for their members. They may involve economic or financial activity, for example in the case of housing co-operatives or credit unions. On the other hand, they can involve campaigns to influence public policy, as in the case of Southall Black Sisters.[91] When self-help groups work well, the experience can reduce individuals' sense of isolation and can create a sense of autonomy and greater control over one's life. They can thus be a means of dealing with social exclusion. The anarchist and libertarian traditions have always valued mutual aid because of its opposition to state aid, with its formal discipline and organisational hierarchy.[92]

Self-help groups present a paradox for outside professionals and agencies. On the one hand they may represent an effective means of organisation, with a strong sense of ownership among members. On the other hand, the involvement of outsiders means the end of *self*-help.[93] In practice, self-help groups do have funding links and other relationships with outside agencies, and this can work well. Self-help does of course have its limitations. It cannot, for example, 'compensate for the effects of highly unequal social systems, which exclude vast numbers of poor people from a reasonable share in the wealth of their society'.[94] At a more practical level, advocating a greater role for self-help, which involves time spent in unpaid work, ignores the reality that people have little time to spare for such activities. In the case of women, disproportionate involvement in unpaid work means that their involvement in mutual help costs more than it does for men.[95] Moreover, self-help organisations may be fleeting, or may become hierarchical and bureaucratic. It is important to recognise that the nature of organisations changes and to avoid becoming fixed on a single model.[96]

Both the possibilities and the limitations of mutual help need to be considered by those who promote them as complementary forms of welfare provision. Mutuals have been regarded favourably by some policy analysts as ways of countering financial exclusion[97] — and for some very good reasons. However, for those concerned primarily with tackling poverty and social exclusion, it is important to focus on identifying the circumstances when mutual organisation is useful and relevant to these goals, rather than setting out with a particular form of organisation as an end in itself.

SUMMARY AND CONCLUSIONS

This book aims to reflect on the potential for microfinancial services to counter poverty and social exclusion. In Britain, microfinance operates in the context of a state social-security system which effectively provides people with a minimum income. It is protective and stands between many people and destitution. Microfinance is not an alternative to state-provided social security. Rather, the implication for those providing microfinancial services to tackle poverty and social exclusion is that they should seek to *complement* the existing social-security system. The way in which social security is provided also carries lessons for microfinance delivery. Targeting of benefits via means tests can socially exclude people, through the stigma with which this method has become associated. If microfinance is to be targeted, which, as will be seen in the following chapter, is relatively common internationally, this needs to be done in a way which does not reduce users' social citizenship.

The present government's efforts to tackle social exclusion have focused on encouraging people back to employment through, for example, increased subsidies on child-care costs, as well as training and enhanced workplace rights. These measures are to be welcomed, because they recognise the changed structures of the labour market, with many more people now in part-time and short-term employment. Microfinance could potentially enable people to manage money better across periods of low earnings from employment. Initiatives focused on credit for self-employment could be relevant to more people, if combined with a 'welfare waiver'. International experience in microfinance, as will be seen in Chapter 4, is characterised by diversity, and approaches developed in the British context should emphasise widening access to financial services, rather than promoting particular models.

National action against poverty is also taken by non-government actors, including voluntary-sector organisations, religious organisations, and trade unions. Some voluntary-sector organisations have a campaigning role; more are involved in service provision; many do both. The 'contract culture' predominates. Microfinance initiatives need to be aware of the dangers of slipping into self-preservation mode where there is a risk of putting the survival and growth of the institution above the requirements of users.

The *Neighbourhood Renewal* report from the government's Social Exclusion Unit has set out a policy-development programme based on integrated work at the neighbourhood level, including work to tackle financial exclusion. There is good reason for the focus on specific areas, given the concentration of multi-dimensional deprivation in some. But there are difficulties in this approach too. Most of all it risks neglecting the many areas of multiple deprivation that are not included, and perpetuating social exclusion through increasing a neighbourhood's local notoriety. This could — unintentionally — lead to the resurgence of behaviour-dominated understandings of poverty and social exclusion and could therefore obscure the underlying structural causes of these problems.

It may be that local authorities can effectively take the lead in attracting money to boost investment in areas of widespread joblessness. Local government has faced major problems of alleged corruption and under-funding over the last two decades, but there is potential for it to develop an enabling local role. Microfinancial services may, in a modest way, have a place in an integrated, locally sensitive, multi-sectoral, and multi-level approach to countering poverty and social exclusion. This potential will be analysed in the rest of the book. However, it is important not to be carried away by what may sound like a good idea, without grounding any assessment in local social and economic realities. Much microfinance emphasises self-help, whether through self-employment, mutual help through social networks, or the formation of new mutual-aid groups. All of these can strengthen people's ability to take control over their own lives. But they do not necessarily do so. The form of organisation — for example mutual ownership — and the type of social network — for example 'family' — are potential means: they should not be mistaken for ends in themselves. In the chapter that follows, international experience is used to illustrate how differing kinds of microfinance intervention have evolved in particular contexts, and an assessment is made of their impacts on poverty and social exclusion.

4 Microfinance and poverty reduction: the international experience*

BEN ROGALY

INTRODUCTION

THE focus of the preceding chapters was on the analysis of poverty and social exclusion in Britain, and responses to them. They explored the links between poverty and finance and showed that poverty in Britain, as elsewhere, is in part about lack of income or wealth. Lack of income and wealth also lead to exclusion from social life and networks, and from societal norms of consumption — in other words, to social and economic non-citizenship. Poverty and social exclusion are connected too to political non-citizenship — to being unable to change the rules. These links are made more acute by financial exclusion. In Britain such exclusion involves the withdrawal of conventional banks from areas associated with large numbers of benefit recipients; the 'red-lining' of certain postcodes, which determines the banks' response to applications for financial services products such as insurance; and the general trend of banks towards seeking up-market customers, who will pay fees for customised services.[1]

Chapter 3 examined deliberate initiatives to combat poverty and social exclusion by central government, local government, and people themselves. Among these schemes, microfinance initiatives have a role to play. There is a long history of providing microfinancial services in Britain, going back two hundred years. Notable among earlier initiatives were the mutually owned building societies, the first of which was set up in 1775 in Birmingham.[2] However, at the turn of the millennium there is much international experience based on new approaches to extending the outreach of financial services, which have been developed in countries as diverse as Bangladesh, Bolivia, and the United States of America.

The purpose of this chapter is to examine contemporary experiences of microfinance in countries other than Britain. The next section explains in more detail what microfinancial services are. The third section illustrates the diversity of international practice in the provision of such services,

* Several of the ideas in this chapter were developed in a previous collaboration between Susan Johnson and Ben Rogaly (*Microfinance and Poverty Reduction*, Oxford, Oxfam 1997). Susan Johnson generously approved this use of the earlier material, but Ben Rogaly remains responsible for all views expressed here.

drawing on the work of five institutions in contrasting national contexts. Distinctions are drawn between different forms of governance and ownership, including user-owned institutions, those primarily donor-driven, and those that rely more on commercial sources of finance. The fourth section considers the extent to which microfinance has reduced poverty or social exclusion. The broad definition of poverty and social exclusion, introduced in Chapter 2, is used in this section to examine the impact of microfinancial services. The fifth section discusses in more detail the lessons for the design of microfinance institutions that are evolving from international practice. Conclusions are drawn in the final section.

WHAT IS MICROFINANCE?

Microfinance is the provision of small loans, saving facilities with no (or a very low) minimum deposit, and other financial services like insurance, money transfer, or bill payment designed for people who live on low incomes or are otherwise excluded from the commercial products of conventional financial institutions.

International attention on microfinance in the 1980s and 1990s has primarily focused on just one category of microfinancial service: credit for self-employment. Behind credit for self-employment lies the idea that poor people lack access to productive capital. If that access is provided (it is argued), it will lead to investment, a new stream of income, further investment, and more income, until the borrowers raise themselves above the poverty line. Credit for self-employment — also known as micro-enterprise credit, or micro-credit for short — is thus about *promotion*: the promotion of poor individuals and households out of poverty.

The international interest in micro-credit has arisen, in part, because micro-credit for self-employment is in tune with the neo-liberal economic ideology of providing opportunities for individuals to help themselves through engaging in market activities.[3] It has also been argued that micro-enterprise appeals to international bi-lateral and multilateral donors, because loans, which are repaid, are a more sustainable strategy than grants, which are not.[4]

However, there is much more to microfinance than micro-credit. Other financial services, particularly savings and insurance, as well as emergency loans and loans for day-to-day needs, can enable people to *protect* themselves from regular or unpredicted drops in income. Vulnerability to a fall in income is most serious for people without wealth. Over time, microfinance may enable people to build up assets which they will later be able to transfer to their children, thus increasing security across generations.

The potential benefits of microfinance, whether of the promotional or the protective kind, are that people without access to banks can obtain the kinds of financial service that banks provide. In our definition, microfinance includes the provision of informal financial products, whether by private money-lenders/deposit-takers aiming to make a profit, or by user-owned groups such as rotating savings and credit associations.

One of the major rationales for *intervention* in the market for financial services at the micro level has been that, because of lack of access to banks, poor people have been left with no choice but to rely for loans on private money-lenders, who may charge extortionate interest rates and insist on interlocked transactions. One example from agriculture is the practice of tying the provision of loans by a trader to the sale of the crop to the same trader at harvest time, when prices are typically at their lowest.

Another rationale is that rural people may not have access to bank branches, and that bank staff may treat poor people with disdain, emphasising their lower status. Some banks charge fees, which makes them inaccessible to people with low incomes, or provide products which are inappropriate to the needs of such customers (for example, savings accounts that do not allow frequent small deposits and withdrawals).

Rutherford has divided financial services into three types:[5]

- Those that build up cash reserves through forgoing income: savings, for example, which are deposits out of income now, forgoing current use to draw a sum in the future; insurance, allowing user access to future lump sums; loans: lump sums given now, in return for income foregone in the future.
- Converting assets into and out of lump sums of cash: mortgages and pawns, for example.
- Cash handling: for example, money transfer and bill payment.

Microfinancial services are therefore about managing money. It is often the people with the least money who also lack access to means of managing what they have, of accumulating assets and wealth, or increasing their incomes through productive investment.

There was a marked increase in the provision of microfinancial services in the 1980s and 1990s. A recent survey by the World Bank suggested that there were 1,000 microfinance institutions with over 1,000 users in existence for at least three years in 1995 in Latin America, Asia, and Africa. Of these, 200 responded to the survey questionnaire. The respondents alone had US $7 billion in loans outstanding to more than 13 million individuals in 1995. In addition, over US $19 billion had been saved in 45 million active deposit accounts.[6]

The trend in microfinancial service provision in recent years has certainly been upwards: between 1993 and 1994, for example, there was a 31 per cent increase in loans outstanding.[7] The volume of savings is particularly impressive, especially considering the attention that has been focused on micro-credit among microfinancial services. Earlier microfinance interventions had been wrong to try to *teach* people the virtues of saving. People *want* to save cash, even in very small amounts. Microfinance initiatives can, under certain circumstances, provide the opportunity to do so securely.

This changing understanding of the role of savings in people's livelihoods illustrates the process of learning about the potential of microfinance for tackling poverty and social exclusion. Moreover, while in countries like Bangladesh and Indonesia there has been a very significant expansion in the number of people with access to loans and to deposit facilities, this learning continues: there is no single 'correct' way of providing microfinancial services to tackle poverty and social exclusion.

The next section therefore illustrates the differing ways in which microfinancial services are delivered by drawing on examples of initiatives focusing variously on savings, credit for micro-enterprises, and insurance. Institutions providing microfinancial services are extremely diverse; they include banks, savings banks, credit unions, and non-government organisations (NGOs). They vary in size from a few hundred users to millions. Some current providers, for example some savings banks, have been in business for several decades; credit unions have a much longer history.[8] The 1980s and 1990s saw a growth in the number of NGOs providing microfinancial services, alongside the rapid increase in interest shown by international aid donors.

There is a range of strategies adopted by NGOs providing microfinancial services. Some emulate banks, confining themselves to the provision of financial services.[9] Some restrict themselves to social intermediation, forming groups of users who may be linked to conventional providers of financial service, and providing business-support services such as training for micro-enterprise.[10] Others engage in both financial and social-service provisioning. The overriding goal of many NGOs is to reduce poverty and social exclusion, and this chapter will review whether and in what ways microfinancial services can contribute to this goal. For some other providers, poverty reduction would be a welcome outcome, but it is not the prime motivator.

What microfinancial services are, and what their providers set out to do, differ not just across institutional types but also across countries and social, economic, political, and agro-ecological contexts. The World Bank study was able to characterise some of the broad areas of similarity within the continents of Latin America, Africa, and Asia. It compared macro-economic environments, population densities, and economic growth rates. Even at this crudely aggregated level of analysis, the following conclusions may be drawn about the two hundred microfinance institutions studied:[11]

- Institutions in Africa are the youngest.
- Three-quarters of the loan volume were disbursed in Asia.
- Social services are prominent in Asian institutions, not in the others.
- Three-quarters of users in Asia were women, as against half in the other regions.
- Median loan size and deposit size were much higher in Latin America than Africa or Asia.
- The African institutions had a higher proportion of donor funding (almost 60 per cent more) than institutions in other continents, but also a higher proportion of funding from savings deposits. The latter is due to the presence of large African credit unions in the sample.

Thus, even at the continental level, microfinancial services involve different things in different places. Within continents, there are also major divergences.

This preliminary review of international experience suggests important themes: the range of micro-financial services, some protective, some promotional; the diversity of institutions providing microfinancial services, which need to be adapted to meet the needs and opportunities of specific contexts; and the on-going learning among practitioners.

It will be argued here that microfinancial services may, in a modest way and in combination with other strategies, be relevant to such an agenda in Britain. The outputs of microfinancial services, such as deposit and loan facilities, may be able to give some people a greater degree of economic citizenship and therefore more control over their lives.

The provision of microfinancial services is, moreover, a *process* as well as an output. Much of the literature on the social impact of microfinancial services in Bangladesh, for example, concentrates on the role they have played in enabling women previously isolated to meet together in groups.[12] Elsewhere it has been suggested that the experience of responsibility and (self-) respect for those users involved in microfinancial institutions has increased those people's capacities to change other aspects of their lives for the better (although involvement in the operations of such institutions is not an option for many users[13]). This implies that the provision of microfinancial services can also potentially influence the social and political citizenship of their users, as well as their economic status.

The rest of the chapter illustrates the diversity of contemporary international experiences in providing microfinancial services, before proceeding to explore the extent to which microfinance has been able to achieve the potentially progressive impact which has been discussed here. Finally it draws out some recent learning on the institutional design of microfinance institutions.

HOW MICROFINANCE WORKS: FIVE INTERNATIONAL ILLUSTRATIONS

In considering the possible relevance for Britain of international lessons in the provision of microfinancial services, it is necessary to outline some of the key technologies that have been used to increase the access of poor people worldwide to financial services. The primary focus here is on savings and loans, although one example is given to show the provision of other financial services (insurance). Because there is no blueprint for microfinancial services, some of the ways in which they are provided are illustrated through examples of initiatives in five diverse contexts:

- *Bank Rakyat Indonesia*, a bank providing microfinancial services to millions of rural people in Indonesia
- *The Grameen Bank*, a specialised financial institution extending micro-loans to millions of poor rural women in Bangladesh
- *The Tequisquiapan Project*, a multi-dimensional initiative addressing poverty among peasants in Mexico
- *SEWA Bank*, owned by women slum-dwellers in Ahmedabad, India, providing a wide range of microfinancial services, including insurance, to its members
- *ACCION*, an international micro-credit network which has recently started lending to micro-enterprises in the USA.

In the course of describing these illustrations, we refer also to other institutions providing microfinancial services, in Bangladesh, Sri Lanka, Indonesia, Bolivia, Peru, and Poland, demonstrating the extent and diversity of such initiatives.

Bank Rakyat Indonesia[14]

The Bank Rakyat Indonesia's Village Units constitute, together, probably the largest provider of microfinancial services in the world. In December 1996 savings worth US $3 billion were deposited in 16.2 million accounts. Bank Rakyat Indonesia (BRI) is a state-owned commercial bank. Arising out of a 1970s government credit programme aimed at expanding agricultural production, the Village Units were transformed in the mid-1980s into commercially viable bank units providing a range of savings and loan services to rural people, many on low incomes, without any need for government or donor subsidies. The Village Units have thus contributed significantly to tackling financial exclusion in rural Indonesia.

There are many more savers than borrowers in the Village Units. But the loan services came first, with 'promotional' loans (known as KUPEDES) offered for any productive enterprise to women and men: loans ranging in 1996 from a minimum sum, equivalent to US $10.50, to a maximum of US $10,500. Although legally there is a collateral requirement, Village Units have been flexible in this, as well as in designing repayment schedules, which have been tailored to the expected cash flow of the enterprise. Character references have been widely used to screen potential borrowers, who are treated as individual clients and are not expected to form into groups. There is no requirement for a borrower to have a savings account with the Village Unit. A financial incentive is given for timely repayment; it consists of a refund of interest on maturity of the loan. Timely repayment is also rewarded by access to larger loans. At the same time, staff of BRI receive annual bonuses based on their performance, and prompt loan collection is given special emphasis in staff-performance assessment.

BRI's Village Units have four main types of savings account. These vary according to rates of interest and restrictions on withdrawal. SIMPEDES accounts, which hold the majority of total deposits, place no limits on the amount or regularity of withdrawals.

Such voluntary savings facilities, developed gradually in response to widespread demand, demonstrate that millions of rural people in Indonesia, many of whom are poor, value a savings facility and access to their deposits more highly than the level of returns (which are higher on the less popular products, which restrict withdrawals to twice per month).

The precedent for village-level financial institutions in Indonesia was set by the Badan Kredit Desa (BKD), which began work over one hundred years ago. These have survived despite periods of national instability, which must give some hope to the BRI Village Units in the face of the recent economic slump in Indonesia. Indeed, as a section of BRI they have, without resources from government or international donors, produced a high level of profitability, which, perhaps ironically, has been used to cross-subsidise other activities of BRI involving loans to larger enterprises. The savings of poor people and their timely repayment of loans have, according to the World Bank survey, enabled BRI to withstand the higher levels of loan default by richer customers. Early indications suggest that BRI has survived the Indonesian economic crisis of 1997 and 1998 relatively well, in comparison with private commercial banks.[15]

The Grameen Bank, Bangladesh[16]

Like the BRI Village Units, the Grameen Bank of Bangladesh, which has become well known for its micro-credit lending, began in the 1970s. The core service offered by the Grameen Bank is loans. Borrowers are also shareholders. By 1996, the Bank had made US$1.5 billion in loans, had a current membership exceeding two million people, and was operating in over half of the villages in Bangladesh. Almost all of Grameen's members are women. Loans are available only to people with less than half an acre of land.[17] The great majority of Grameen Bank's loans are therefore made to poor women.

Grameen Bank was established by a statute of the Government of Bangladesh as a specialised financial institution in 1983, around the same time as the BRI Village Units were being transformed in Indonesia. The Grameen Bank's innovative way of working had been established through the experiments begun seven years earlier by an economics professor, Muhammed Yunus, who remains in charge of the Bank today. Also like the BRI Village Units, the Grameen Bank has high repayment rates on loans, reported to be 98 per cent.

There are two central innovations involved in the Grameen approach. The first is the organisation of borrowers into groups of five; members are expected to bring pressure to bear on each other for timely repayment. The idea is that loans are made to individuals via the group, which has a quota of two loans at a time. The group's eligibility for further loans depends on its members' repayment performance. This is also intended to serve as a screening mechanism. In the forming of groups, which borrowers are expected to do themselves, people who are unlikely to repay loans are not invited to join, which may itself be a form of exclusion. Similarly, potential members who doubt their capacity to take on more debt may exclude themselves. The Grameen Bank thus relies on peer pressure to involve poor borrowers themselves in both screening and enforcement of loan repayment.

If peer-group lending is effective in Bangladesh, it is because rural people in a particular locality know each other well and are therefore best placed to assess each other's debt-repayment capacity. It is also because many consider the risk of damaging potentially supportive social networks through not honouring a commitment made to other members of the group to repay to be greater than similar behaviour towards an institution from outside the locality. As will be seen in Chapter 5, peer groups for micro-enterprise lending have been put into practice in the British context, although it is too early to judge their impact.

The second major innovation is the Bank's weekly meetings, which are compulsory for all members, and, like peer-group lending, may be of relevance for the British context. The meetings involve a high degree of ritual and discipline,[18] which have proved important in ensuring that loan instalments are repaid on time; the meetings enhance transparency, as all cash transactions for loans and savings are conducted at these weekly meetings in the presence of the whole membership of a 'centre'.[19] The meetings may also serve an important screening function: along with the small loan sizes available, they are likely to act as a disincentive to relatively rich people to try to find ways around the eligibility criteria.[20]

A member's first loan can range in size from US$75 to US$100, repayable in weekly instalments over one year. The intention of small, regular, and equal instalments is to strengthen borrowers' ability to repay. It is, in effect, a recognition that repayment instalments are akin to savings, with the loan taken as an advance against savings capacity.[21] This is not explicitly stated, because the promotional idea still reigns — that the loan will lead to new income through expansion of an existing micro-enterprise.[22] Like BRI, Grameen offers future larger loans as an additional incentive to timely repayment.

However, there are substantial and important differences between BRI and Grameen. Unlike BRI's Village Units, Grameen continues to rely for a proportion of its funding on external donors. Moreover, Grameen's approach to savings has been to make them compulsory, both as a condition of loans and to raise capital for the Bank. Members have to save one taka per week to build a group fund, and 5 per cent of the value of the first loan is also placed in the group fund. Once the group fund has reached a certain level, the group is required to purchase shares in the Grameen Bank. The Bank is thus largely owned by its members: members take nine of the thirteen seats on the board.[23] Members have access to their savings only when they relinquish their membership. Voluntary savings have come only lately and in a very limited fashion for long-standing members.[24]

Other big Bangladeshi microfinance institutions, such as BRAC and ASA, may also be on the verge of introducing flexible savings facilities. But to date, the emphasis in the savings policy of these institutions has been to 'secure and safeguard capital funds', rather than responding to the demand of their members.[25] The authors of this interpretation argue that among poor people there is widespread demand for flexible savings services. However, they also caution against the expansion of savings facilities by inexperienced providers of financial services. The provision of savings facilities requires regulation in order to protect savers' deposits and to enable people to identify trustworthy institutions.

Grameen's model, which has been adapted in many different national contexts,[26] represents a major innovation in lending to poor people by making use of potential borrowers' local social and economic ties to aid screening and enforcement of loan repayment. As a result, small amounts of capital have been provided to millions of Bangladeshi women, who had no access to formal-sector finance. Like BRI, Grameen's contribution to addressing financial exclusion among poor people has therefore been significant. Moreover, new types of village-level organisation, such as the five-member groups and the Grameen centres, have enabled women, many of whom were relatively confined within their households, to meet together regularly. However, while savings have allowed individuals to become members of the Bank, such savings have not served as protection against income fluctuations and emergencies, because they cannot be withdrawn on demand.

The Grameen Bank, like many NGOs involved in providing credit for micro-enterprise, has continued to rely in part at least on external sources of capital. While international donors have emphasised financial sustainability as a central goal for microfinance institutions, they have also continued to subsidise their operating costs and, in many cases, to provide loan capital. Following the 1998 floods in Bangladesh, Grameen Bank sought a loan of US $100 million to recover from the inability of its borrowers to repay loan instalments, by freezing outstanding loans and making bridging loans to enable people to rebuild their homes.[27]

Credit Unions and the Tequisquiapan Project, Mexico

Both the BRI Village Units and the Grameen Bank are large-scale institutions providing microfinancial services. Most institutions providing such services are far smaller. Some of these are similar to credit unions, in that user-members buy shares on joining and can vote at meetings; savings are voluntary, but eligibility for loans depends on amount saved; and loans are mainly non-directed: they are not made for a specific purpose, but rather relate to a demonstrated capacity for regular saving. According to the World Council of Credit Unions, there are 37,078 registered credit unions worldwide, with assets of $418 billion, serving 88 million members.[28]

About three-quarters of credit-union members are in the United States. Of particular interest are about 300 Community Development Credit Unions (CDCUs),[29] which, although owned by their members, are permitted to accept deposits from non-members up to 20 per cent of their total shares. Because of community reinvestment legislation in the USA which requires commercial banks to report the geographical pattern of their lending, the CDCUs often work in partnerships with banks to provide services to people who are on low incomes or who are effectively excluded on grounds of race (including many African-Americans, Hispanics, and Native Americans). However, the failure of a number of credit unions set up in the 1960s as anti-poverty vehicles under President Johnson's 'War on Poverty' Programme has led to an emphasis on creating CDCUs with a mixed membership of low-income and moderate-income savers. CDCUs offer a wider range of services than credit unions in many other countries, including loans for micro-enterprises.

Some features of the Tequisquiapan Project (TP) in Queretaro State, Mexico are similar to those of community credit unions. However, TP does not view itself as a microfinance institution. The provision of savings and loan facilities is a means to the end of creating a more integrated regional society and economy, in which the wealth that is created is retained locally, and poor people develop the capacity to control their own lives, partly through the structures of the *campesino* (peasant) organisation, Union Regional de Apoyo Campesino (URAC), which is at the heart of the project.

In 1997, URAC had over 9,000 members, spread across the 30 rural localities in which it works. There has been steady and continuous growth in membership since it began in 1987. The work of URAC is built around its dynamic relation with the four community-development workers and one agronomist who make up the membership of the sister organisation Union de Esfuerzos para el Campo (UDEC). These workers divide up between them the localities where URAC works. Each locality is visited monthly, to facilitate meetings and the building of locally based organisations. Representatives of the localities meet regularly to decide on policy, in dialogue with the UDEC workers.

The financial work which TP carries out in the localities where it operates involves groups and joint liability, but in a very different way from Grameen. Groups vary in size from 20 to 70 members. Each has a cashier, who is responsible for collecting savings and depositing them weekly at the Tequisquiapan office of TP. Loans are made only to groups in which all members are keeping up with their repayments. This is the joint-liability aspect. Cashiers receive incentive bonuses for timely collection of savings and loan instalments. Almost all of the members and all of the cashiers are women.

Since 1994, there has been more saved than borrowed: savings are a highly valued service used in a range of ways by members to manage fluctuations in income, or sudden expenditure crises. They are also used for expenses associated with children's schooling; and for some they are seen as ways of accumulating assets to pass down across generations.[30] Because loans are available as advances against savings rather than for any expressed productive purpose (though TP has these as well), some members prefer to manage their money by taking loans, rather than withdrawing savings. The flexibility of both savings and loans in TP means that it is able to respond to various methods of money management.

TP does receive support from international donors, which has funded the salaries of the UDEC development workers. However, loan capital is funded entirely from the pool of savings deposits, interest earned by TP on that pool, and interest earned on loans. The former is maximised via investment of the savings pool in a mixture of accounts, following the principle of low risk and high returns — in that order. Rates of interest on members' savings and loans do not move with the market, so that from time to time savers' interest rates are negative in real terms (less than the rate of inflation). There has been no massive increase in withdrawals at such times, suggesting that member-users place a higher value on having their savings available in the form of a deposit account than on the specific rate of return.

SEWA Bank, India

The above three examples, which point to the many different ways in which microfinancial services have been made more accessible to poor people in the South, are all rural. Many microfinance providers operate in urban areas: for example, BancoSol in Bolivia, which uses a 'solidarity group' methodology for micro-enterprise loans in a similar way to Grameen, and the Colombo Women's Thrift and Credit Co-operative Society.[31] Only 5 per cent of BancoSol's clients are rural, as compared with 100 per cent of Grameen Bank's and URAC's memberships, and 80 per cent of BRI's.[32]

SEWA Bank, a co-operative bank in Ahmedabad, India, is another example of an urban institution providing microfinancial services (although it has more recently also begun operations in rural areas surrounding Ahmedabad city). The Bank was set up in 1974 by the Self-Employed Women's Association (SEWA), a trade union of women working in the informal sector, which had been established to campaign for recognition and the rights of its members. The trade union now has over 250,000 members, and has also set up educational and housing trusts, and an academy for research and training.[33]

At first, SEWA union collaborated with a commercial bank in seeking to gain access for its members to financial services, but this strategy proved ineffective, because of the inappropriateness of products provided by the bank, and the attitudes of bank staff to SEWA members, many of whom were poor and illiterate. The union therefore decided to establish its own bank, which now has about 60,000 women savers, 20,000 women shareholders, and a board of 15 directors, all women, nine of whom are elected by shareholders engaged in different trades, such as vegetable vending, cloth weaving, or rag picking. SEWA Bank is therefore remarkable in being a formal and regulated financial institution (particularly important for protecting deposits) which is owned by thousands of low-income women.

SEWA Bank provides a range of banking services, but in particular various savings, loans, and insurance products. Its strategy involves both promotional and protective services. For example, a new member might first take a loan specifically designed to allow her to repay existing high-interest debt, for example to money-lenders. Thereafter the member is encouraged to build up savings and take out insurance, to protect her from slipping back into debt, for example in the case of illness in the family or a crisis such as flooding. At the same time, the member will also be taking small working-capital loans to stabilise the cash-flow of her business. It is usually only later that she will take larger loans to invest in and expand her business.

This integrated mix of microfinancial services may be of some relevance for those considering microfinance as part of a strategy for tackling poverty and social exclusion in Britain. As was shown in Chapter 2, many low-income people in Britain face high levels of debt, as well as difficulty in managing cash-flows in the face of fluctuating incomes and expenditure. At the same time, for a small proportion of such people, self-employment may offer a potential route back into the labour market. SEWA Bank has also learned from informal financial markets, for example providing loans secured against gold or other jewellery, just like pawn-brokers, but at more reasonable rates and with far less risk of losing the assets pledged.

SEWA Bank is one of the few microfinance institutions that offers insurance services to its members. The bank provides life, accident, and health insurance, as well as maternity benefits and basic pensions. In the case of life, accident and health insurance, SEWA purchases bulk insurance coverage from national insurance companies for members who open a fixed-deposit account or pay regular instalments into a special savings account. Purchasing wholesale reduces the costs of individual premiums, which can moreover be spread over time, making payment possible for poor women who may not have sufficient savings for the fixed-deposit option. Husbands of members can also be included under the life and health insurance. The Bank then assists members in making claims to the insurance companies concerned. There still remain difficulties in making claims, however, and for health care the Bank now intends to provide its own health-insurance policy internally, as it does already for maternity benefits and pensions. The pension scheme is a specially designed savings (not investment) product which guarantees a member a minimum income when she can no longer work.

SEWA Bank therefore demonstrates the potential for microfinancial institutions to provide insurance services, which may be critical for protecting low-income users against illness and crises. Purchasing bulk insurance coverage is clearly a way of reducing the costs of insurance to individuals, as social landlords have successfully done in Britain in the case of home-contents insurance (see Chapter 5 below). However, the breadth of SEWA Bank's insurance services is necessitated by the lack in India of any state provision for SEWA's members; the number of women covered is very limited in comparison with the need; and, as a private institution, it cannot achieve any redistribution of income or wealth. There are no grounds, therefore, to extrapolate from SEWA Bank's experience in India that state welfare provision in Britain should be privatised. Indeed the evidence reviewed in Chapters 2 and 3 suggested that public provision should be strengthened, because many of the poorest people rely on benefits, levels of which are often inadequate for a full sense of citizenship. At the same time, aspects of SEWA's strategy adapted for the British context may be able usefully to complement state welfare provision.

ACCION, USA[34]

Founded in 1961 as a private non-profit organisation, ACCION today supports an international network of micro-credit partner organisations in 14 Latin American countries and six US cities. Its first micro-credit programme was established in Brazil in 1973, while it began its US operations in New York City only in 1991. Table 4.1 highlights the financial turnover of both ACCION's Latin American and US operations in 1997, suggesting that the latter are still small.

Table 4.1: ACCION International Network (1997)

	Latin America	USA	Total
Active clients:	341,107	998	342,105
Amount disbursed:	$503.3 million	$3.5 million	$506.7 million
Active loan portfolio:	$226 million	$2.6 million	$228.7 million
Number of loans:	621,721	1,194	622,915
Average loan size:	$809	$2,955	$813
Average loan balance:	$633	$2,672	$699
Proportion of women members:	61%	37%	61%

As in Latin America, ACCION (USA) works through a partner network of local non-profit institutions, which now operate out of six cities. With capital offered below market-rates and guarantee funds from ACCION, the local partners negotiate lines of credit and loans from commercial banks for lending, and raise operating grants from the federal and state governments, as well as foundations.

ACCION's partners primarily focus on credit for micro-enterprises. ACCION's borrowers in the USA typically run so-called 'lifestyle' and retail businesses: 39 per cent work from home, 30 per cent from a shop, and 23 per cent from the street or a market stall. Many of the women entrepreneurs need to work from home because of the high cost of child-care. Most enterprises financed have been trading for three years or more. Few businesses supported are pure start-ups, but 25 per cent have been trading for less than one year. ACCION has to date targeted ethnic-minority businesses: 87 per cent of borrowers are either Hispanic-American or African-American. As existing entrepreneurs, ACCION's borrowers are clearly not among the poorest people, although they may be poor and socially excluded, for reasons that include racial discrimination. As we saw in Chapter 3, for some people from ethnic minorities, self-employment may be a refuge from discrimination in the workplace. Part-time self-employment may also be suited to women's greater needs for flexibility in employment, although there is some evidence from the USA that it can result in women getting stuck in the 'pink collar' sectors.[35]

ACCION (USA) lends both to individuals and to peer groups. For loan-security, individuals are asked to post whatever physical collateral they can, including a car, television set, or business equipment. Groups provide joint and several guarantees on each other's loans and are not asked for other collateral. Interest charges are well above bank overdraft rates, and similar to that on credit cards (i.e. 24–27 per cent APR). ACCION justifies these costs as necessary to cover the service provided and to enable it to achieve self-sufficiency in due course.

ACCION is one of the microfinance networks that has placed considerable emphasis on self-financing and sustainability. In Latin America, nine out of 19 ACCION network institutions are self-sufficient to the extent that they can access and pay for commercial funds. Sixteen out of 19 cover all their operational (but not capital) costs with fee and interest income generated. Indeed, two of the most financially successful ACCION partners have achieved banking status since 1992 (BancoSol in Bolivia and MiBanco in Peru).

In contrast, none of the six partners in the USA, all relatively young, is able to cover its operational costs. Indeed, to date none of the US partners can be considered successful in meeting the needs of micro-enterprises just beyond their start-up phase. Operations remain small, costs remain high, and group lending has proved difficult, although other organisations like Working Capital have had greater success with group lending.

To some extent, ACCION started operations in the USA because of the wide recognition of its achievements in Latin America and political pressures to do the same in the USA, where ACCION International is based. However, it failed to develop a carefully considered strategy to begin work in the USA, and, in reviewing its operations to date, ACCION recently isolated numerous inefficiencies. A new strategy and development plan agreed in 1998 seeks to address these weaknesses. To date, however, the case remains a salutary warning that experience from one or more countries cannot simply be transferred to another without adequate attention to the local context and careful experimentation through well-planned pilots.

Fundusz Mikro, a micro-credit programme set up in Warsaw in 1994 to target a similar clientele of existing micro-enterprises (operating in the grey economy), has expanded much more rapidly and is now covering its operational costs. In contrast to ACCION USA, Fundusz Mikro experimented with nine different credit-delivery mechanisms in order to identify the most popular and cost-effective ones. The speed of its growth was enabled by access to US$24 million in capital from the outset. At the time of writing, no independent study of the impact of Fundusz Mikro on poverty and social exclusion was available to the author.

HAS MICROFINANCE REDUCED POVERTY OR SOCIAL EXCLUSION?

In Chapter 2, relative poverty was defined in terms of wealth and income, both low annual income and vulnerability to fluctuations in it over the year. Wealth was seen as a prime determinant of people's capacity to withstand periods of low or fluctuating income, as well as a key to privileged education and networks, which could perpetuate economic inequalities. Reducing poverty meant not just raising incomes, but also reducing inequality and enabling people to accumulate wealth for transfer across generations. Initiatives to combat social exclusion overlap to a significant degree with the agenda of reducing poverty, but they are wider in their range. Chapter 2 argued that social exclusion was about social, economic and/or political non-citizenship and that reducing social exclusion involved people taking greater control over their own lives.

In this section the intention is to illustrate the impacts that microfinancial interventions can make on poverty and social exclusion. Because poverty and social exclusion have been defined so inclusively in this book, it is likely that the process of microfinance intervention will have a progressive impact on some variables and a neutral or even regressive one on others. For example, loans for micro-enterprises may increase the incomes of borrowers. It may be, for instance, that a loan for self-employment to a person on a relatively low income leads to an increase in his or her income (good). However, unless this leads to an increase in employment for other, poorer people, inequality could increase (bad). It is because of this complexity that microfinance aimed at achieving the progressive goals we have outlined should be practised with care.

Microfinancial services have certainly increased *access* to formal financial services for many people who did not previously have it. In Bangladesh and Indonesia millions of people, whether poor or not, now have access to certain types of microfinancial services. It has been estimated in Bangladesh, for example, that up to one-fifth of those without access to micro-enterprise loans (before the increase in micro-credit through the Grameen Bank and Bangladeshi NGOs) now have it.[36] In many other countries access has also increased, although, unlike in Indonesia and Bangladesh, the number of users of microfinancial services remains a small fraction of the total number of people living in poverty.

Microfinancial services may not be limited to savings, loans, and insurance. Services to help people to manage money may be just as important. For example, pilot microfinancial projects in Central America are developing mechanisms to transfer remittances from migrant workers (in or outside the country) more cheaply than mainstream commercial operators (such as Money Express or Western Union). Such remittances are an important means for poor families to smooth their consumption patterns, manage in times of crisis, and pay for education and health care.[37] Remittances are important for minority groups in Britain as well, such as those of Pakistani origin, who transfer money to their families in Pakistan, and also frequently borrow money from the foreign-exchange agents involved in such transmissions.[38]

The association of credit unions in El Salvador, moreover, argues that allowing low-income families to channel remittances through a credit union will lead many to open savings accounts, which may encourage the families to use the money received for investments rather than consumption, and allow the credit union to invest the money in productive capacity within the low-income locality. Banks that capture remittances may charge more and tend to invest in commerce, or even currency speculation. Money transfers may also be an important service for people who travel in insecure areas. CARUNA in Nicaragua, for example, allows people in the town of Siuna (which has no phone communication to Managua, the capital city) to deposit money in the bank account, then get a notarised letter from the manager to withdraw it one day's travel later in Managua.[39]

There are, however, few studies of the *impact* of loans for consumption or for emergencies, savings-based microfinance, insurance, bill payment, or money transfer. Most studies of the impact of microfinancial services have examined the impact of loans for micro-enterprise. Nevertheless, some of the most thorough research on micro-enterprise credit, much of which has been undertaken in Bangladesh, found that borrowers may not necessarily use the loans directly for their own businesses. Especially given the 'fungibility' of funds within a household, which we describe below, micro-enterprise loans are in fact used for a number of purposes, including non-business ones, and often by other members of the same household. Such apparently unpredicted and unintended outcomes can of course remain consistent with progressive impacts of microfinancial services, in terms of the reduction of poverty and social exclusion. However, it will be important to ask whether micro-enterprise credit, as opposed to savings facilities, loans for consumption and emergencies, and insurance products, are the most effective way to enable poor people to protect themselves, for example against seasonal stresses and sudden shocks.

In the following sub-sections I consider in turn the impact of micro-enterprise credit on absolute levels of income and on social relations, including class and gender relations. This will be followed by a brief report on studies of the impact of savings and insurance services on poverty and social exclusion.

The impact of micro-enterprise credit

Income

A study of 13 microfinance institutions in seven countries in the global South by David Hulme and Paul Mosley found that credit for investment in micro-enterprises had led to increased incomes.[40] Individuals living below the poverty line increased their incomes by 18 per cent and 12 per cent in the two groups of institutions examined, while individuals above the poverty line increased theirs by 116 and 55 per cent.

Evidence from micro-enterprise credit services in the USA suggests that while they 'can help a few people to beat the odds', care should be taken not to over-promote them, because '[m]ore people will be hurt than helped if the safety net is withdrawn and replaced with mandated self-employment' … '[Micro-enterprise programmes (MEPs)] may or may not end up as part of the best mix of ways to help the poor. Funds spent on MEPs are not spent on other ways to help the poor.'[41] The numbers of people raising their incomes via micro-enterprise loans in the USA are likely to remain small, because micro-enterprises in that context involve 'high effort, high risk, and low profits. Few people ride [micro-enterprises] from rags to riches.'[42] Indeed, for micro-enterprises which survive in combination with wage work, the 'main effect in both the US and abroad seems to be not more income but rather smoother income in the face of shocks'.[43]

The evidence therefore suggests that, depending very much on context, micro-credit may enable small numbers of people to raise their incomes. Moreover, for those in countries like the USA, who combine wage work with micro-enterprise, the latter may enable them to reduce their vulnerability to income fluctuations. This has relevance for Britain, where, as we have seen in Chapter 2, such vulnerability is often an important part of the experience of poverty. However, the US experience in terms of the impact of micro-enterprise credit on the incomes of poor people, and the evidence on other impacts of such loans, reviewed below, clearly points to a cautious approach to using this strategy in programmes to counter poverty and social exclusion.

Income and inequality

The evidence from Hulme and Mosley cited above makes clear that those who are less poor benefit more in terms of proportionate increases in income than the poorest micro-credit borrowers. This is not surprising. Relatively better-off people, by definition, have greater access to other forms of capital, and can therefore make higher returns on their businesses per unit of loan.

Micro-enterprise credit for the poorest people should therefore be practised with particular caution, both because they are less likely to have access to the necessary inputs to set up successful businesses, and because business failure is most devastating for those with nothing to fall back on. For example, a study of micro-enterprise among welfare recipients in the United States found that fewer than half of those who started a business made a profit in a normal month, and some 25 per cent reported a negative net worth.[44]

There is now a large body of evidence confirming that this particular type of financial service, micro-enterprise credit, is relatively less useful to the poorest people, and that larger microfinance institutions are increasingly making loans to those who are less poor.[45] An interesting exception to this body of evidence is a survey by ACCION of the impact of micro-loans on the incomes of 849 of its US borrowers. After the first two loans over 17 months, average take-home income increased by 38 per cent, or by an average of US$455 per month. ACCION does not lend to the very poorest people. However, the survey suggests that, among ACCION borrowers, the gain in income for those on lower incomes was higher than for those on relatively higher incomes. For the lowest-income ACCION borrowers, the mean rise in income per month was US$515 (54 per cent).[46]

The ACCION study illustrates the dangers of unquestioningly extrapolating from the evidence in one context to draw conclusions for another. Moreover, the nature of financial exclusion is different in Britain from Bangladesh, Bolivia, and the USA. The proportion of people lacking access to current and savings accounts in High Street banks is relatively low (6 to 9 per cent, according to one authoritative study[47]), and many such people suffer from multiple disadvantage. There may be other reasons for caution in lending for micro-enterprises to people in multiple deprivation in Britain (see Chapters 3 and 5), but increasing inequality within the group of the financially excluded is not one of them.

However, in many other contexts internationally, where much larger numbers of people rely on microfinance institutions as their sole sources of business credit, poor people with relatively higher initial endowments may be enabled by micro-enterprise credit to widen the gap between themselves and the very poorest people. The resulting inequality may drive more of a wedge between different classes of poor people.

In Bangladesh, micro-enterprise loans have deliberately been targeted at the poorest people, often using a landholding ceiling: for example, individuals from households with more than half an acre of land would be ineligible. Although by the standards of many other countries this would be a very low ceiling, because of the density of population in rural Bangladesh and the way land-ownership is distributed, many millions of people qualify for loans. Nevertheless, studies of microfinance interventions have found that in recent years there has been an increase in the number of 'non-target group' households that access such loans.[48] The process of targeting according to land-holding is similar to means-testing in the British context, which was discussed in Chapter 3. However, there is no evidence available to the author that being in a target group bestows the kind of stigma that has become commonplace in the context of means-tested welfare benefits in Britain.

Employment

The dilemma is not, however, a simple trade-off between income and equality. Micro-enterprise loans can make an impact on employment. The study by Hulme and Mosley found that, although the impact on employment was modest, with borrowers over time increasing employment in their enterprises by one job per enterprise since taking the first loan, 'they frequently increased inputs of labour from, and payments to, persons within the family, and this turned out to be an important channel of poverty reduction'.[49] Loans for micro and small enterprises,[50] which are potential employers of poor people, may more directly and positively impact on poor people's incomes than loans focused on self-employment.

Exclusion of the poorest from micro-enterprise loans is thus not necessarily a problem if those people gain employment as a result. This will depend on the type and conditions as well as quantity of employment. The Hulme and Mosley study found that it is the wealthier borrowers who tend to hire more labour on taking out loans. With BancoSol, for example, no borrower below the Bolivian poverty line had hired additional labour, while more than half of borrowers with an income four times the poverty line had hired labour from outside the family.[51] Likewise, evidence from a business credit programme in Nicaragua suggests that small and medium-sized businesses generate more employment per loan amount than micro self-employment does.[52]

It was argued in Chapter 3, for the British social policy context, that generating employment, especially in poor neighbourhoods, was an overriding priority in tackling poverty and social exclusion. The evidence on micro-enterprise credit suggests that sole trading may have only a limited role to play in this. This points to the need for more integrated approaches, both to increase local economic activity and to attract inward investment in order to generate local jobs.

Dynamic social relations

According to Imran Matin's research, the poorest gain from the inclusion of less poor households as users of microfinancial services in other ways.[53] The latter take larger loans, through which they are not only likely to contribute more to local economic activity and employment, but also to make larger interest payments, thus enhancing the capital available for others. Better-off households are encouraged to 'buy in' to the existence of microfinance institutions, making them more sustainable as institutions, and allowing the poorest households to retain essential ties with the less poor, who may provide access to informal loans. Avoidance of the 'ghettoisation' of poor people, through which services for low-income people alone tend to become poor services, is especially important for the British context, given the growth of inequality in Britain since the 1970s.

At the same time, microfinance interventions that seek to reduce poverty or social exclusion need to be aware of the dynamic social relations, the structures of class, gender, race, and ethnicity within which they are operating, and the ways in which these relations are influenced by the interventions and *vice versa*. Monitoring and reflecting on impact is essential: there is no necessary link between outreach (large numbers of users) and progressive change, between outreach and impact.

For example, if the provision of microfinancial services reinforces unequal power structures by further strengthening those who already dominate economic and social life, then it may be doing more harm than good. This does not appear to be the case among BRAC borrowers in Bangladesh, where a study by Zaman found that many of the non-target group households which accessed credit were still poor 'marginal farmers', and that the leakages were not going to local elites.[54]

On the other hand, micro-enterprise programmes for low-income women in the United States have been criticised because they 'encourage women to partake in undercapitalized, small-scale businesses that maintain [the women's] economic vulnerability and social peripheralization in a gender-biased world'.[55] While women on low incomes may have little choice about the type of business they take up, overemphasising the potential for them to take up micro-enterprise may contribute to the continuing exclusion that some of them face. Micro-enterprise credit, and even business training, may enhance incomes, but these are clearly not adequate to address the disadvantage of the 'reproductive tax', and socially constructed notions of what women and men should be or do, referred to in Chapter 2. Evidence on gender relations is reviewed in greater detail below.

Diversity of loan purposes

Assumptions about impact based on outreach are especially problematical in the case of micro-enterprise credit, because of the so-called 'fungibility' of credit: borrowing for one purpose to use for another. Recent studies have shown that many borrowers do not use their business loan for the stated purpose. Instead, the cash often enters the pool with which people manage their various spending needs and obligations. According to one study, the main uses to which loans are put are in fact for repaying debts and for 'consumption smoothing',[56] which, as we saw above, are likely to be of particular importance for the poorest borrowers.

> *Through a detailed study of informal credit transactions in a village in northern Bangladesh, the research empirically establishes that [microfinance institution (MFI)] -member households borrow as much from informal sources as non-members of comparable groups. Target-group households, in particular, resort to extensive cross-financing of their loans: they use 89 percent of informal loans and more than 78 percent of MFI loans for current consumption and debt-servicing. The non-target group households, on the other hand, use 60 percent of informal loans and 61 percent of MFI loans for these two purposes.[57]*

In the British context, enabling poor people to manage their money better and also to enhance their credit-worthiness would be positive outcomes. But are there better ways of enabling people, especially the poorest, to smooth consumption and guard against shocks than providing micro-credit loans? According to Sinha and Matin, the answer is yes, particularly in the long term. In current practice, micro-credit providers in Bangladesh encourage *all* members to take larger and larger loans. These loans are beneficial to people seeking to smooth out consumption in the short term, because they make people credit-worthy. 'Informal' lenders, such as private money-lenders, employers, and landlords are more willing to lend if they know that the borrower has a source of money for repayment; a micro-credit loan could count as this.

However, in the longer term, the cycle of larger and larger loans becomes unwieldy and stretches poorer people beyond their capacity to repay. At the same time, better-off borrowers who may be able to invest in productive businesses would be better assisted by larger loan sizes, and proper business appraisal. Sinha and Matin suggest that providers of microfinancial services should learn from the flexibility of the informal sector in designing their loan products for very poor people, and from the more rigorous business-appraisal and advice of the formal sector for better-off people.

Their point is that the diversity of loan products should be increased to acknowledge both the protective and promotional needs for credit, thereby more directly helping poorer borrowers with consumption-smoothing and better-off borrowers to build successful businesses.

Gender relations

The impact of micro-enterprise lending on the relative power of women in households and communities has been studied intensively in Bangladesh. That access to micro-enterprise credit empowers women and changes gender relations in the household and the community is claimed by several of the major microfinance institutions.[58] Researchers who have examined this claim have acknowledged the difficulty of defining and measuring empowerment and have used different definitions in parallel to explore exactly how, if at all, women have been empowered by microfinancial services. Linda Mayoux has shown that, among those concerned with the impact of microfinancial services, understandings of empowerment vary according to paradigm. Many of those whose main concern is with financial sustainability define empowerment as being about 'expansion of individual choice and capacities for self-reliance'. On the other hand, those more involved with microfinancial services because of its potential for poverty alleviation argue that targeting women is important 'because they are seen as poorer than men and also more likely to spend income on the welfare of their families'. Empowerment is understood in terms of 'collective community development and self-sufficiency'. The third paradigm in Mayoux's typology, the 'feminist empowerment' perspective, sees empowerment as the 'transformation of power relations throughout society' and the rationale for targeting women as promoting 'equity and the human rights of women'.[59]

It is clear from one major study, by Goetz and Sen Gupta, of the control of loans taken by 275 women from four different credit programmes that the women in whose name loans are taken often do not retain control of the businesses in which they invest.[60] It was found that only in 37 per cent of cases did women borrowers retain significant control; 63 per cent fell into the categories of partial, limited, or no control over loan use. The study found that single, divorced, and widowed women were more likely to retain control than others. Control was also retained more often when loan sizes were small and when loan use was based on activities which did not challenge ideologies about which types of work were appropriate for women and which for men. In some cases women were able to use the fact that the loan had been disbursed to them *as women* to increase their status and strengthen their position in the household. In a few cases, women reported an increase in domestic violence because of disputes over cash for repayment instalments.[61]

The findings of the Goetz and Sen Gupta study are supported by others: within replications of the Grameen Bank in Asia, 'pipelining' of loans from borrower women to male relatives is common;[62] women's access to credit from Grameen and BRAC has enabled them to negotiate within the household to improve their position.[63] Goetz and Sen Gupta make a similar point: that control of loans by men or women other than the original borrower could be seen as part of a bargain inside the household — in some cases women may lose control of the loan, but negotiate higher status or less involvement in manual work instead.

Lutfun Osmani has considered in some detail the effect of Grameen Bank micro-enterprise loans on women.[64] Her one-off questionnaires included indicators of changes in women's 'breakdown position': what women would have if the household broke up, which is a key determinant of their bargaining power and thereby their well-being. In comparison with a control group of non-borrowers, Osmani found that women who had taken Grameen Bank loans had enhanced their breakdown positions, although they had not changed their perceptions either of their own contributions to their households or of their own self-interest. Osmani also found that Grameen women borrowers' relative well-being in relation to men had increased in terms of their autonomy and their access to resources (measured by the way food and health care was allocated within the households). There was no change in women's role in decision-making, except, importantly, in terms of contraceptive use, where Grameen Bank members had more say than women in the control group.

This detailed evidence makes clear the complexity of determining the influence of micro-credit on gender relations. On the one hand, there is evidence from Bangladesh that a relatively high proportion of micro-enterprise loans made in a particular woman's name is controlled by another woman or a man. On the other, researchers have argued that this may be part of a bargain inside the household, and that the woman named as borrower may turn out to be better off having taken the loan than if she had not, even if she cedes control of the business. Overall the evidence from Bangladesh suggests that micro-credit has not led to a transformation in gender relations, but has become an additional resource, around which negotiation occurs.

Savings and insurance

Loans for consumption and emergency may be the credit products best suited to the poorest users of microfinancial services. These are likely to help people to deal with both regular down-swings in income and with sudden shocks. Savings can perform a similar function, once sufficient funds have been built up. This requires savers to be able to withdraw on demand — the system practised by Bank Rakyat Indonesia Village Units, the Mexican Tequisquiapan Project (TP), and SEWA Bank in India. There have been few studies of the impact of savings-based microfinance schemes. However, research was carried out on the impact of TP in early 1996.[65] The indicators of impact used were the relevance and usefulness of TP's financial services products to the members of the Union Regional de Apoyo Campesino (URAC), most of whom were poor women.

Nineteen members of URAC from one of the localities where it worked — La Laja — were interviewed for the study.[66] Eighteen of those interviewed were women, the other a thirteen-year-old boy. The incomes of people in La Laja had been squeezed drastically by reduced opportunities for industrial employment, following the peso crisis of 1994-95 and escalating prices, especially for health care and education. The URAC services enabled members to survive in times of difficulty and to cope with unemployment following the crisis. Members used URAC to maintain economic security, despite savings deposits losing their purchasing power through the operation of a negative real interest rate. Its savings and loan components offered ways of saving that worked out cheaper than alternatives such as *abonero* (collecting payment instalments towards purchase of consumer durables selected from a catalogue), and less embarrassing than borrowing from relatives.

Most of the households operated more than one savings account. Often women had accounts for themselves and each of their children, to which they contributed regularly. Most saved weekly, although the amount varied. Savings were withdrawn for medical expenditure (including urgent treatment), survival in hard times (including sporadic unemployment), utility bills, raw materials for making household adornments, consumer durables (fridge, cupboard), clothes, shoes, school fees, and registration of a truck. According to the members interviewed, the advantages of the URAC microfinancial services were the freedom of not having to save a fixed amount weekly; easy access to loans, with minimal regulations and red tape; easy access to savings (including withdrawals for urgent requirements); and the fact that individuals could safeguard cash without informing other household members.

Members adapted their use of the services to their preferences. Thus some people liked to save and withdraw but would never consider borrowing; others took loans because they liked the additional incentive to keep up payments. People who were very indebted could not normally save and were therefore unable to join the scheme.

Just like the users of microfinancial services in the Bangladesh study by Sinha and Matin, URAC members made use of several financial services simultaneously. They used URAC services for cross-financing. For example, one household reported paying school fees under a credit arrangement with monthly instalments. If the instalments were paid late, they increased by 10 per cent. A loan from URAC was used to ensure that payments did not fall behind. In some cases, credit taken from local grocery shops was repaid from URAC savings. URAC savings were also used for instalments to *tandas* (rotating savings and credit associations, alternative providers of microfinancial services to which half of those interviewed belonged).

URAC's flexible savings facilities were clearly appreciated by its members and used by them to support a wide range of livelihood needs, including food purchases, emergency health care, and insurance for periods of unemployment. In this way, the services have demonstrated their usefulness and relevance to members and enabled them to protect their livelihoods.

The case study of the Tequisquiapan Project shows that there are ways in which organisations can use microfinancial services to respond to poor people's need to survive times of no income without becoming further indebted. Such organisations have tended to keep broader needs in mind, apart from the mere provision of financial services. There is a danger that the emphasis of international donors on financial sustainability (see further below) has reduced the grants and investments available for social organisation and services, and pushed some NGOs and membership organisations engaged in microfinancial services away from other forms of intervention to become more narrowly focused on financial services.[67]

Where other interventions exist, for example in health or education, it is difficult to separate out the impact of microfinancial services on well-being. However, a recent review of the experience of Save the Children Fund with microfinancial services reported that the children of users were healthier and ate better than when the project started monitoring such variables.[68] A study by the International Food Policy Research Institute led to similar findings.[69] As suggested in Chapter 3, in such cases it is important to ask whether and under what circumstances money spent on financial services provision aimed at the reduction of poverty and social exclusion is more effective than money spent on other kinds of intervention[70] (just as it was important above to ask whether micro-credit loans, as opposed to savings facilities, loans for consumption and emergencies, and insurance products, were the most effective way to enable poor people to cope with seasonal stress and sudden shocks). This is not to suggest that any single intervention is superior, but rather to encourage the most effective mix.

LEARNING ABOUT MICROFINANCIAL SERVICE PROVISION[71]

The illustrations of institutions providing microfinancial services given earlier in this chapter suggested a wide diversity of approaches, depending on context and objectives. These examples, together with our review of the available evidence of the impact of microfinancial services on poverty and social exclusion, point towards an ongoing process of learning about the design of microfinance initiatives. We consider this process under three heads: diversity; innovation; organisational and financial sustainability.

Diversity

There is no blueprint for an institution planning to provide microfinancial services: no two institutions are the same. Organisationally, initiatives range from small savings and credit groups to large commercial banks. Some use highly standardised operations to reduce costs; others allow great diversity in order to meet local needs. It is clearly inadvisable to consider transplanting a replica of the design of an anti-poverty intervention in one country or region into another, without allowing for major differences in context.

Differences may be demographic and topographical: for example, Bolivia is sparsely populated, mountainous, and largely urban, whereas Bangladesh is very densely populated and mainly flat. These factors have implications for the number of group meetings that can be conducted by a single bank officer in one week.

Differences in social relations, including gender relations, mean that microfinancial services designed to work with or change particular institutions in one place are much less relevant in another. For example, a recent comparison of a microfinance project in Indonesia with the Grameen Bank in Bangladesh pointed out that Indonesian women had relatively greater autonomy inside the household, and that the benefits of the process of meeting together, which Grameen has developed, are less of a priority for them.[72]

The wider context also causes strategies for microfinancial services to diverge. For example, in Islamic countries, such as Pakistan, it is forbidden to charge interest. In such contexts, Islamic banking has developed its own methodologies.[73] In the United States, community development finance initiatives have partly grown in response to diminishing social and welfare provision by the state. In recognition of this role, the state has nevertheless provided a supportive legislative environment, particularly the Community Reinvestment Act, which has enabled microfinance initiatives to develop. Often regulation of financial services is very thorough and thus stands in the way of semi-formal providers. In several countries, for example, NGOs are not permitted to collect savings deposits. On the other hand, as we have already seen, secure savings clearly require an adequate regulatory framework.

As suggested in Chapter 3, politics and ideology both of institutions and of wider environments also cause divergence in design. Microfinancial services are provided for very different reasons by different organisations. For example, at the 1997 Micro Credit Summit in Washington, DC, banks were encouraged to get involved in a new relatively untapped market — a source of potential profit. On the other hand, organisations such as the Tequisquiapan Project and many NGOs involved in microfinancial services are motivated by other goals, including building organisations of the poor, and retaining and circulating wealth locally.

Susan Johnson has contrasted the ideologies behind emergent microfinance initiatives in Northern and Southern contexts. Those in the former case were seen as counter-cultural — part of a 'green' agenda of keeping wealth local. The latter, on the other hand, were seen as driven by rich-country development donors and their ideologies of promoting neo-liberal economics. As Johnson points out, this caricature of microfinance initiatives in both North and South does not adequately capture the divergent motivations of many microfinance practitioners. What *is* clear is that institutions not concerned primarily about financial sustainability and using 'market' interest rates have to justify their stance.[74] Financial sustainability is further discussed below.

Innovation

Microfinance, including micro-credit, has a long history.[75] Yet the recent mushrooming of initiatives has also been based on a number of new and important innovations. These have served to demonstrate to mainstream microfinancial-service providers, in case they had been in any doubt, that poor people are as likely to be reliable and responsible users of financial services as anybody else. For example, Hulme and Mosley conclude on micro-lending: 'What has now been established beyond all doubt ... is that the option of lending at the bottom end of the capital market exists, and is not a financial black hole, if design is correctly done and the accompanying policy environment is not actively adverse.'[76]

Learning continues on the best ways to deliver microfinancial services. Hence, providing an illustrative list of innovations runs the danger of appearing static.[77] Moreover, microfinance as a means should not be confused with the goals of many of its practitioners — tackling poverty and social exclusion. For example, providing micro-enterprise loans, which are relevant and useful to poor people, is about understanding the market in which they operate. However, an illustrative list, which now follows, is nevertheless helpful in pointing to important international lessons for the design of microfinancial services.

- *Mechanisms encouraging self-selection by poor people:* for example, many credit-oriented schemes now practise 'self-selection' through keeping loan sizes small, and demanding regular attendance at meetings, which better-off people might regard as not worth attending.

- *Financial services appropriate to the poor:* BRI and TP have developed voluntary and flexible savings facilities, which have been a largely unmet need of poor people; SEWA Bank is one of the first institutions to develop insurance services suitable for the poor, such as women slum-dwellers, who do not have access to state provision; micro-loans (often with tiny and flexible repayment instalments), including those available immediately for the emergency needs of poor people, are another innovation among formal financial-service providers. Institutions providing microfinancial services often use very simple procedures, such as one-page loan formats, with approvals taking from a few hours to a fortnight.

- *Mobile banking and the use of intermediaries:* microfinance initiatives have gone out to their customers to provide convenient and accessible services, for example savings and credit groups in villages, or financial services through mobile extension centres at weekly markets. Some initiatives are also beginning to lend through intermediaries, such as co-operatives, agricultural traders, and even money-lenders, who have access to many local borrowers.[78] The author has not seen evidence on the impact of these innovations.

- *Use of groups:* some providers of microfinancial services extend services to individuals. Others, however, such as the Grameen Bank, use peer groups. The impact of peer groups in different contexts is still debated: they may help with transparency, screening of potential borrowers, incentives to repay, and enforcing repayment. On the other hand, they may also exclude the poorest and most vulnerable members of the community.[79]

- *Incentives to repay loans:* in addition to peer-group monitoring, microfinance initiatives have developed a series of incentives for borrowers to repay, for example, by ensuring extensive supervision by staff at regular meetings of borrowers; offering interest rebates on loans repaid on time; and allowing repeat lending to borrowers who build up a good repayment history. These incentives are in some cases complemented by similar incentives to staff, who may, for example, be evaluated on their performance in collecting loans.

- *Interest rates:* although most micro-credit programmes rely on subsidies,[80] there is obviously a question about the length of commitment of grant-making bodies including international donors (see sub-section below on financial sustainability). Partly because of this concern and partly because of the capture of much more highly subsidised loans by the relatively better-off in some credit schemes in the 1960s and 1970s, there has been a move towards charging interest rates that cover inflation and make a contribution to the cost of providing the service. Some argue that this is necessary, because availability of credit is more important to poor people than its price (although, as we saw earlier in this chapter, high private-sector interest rates were one of the rationales for microfinance). Others argue, drawing on historical evidence, that relatively high interest rates are essential to attract savers, and that among loan schemes it is those which use the capital of their depositors that have been the most successful.[81] It is important to note at the same time that charging high interest rates to very poor people may be counter-productive to the goals of reducing poverty and social exclusion.

Organisational and financial sustainability

There is widespread debate among microfinance practitioners about the importance of the goal of financial sustainability. While some argue that this goal should be paramount in order to ensure the continued delivery of financial services, others have found that aiming for financial sustainability diverts organisations away from providing services of greatest relevance to the poorest people.[82]

Experience has shown that full sustainability — defined as the ability to cover the full market cost of funding the portfolio of services (as well as all operational costs) — is very rare among microfinance organisations. Yet historical evidence based on an analysis of loan funds in nineteenth-century Europe suggests that such initiatives can have long lives (of at least several decades), but that the nature and structure of the organisation and its sensitivity to the local environment are the critical factors in bringing about such longevity.[83]

Among some donors involved in international microfinance, the emphasis on the financial sustainability of the institution has diverted attention away from the issue of organisational form and also from the issue of 'borrower sustainability' (what kinds of impact are made by microfinance on its users, and how long the impact lasts).[84] As we have seen, microfinance initiatives take a wide range of forms, from small savings and credit groups at one extreme to commercial banks at the other. Large commercial financial institutions may appear to be the most financially sustainable, and they have the capacity to provide microfinancial services to a large number of people. However, they are unable to provide complementary services, which may be just as important, if not more so, for addressing poverty. Moreover, commercial objectives may cause them to take decisions which do not serve the needs of poor people. Indeed this has been one of the causes of the economic decline of neighbourhoods in the United States and Britain, as banks and other financial-service providers have refused to reinvest in their locality or have withdrawn from disadvantaged areas altogether.

Local membership-based financial institutions, such as community credit unions, seem then to be more appropriate to the needs of poor people. Because of their ownership structure, they are less likely to abandon their locality and more likely to recycle capital locally, rather than investing it outside the neighbourhood. However, such institutions may suffer from the difficulties set out at the end of Chapter 3; they may not achieve adequate scale to be run professionally; and they may be less secure in terms of providing safe savings facilities, unless they are adequately regulated.

There are no ready-made answers to such organisational dilemmas. Instead the answers must again depend on the objectives and context for the provision of microfinancial services. Whatever the answers, the challenge remains great. As Hulme and Mosley express it:

> *the success of institutions such as the Grameen Bank and BancoSol in 'walking the tightrope' between ineffective targeting and financial failure comes to be seen as something straight-forward and inevitable, their many experiments and changes of direction are obscured and the failure of many institutions who have tried to emulate them have been cast into outer darkness. Walking a tightrope is what micro-finance remains, and it is right to emphasise the risks run by those who undertake it and to salute the achievement of the institutions ... who have done so successfully. They have achieved something thought by most people, until about ten years ago, to be impossible.*[85]

SUMMARY AND CONCLUSIONS

In 1998, many Grameen Bank members were threatened by a natural catastrophe. Widespread floods made it impossible for them to continue with repayment instalments, and the Bank, along with other micro-finance institutions, was forced to appeal to international donors and others to enable it to make bridging loans.[86] This was a tragic demonstration of the impact of the wider environment on the performance of microfinance institutions. In other Asian countries, other kinds of warning came from the collapse of formal financial institutions. The plummet of the Russian rouble caused a rush to withdraw savings to which banks could not respond. The prospects and capacities of microfinance institutions to reduce poverty and social exclusion are dependent in part on macro-level processes and events. While access to deposit facilities makes an important difference to the lives of many poor people, the expansion of savings requires proper attention to regulation and the wider economic and political context.

International experience demonstrates the possibility of broadening access to financial services for many more people than can currently access formal banks. Loans provided for micro-enterprises in Bangladesh have enabled millions of women either to make productive investments or to smooth consumption. Even for the many women who have passed control of a loan-financed investment to another (often male) household member, there may be benefits in terms of their status and autonomy within the household. The process of organising collectively, indeed being involved in organisation building at all, can be constructive and may enable people to take greater control over other aspects of their lives.

Microfinance can and has helped many people to cope with poverty and social exclusion better. For some, not generally the very poorest, poverty and social exclusion have been reduced. On the other hand, microfinance interventions have not changed the shape of demand for what people produce, nor the unequal structures of social and economic relations which determine, to a large degree, the opportunities and constraints that operate in people's lives. A careful, context-sensitive approach is required to avoid making exaggerated claims for microfinance: lending beyond people's capacity to repay, for example, only compounds their problems. An approach attuned to reducing poverty and social exclusion will examine at each stage the impact of microfinance on inequality and on livelihood possibilities.

It may be that the most effective way of expanding the latter involves larger loans to employment-generating business, rather than attempting to make individual entrepreneurs of the poorest people. Alternatively, as suggested by Sinha and Matin, products should be differentiated, so that poorer people can use microfinance to smooth consumption without getting into greater debt, and the relatively better-off among the poor are enabled to start their own businesses (although this may enhance inequality among the poor themselves). Both of these approaches involve an acknowledgement that microfinance practice needs to keep learning from experience and that there is no blueprint for success.

5 Microfinancial services in Britain

THOMAS FISHER

INTRODUCTION

CHAPTERS 2 and 3 of this book described the dimensions and causes of poverty and social exclusion, including rising inequality, in Britain, and current policies seeking to combat them. Chapter 4 reviewed international experiences of providing microfinancial services to see to what extent they have been able to tackle such issues in other countries. This chapter seeks to draw these strands together, to consider the potential of microfinancial services to combat poverty and social exclusion in Britain.

There are many different types of institution that provide microfinancial services in Britain, or which could potentially do so. In analysing ways in which microfinancial services can contribute to reducing poverty, financial exclusion, and social exclusion, it would be inappropriate to focus solely on those institutions that directly seek to address these issues (generally known as 'community finance initiatives' or CFIs). Even with the decline of bank branches, for example, mainstream financial-service providers still have a much wider outreach in Britain than in many countries in Africa, Asia, and Latin America, and often remain the largest providers of microfinancial services. Therefore the need for mainstream providers to take seriously their social responsibilities to poor and socially excluded individuals and neighbourhoods[1] is as important as the need for CFIs that may exclusively serve such individuals and neighbourhoods. Just as in most of the rest of the world, informal and semi-formal financial services (such as money-lenders) are also a major source of microfinancial services in Britain. The second section of this chapter therefore introduces the main types of financial institution that provide microfinancial services, and elaborates more specifically on the different types of CFI.

Previous chapters distinguished between microfinancial services for protection (for example against income fluctuations) and promotion (for example of micro-businesses). Money-transaction services, such as bill payment and cheque cashing, which help poor and socially excluded people to manage money better from day to day, and at less cost, are equally important. This chapter obseves these distinctions. The third section discusses institutions that provide access to personal financial services which can perform a protective role and enable better money management. The fourth section turns to promotional micro-credit for micro and small business, as well as introducing an approach to community finance based on neighbourhood regeneration, rather than just microfinancial services for individual poor and excluded people.

Two further sections review the sustainability of initiatives providing microfinancial services and the extent to which they can effect wider change beyond providing their immediate users with microfinancial services (thus directly addressing the last of the three questions set out in the introduction to this book). A final section summarises the chapter.

To address the complex issues of poverty, financial exclusion, and social exclusion, money-advice services[2] and financial literacy are clearly as important as microfinancial services. Over-use of financial services may lead individuals into excessive debt in particular: debt enquiries are now the second largest area of work for the Citizens' Advice Bureaux, for example.[3] As the evidence from this chapter suggests, greater financial literacy could help those on low incomes to gain access to more appropriate and cheaper financial services.[4] Clearly, the provision of microfinancial services and of money-advice and financial-literacy services needs to be integrated into initiatives to tackle poverty and social exclusion.[5] Given the focus of this book, however (on microfinancial services to address poverty and social exclusion, and what lessons can be learned for Britain from international experience), this chapter concentrates primarily on microfinancial services. Indeed, in spite of the growth of microfinancial services in the South in particular, there is little relevant experience of complementary money-advice services and financial literacy to draw on. This is an area in which learning is as likely to flow from North to South, reversing the broad direction of learning on microfinancial services from South to North, which underlies the structure of this book also.

INSTITUTIONS PROVIDING MICROFINANCIAL SERVICES IN BRITAIN

Table 5.1 sets out the range of financial institutions and the services they provide that are of potential relevance for an agenda to reduce poverty, financial exclusion, and social exclusion. The table illustrates the wide range of institutions, including 'mainstream' financial institutions, non-bank credit, offered for example by money-lenders, and community finance initiatives. The table also illustrates the wide range of financial services: money-transaction services, such as bill payment and cheque cashing; protective financial services, for example savings and insurance; and promotional services, for example credit for micro-business.

The table does not include more informal sources of financial services, such as family and friends, credit accounts at the local corner shop, and informal community-based savings and loan schemes. All of these providers of financial services are important for poor and socially excluded people and they demonstrate the enormous diversity of financial services that may be available, and the multiple sources that a low-income household may be using at any one time. In this chapter, however, the focus is on those institutions and services set out in Table 5.1. Herbert and Kempson provide a detailed description of the use of credit, including credit from informal sources, among three ethnic minorities.[6]

Table 5.1: Financial institutions and microfinancial services with potential for addressing unemployment, poverty, financial exclusion, and social exclusion

Type of financial institution	Existing or potential microfinancial services
Banks and building societies	Basic banking service for those on low incomes[7] Personal loans (including credit-card facilities) Micro-business loans Small home-improvement loans Insurance services for those on low incomes
Post Office	Cheque cashing, including benefits and state pension payments Micro-savings and other financial products through Girobank and National Savings Bank Bill-payment and money-transmission services
Social Fund	Emergency loans at no interest for people on state benefits, but with repayments deducted directly from benefit payments
Local-authority and other public-sector loan funds	Grants and small loans for business start-ups in particular
Small Firms Loan Guarantee Scheme	Loan guarantees for bank loans to businesses (although currently restricted to loans over £5,000)
Money-lenders, pawnbrokers, cheque-cashing bureaux	Micro-loans for paying bills; purchasing goods and services; smoothing income fluctuations; emergencies Cash advances against cheques

Table 5.1: Financial institutions and microfinancial services with potential for addressing unemployment, poverty, financial exclusion, and social exclusion (continued)

Type of financial institution	Existing or potential microfinancial services
Hire-purchase companies, mail-order firms, local shops	Goods on credit
Credit unions	Savings in the form of shares Micro-loans (as a multiple of savings) Some other services, such as home-contents insurance Potentially, more micro-business loans from credit unions for micro-businesses
Micro-credit funds	Micro-loans for setting up new businesses, as well as for existing micro-businesses
Community loan funds	Loans for start-up and existing businesses Loans for charities, social and community enterprises[8] Loans for worker co-operatives Potentially, loans for home-improvement
Mutual-guarantee societies	Pooling savings of member businesses Accessing business loans from banks
Social banks	Loans for charities, social and community enterprises
Local Exchange Trading Systems (LETS) and other alternative currencies[9]	Local currency for trading services and some goods without cash among members

The rest of this section elaborates in greater detail on the different types of community finance initiative (CFI) in Britain, which are likely to be less familiar to the reader. While the response of recent developmental initiatives that seek to provide financial services to the poor and socially excluded in the South can be broadly categorised as microfinance, this is not the case in Britain. In Britain there has been a growth in community finance initiatives,[10] only some of which provide, for example, loans which could be classified as microfinancial services in terms of their size.

The recent origins of community finance in Britain date back to the 1960s and 1970s, when pioneers in the co-operative sector established the first credit union and the first community loan fund.[11] These differed from previous state-led initiatives by being market-based and led typically by the non-profit sector. Pioneers in Britain include Mercury Provident (now Triodos Bank), Industrial Common Ownership Finance (ICOF), Hackney Business Venture, and The Prince's Youth Business Trust (now The Prince's Trust). Their experience over 10 to 25 years has inspired a second wave of initiatives from the early 1990s onwards.

Community finance initiatives in Britain are diverse. They address differing needs and sectors, using differing financial mechanisms and organisational structures. Most, however, can be grouped into six models, as follows.[12]

Credit unions are not-for-profit, co-operative institutions for saving and borrowing, whereby members with a common bond save in the form of shares, which are then re-lent to members. There are three types of common bond: the work place (employee credit unions); a locality (community CUs); or an association such as a church group (associational CUs). Some 220,000 people now benefit from the services of 530 credit unions in England, Scotland, and Wales; 152 credit unions serve a further two hundred thousand members in Northern Ireland, which has seen the fastest growth of credit unions. While primarily geared to personal finance, a few credit unions are beginning to provide loans for self-employment and micro-enterprise.

Alternative currencies: Local Exchange Trading Systems (LETS) allow members in a local area to trade services and goods among each other, using a local currency rather than the national currency. The currency consists not of coins or notes, but of credits and debits which are recorded against members' accounts. There are now about 450 LETS in Britain, with an estimated membership of 40,000.[13] 'Time money', recently introduced in Britain, is an alternative currency based on the exchange of time.[14]

Micro-credit funds make very small loans to micro-entrepreneurs, typically working as sole traders, or in business with family or friends. The Prince's Trust, which lends to unemployed youth, is the largest initiative in the UK providing micro-loans. Three initiatives to extend micro-loans, as well as some pooled savings, to women on low incomes or welfare are currently being developed.[15] There are also draft proposals for a new national micro-credit initiative to serve existing micro-entrepreneurs, especially those just beyond the business start-up phase.[16]

Community loan funds serve community regeneration initiatives by making capital available. Such loan funds are usually charitable, but not exclusively so. There are currently 11 community loan funds in the UK, with assets of over £74 million, about half available for loans (as opposed to equity); further loan funds are under development.[17] Community loan funds have helped to lever in additional commercial investment (in ratios of up to 1:10), as well as subsidies.

Mutual-guarantee societies are formal associations of small and medium-sized enterprises which pool their savings in banks, so that they can offer collective guarantees which help them to obtain bank loans and achieve better lending and deposit rates. Their aim is to enhance the members' growth and stability. Over the last four years, eight mutual-guarantee societies have developed in Britain.

Social banks are for-profit financial-service providers dedicated, typically in their constitution, to social or environmental objectives. Triodos Bank is the largest of these in the UK, though still very small by mainstream banking standards. Unity Trust is a bank established with a focus on trade unions, which also lends to community initiatives. In the USA, mainstream banks have also established social and community development banking subsidiaries, largely to meet the requirements of community reinvestment legislation.[18]

Together, CFIs in the UK serve directly or indirectly around half a million people and are worth over £400 million (£240m with credit unions; £96m with loan and micro-credit funds; and £74m with social banks[19]). The number of CFIs has risen fourfold over the last five years. Of these, only the credit unions, alternative currencies, the micro-credit funds, and some loans extended by the community loan funds can be defined as microfinancial services in terms of their loan size. Moreover, except for the credit unions, none of the above community finance initiatives provides other microfinancial services (apart from loans) to directly address financial exclusion from personal financial services. Mutual-guarantee societies pool their members' savings, and social banks provide savings products, but the former generally serve small and medium-sized enterprises, which may be excluded from business finance, and the latter serve social investors,[20] who are generally larger or wealthier than the typical user of micro-deposit services.

However, we should not ignore many of the CFIs in Britain because they do not provide microfinancial services. In Chapter 4 Ben Rogaly questioned the sometimes exclusive focus of microfinancial-service providers on promoting self-employment among the poorest, suggesting that generating employment might be more appropriate. The tradition of community finance in the North has much to offer to practice in the South, in terms of the value of neighbourhood and local economic reinvestment and regeneration, rather than a simple focus on individual users. Many of the loans extended by CFIs in Britain seek to promote employment by supporting new or existing businesses. Some loans also support charities and community enterprises, for example, that seek to address issues of poverty and social exclusion directly.

Access to personal financial services

Earlier chapters explored the potential not only for micro-loans for business to raise incomes (promotional microfinancial services), but also for financial services to smooth fluctuations in incomes and provide protection against sudden falls (protective microfinancial services). Such services include providing a place to save; access to micro-loans, for example in a crisis; and insurance. In modern Britain most people also need other key 'lifeline' financial services, for example for paying bills and cashing cheques. This is particularly important for poor and socially excluded individuals, who have to devote considerable time and energy to managing their meagre resources. The impact on people of not having access to these financial services, so-called financial exclusion, is an issue of increasing seriousness. It is not simply a question of cost or inconvenience. It is part of the interlocking dimensions of powerlessness and constraints that people face in poverty.

The providers of such 'lifeline' financial services are often the banks, building societies, the Post Office, and credit unions, as well as other financial-service providers such as money-lenders, pawnbrokers, mail-order firms, and cheque-cashing bureaux. Kempson suggests that the first group provides up-market (or mid-market) financial services, while those in the second provide down-market services.[21] The performance of each of these is considered in turn below.

However, it is not just a matter of access, but also a question of the *use* of financial services. There has been a significant rise in the number of low-income households taking credit, from 22 to 69 per cent between 1980 and 1989. Over the same period, the number of households reporting debt problems rose from 1.3 to over 2 million.[22] 'The growth in consumers' use of credit has coincided with a huge increase in the numbers of consumers who can no longer manage their debts.'[23] It is in this context that money-advice services and greater financial literacy are so important, as suggested above.

Banks, building societies, and the Post Office

Six to nine per cent of adults in Britain do not have a current or savings account, and these are often the individuals who suffer from multiple disadvantages.[24] In some cases this lack of access is a result of self-exclusion; for example, more people expect banks to refuse them an account than are actually turned down. In most cases, however, the banks and building societies are failing to provide an appropriate service which would allow such people to manage money cheaply without the danger, for example, of overdrawing their account and being charged heavily as a result. In Chapter 4 Ben Rogaly cites the example of Bank Rakyat Indonesia, a large public bank which discovered a profitable way of introducing appropriate financial services (in this case savings) to the rural population of Indonesia. In Britain, however, bank-branch closures are affecting disadvantaged areas most,[25] in some cases removing local access to banks altogether.

Kempson and Whyley, Lynch and Haidar, and the Office of Fair Trading have all argued for a basic banking product appropriate to the needs of low-income customers.[26] Because such a product would not provide access to overdraft facilities, the banks would face little risk, although such customers may not be particularly profitable.

Even without a basic banking product at present, banks need to deal more appropriately with existing customers who fall on hard times. In Chapter 2 Ben Rogaly suggested that moving in and out of income poverty is common, and partly caused by adverse shocks, such as losing a job or separating from a partner. The National Consumer Council's assessment of how banks deal with their customers at such times is disturbing, in spite of significant improvements in the code of banking practice. In the worst cases, banks can push customers into 'an ever-increasing spiral of debt', put their housing and access to utilities in jeopardy, and leave them with 'no income ... for day-to-day living expenses'.[27]

For many living on low incomes or benefits, or lacking access to personal banking services, the Post Office is a major supplier of microfinancial services. In particular, it encashes benefit cheques and state pension cheques, as well as providing services for paying bills and transmitting money, for example through postal orders. In this way the Post Office provides key 'lifeline' financial services for poor and socially excluded people. The Post Office also acts as agent for Girobank and National Savings, and has recently been developing personal banking and insurance services. 'In 1996 the Post Office began to trial a range of low-cost financial services within a number of English regions. The products included a personal banking service (as part of a joint venture with the Co-operative Bank), life assurance, as well as health and critical-illness insurance.' As the Managing Director of Post Office Counters has suggested, 'in many communities post offices are replacing banks to meet customers' needs'.[28]

Kempson suggests that the Post Office is best placed to manage what might be called a 'benefits bank', which could also provide low-cost micro-loans to low-income households.[29] However, the Post Office is not servicing some of the neighbourhoods suffering the worst disadvantage. A survey of 20 of the most deprived local-authority estates in 1994 found that only five of them had a post office;[30] post offices in rural areas are also being closed. This is partly because benefits are increasingly being transferred directly into bank accounts, thus threatening the viability of post offices which provide weekly or fortnightly payments in cash. However, if the Post Office were to operate a 'benefits bank', which continued to make regular cash payments, as well as providing micro-loans, financial viability might be better assured.[31]

Some of the remaining building societies may also seek to develop products for low-income customers as part of developing their mutuality in practice. Lynch and Haidar[32] cite the case of the Cambridge Building Society Limited:

> *Launched in 1997 with the Cambridge Housing Society, a local housing association, the New Horizons Savings and Loan Scheme [of the building society] offers a savings and loan account to tenants of [the association]. A person can open an account with £1, getting round the high minimum balance account problem caused by carpetbagging. Savings can be made by post or at an office of the building society or the main office of Cambridge Housing Society. A loan can be applied for after saving regularly for 12 weeks up to twice the amount saved with a first time maximum of £500. If this is repaid over a period of 24 months then a person will be entitled to a loan up to three times the savings balance with a maximum of £1,000. A loan committee comprising tenants and staff from the building society and the housing association will decide whether the loan criteria are met. The interest rate on the loan is 1% a month, the same as that of a credit union. ... It is important to note that there is a carrot for the building society in a deposit of an interest earning lump sum by the housing association with the building society to act as a guarantee fund. The interest rate differential between the savings and loan rates will be apportioned between the building society and the housing association as a contribution towards running the scheme.*

It is possible that the recent tendency of supermarkets to offer banking services may also extend the outreach of financial services in low-income areas. 'The loyalty cards that form the basis for the entry of firms such as Tesco and Sainsbury's into the retail banking market provide databases rich in information on the spending behaviour of customers. The information from such cards, linked to ... other ... information, might make it possible to produce the kind of detailed characteristic information which is currently unavailable for poorer members of the community and might in turn make it easier to identify who are good loan risks.'[33] However, it is yet to be seen whether the supermarkets will target poor neighbourhoods and accept low-income customers for their financial services. Kempson and Whyley argue that supermarkets providing banking services are often 'some distance away from where people on low incomes live. And the cut-price supermarkets used by such households are not the ones offering banking facilities.'[34] Likewise, investigations by the Office of Fair Trading into supermarket pricing policies, including stores in low-income areas, suggest the need for caution in assuming a strong commitment by supermarkets to poorer consumers.

The examples of the Post Office and some building societies demonstrate that it is possible to provide financial products and services that can facilitate the access of low-income households to basic banking services. However, initiatives for this have been few and far between among mainstream financial-service providers, and even the Post Office faces difficulty in providing financial services in some of the most disadvantaged areas. There may well be a case for a right under legislation to have a basic banking facility, as exists in Sweden and France.[35]

Money-lending, mail-order firms, and cheque-cashing

Because banks and building societies do not offer a suitable product for potential low-income customers, and because of bank closures in disadvantaged neighbourhoods, low-income households are increasingly resorting to money-lenders, pawnbrokers, mail-order firms, and cheque-cashing bureaux (the down-market sources of credit). As the Chief Executive of one of the largest money-lending companies puts it: 'The banks are all leaving this market. Every time they close a branch, every time they cut staff, there are more people dropping into my market.'[36]

The popular image of money-lenders is of loan sharks who encourage the poorest and most vulnerable to get into debt, and who resort to threats and violence if borrowers do not repay. There are undoubtedly examples of such practices, especially among unlicensed money-lenders, and all money-lenders charge very high interest rates. (APRs often range from 100 to 500 per cent.[37])

However, research conducted by Rowlingson[38] suggests that licensed money-lenders provide an essential service to those who have few alternatives, and they rarely resort to threats and violence. This section draws on Rowlingson's research. However, because that research focused only on licensed money-lenders, it cannot reflect adequately on the extent of bad practice within unlicensed money-lending.

Rowlingson estimates that at least three million people borrow money from licensed money-lenders, making such lenders one of the main providers of microfinancial services in Britain. Most customers are from low-income households, and many are women. The majority are employed in paid work, although it is often low-paid manual work, while a sizeable minority are either unemployed, 'economically inactive', or retired. Most are council tenants. Most of the money-lenders' collecting agents are women, and it is often the women in borrower households who interact with them.

However, money-lenders do not lend to the poorest: 'Money-lenders were reluctant to take on very poor people as customers. Those groups with a restricted access to licensed money-lending included the long-term unemployed, lone parents, pensioners and those living in areas with a crime problem. ... The least attractive customers were people who were desperate for money or living in particular areas.'[39] Likewise, Kempson found that about half of money-lenders' customers had a bank or building-society account.[40] These facts suggest that some of the individuals facing the worst multiple disadvantage do not have access even to licensed money-lending.

Rowlingson found that customers borrowed from money-lenders to buy consumer items, often clothes for children, for example, although also some 'luxury' goods such as foreign holidays; to smooth income levels that fluctuated because of insecure jobs and periods in and out of employment; to manage their meagre resources: 'They were living long-term on low income and found it difficult to save up for bills and provide any basic household goods' (p71).

These uses demonstrate that money-lenders are meeting immediate needs of low-income households for protective credit. A typical loan may average £100, although customers may take more than one, so that the average loan balance is around £300 to £400. In spite of paying very high rates on such loans, borrowers continue to use and repay money-lenders regularly, partly to ensure that they retain access to such credit when needed.[41]

Why then do poor people use money-lenders? Ford and Rowlingson point to three reasons.[42] The first is financial exclusion, where some households are denied access to cheaper alternative sources of credit (or believe they will be denied such access). However, other households do have access to alternatives, and may select money-lenders by preference, 'in particular a preference for cash transactions,[43] for a weekly budgeting cycle, and for processes that were informal and nonbureaucratic', including friendly relationships that develop between borrowers and collecting agents, especially when both are women. Money-lenders are willing to provide very small loans, and collect payments on a weekly basis at a convenient time.[44] In a sense, borrowing from a money-lender was seen as an alternative to saving, because, while it was always difficult to put money away each week, the knowledge that a collector would be knocking at the door was an extra incentive to ensure that the money was there. But if they did miss the odd payment, there were no default charges.'[45] This suggests that money-lenders have successfully adapted their services to meet the complex day-to-day financial and money-management needs and preferences of low-income households, as described in Chapter 2. For alternative microfinancial-service providers to compete against such well-adapted services will clearly be a challenge.

The third reason advanced by Ford and Rowlingson is that money-lenders seek to promote and maintain their business markets, and many agents are paid on a commission basis, giving them strong incentives to push loans on to customers[46] (incentives restrained only by the risk of customers defaulting). This is another factor, in addition to interest costs, that often makes the services of money-lenders damaging to low-income customers, who may be encouraged to take on too much debt. In most cases this does not involve physical intimidation; however, agents manipulate the close social relationships they have with borrowers.

There are more than 1,000 licensed money-lenders in the UK. In 1996 the largest enjoyed a rate of return on equity on its lending business of 43 per cent and a bad-debt ratio of 5 per cent.[47] The profitability of such lending suggests that there might be room in the market for alternative, socially responsible providers of microfinancial services to low-income households, offering lower rates of interest.

In addition to money-lenders, many low-income households also use mail-order firms, which are in fact their main source of credit. 'Mail order frequently allows a large number of very small payments over time, so that the purchase of goods becomes possible out of a very low income.' The mail-order industry, used by low-income and middle-income households, is growing rapidly.[48]

Cheque-cashing bureaux are also expanding, especially since the 1992 Cheque Act, which has meant that most cheques are crossed 'account payee only'. Cheque-cashers 'operate through pawnbrokers, insurance companies, weekly collected credit companies and letting agents as well as shops that concentrate on cheque cashing. ... Charges are typically around 7 per cent of the value of the cheque, plus a handling charge of £2, although they vary from company to company. ... Prospective customers need only provide official proof or their identity ... and of their address.'[49]

The growth of money-lending, mail-order and cheque-cashing facilities demonstrates that outreach and access to financial services are at least as important as costs. They provide a service which meets the needs of many on low incomes who may also face unstable patterns of work and income and who have access to few alternative sources of credit. Such protective credit can be critical for smoothing income fluctuations or allowing borrowers to purchase essential or basic consumer items.

However, costs are very high, often well beyond what people on low incomes can reasonably afford. The unequal power relationship between money-lenders and their clients is equally problematic. Not only can collection agents encourage borrowers to take on excessive debt, they can also choose to enforce repayment, for instance by having household goods repossessed (or threatening to do so), in a way that is severely damaging to those who can least afford such losses. Moreover, these credit sources are not available to the poorest and most disadvantaged, often excluding the long-term unemployed, lone parents, the elderly, and those living in areas seriously affected by crime.

Lack of competition is probably the primary reason why money-lenders can charge such high interest rates and enjoy such high returns. There is clearly room for competing products supplied by the banks, building societies, the Post Office, credit unions, and socially responsible money-lending.[50] The high profits enjoyed by the larger money-lending companies suggest that there are sufficient margins for a socially motivated initiative to provide microfinancial services targeted at these markets, especially for potential borrowers who may not want to commit as much time as is needed to set up credit unions — which are the subject of the next sub-section.

Credit unions[51]

Credit unions can potentially provide an alternative source of micro-loans. They provide incentives for members to save (in the form of shares). Members can then borrow a multiple of their shares (for example, up to four times the value of their shares). The most obvious advantage of credit unions over money-lenders is the cost of their loans (1 per cent a month, equivalent to 12.68 per cent APR). Loan amounts can also be very small, and can be secured with relatively low transaction costs, thus potentially acting as protective credit in times of crisis. As mutual institutions, in contrast to banks or money-lenders dealing with individual customers in isolation, credit unions also have the potential to provide opportunities for inclusion within new social networks, while the volunteers who sustain the operations of many credit unions may also benefit in terms of personal growth and new skills. Credit unions are therefore, in principle, ideally suited to address some of the multiple dimensions of poverty, financial exclusion, and social exclusion set out in Chapter 2.

The origins of credit unions go back to some of the earliest attempts to address financial exploitation and poverty. The credit union movement traces its origins to a co-operative loan bank set up by the burgomaster of Weyersbuch in Germany, Friedrich Wilhelm Raiffeisen, who was appalled by the activities of money-lenders who 'fastened like a vampire on the rural population' during a famine in 1846-7. Samuel Smiles, the Victorian doyen of self-help, argued for 'penny banks' to help poor households to save on a regular basis. And in France the Caisses de Credit Municipal, which serve one million, mainly low-income consumers, date back to the example of an Italian monk in 1462, who established the 'Monte-di-pieta' bank (still in operation) to fight usury.

While currently credit unions are typically not a 'poor person's bank' in Britain, their record is sufficient to demonstrate the following facts:

- low-income consumers can and want to save;
- there are effective, mutual ways of organising the delivery and recovery of credit which reduces operational costs;
- given appropriate financial services, low-income households are able to use them effectively, both to reduce their economic vulnerability and to increase disposable incomes.

The most successful credit unions have been able to establish an efficient and reliable saving and lending service based on convenient opening hours, accessible collection points, and a quick response to enquiries for information, loans, and services on offer. Some of the longer-established and larger credit unions are providing additional services, such as home-contents insurance; debt consolidation and rescue loans; specific savings and budgeting accounts (for Christmas, holidays, weddings, and funerals, for example); and bill-payment services.

More and more Citizens' Advice Bureaux, which devote so many resources to debt advice, 'are helping to set up credit unions ... as a forward-thinking and sustainable response which supplements the crucial remedial and bread and butter work of debt advice. ... Established credit unions can perform a valuable role in buying up debts attracting high interest rates.'[52]

However, the credit-union movement is held back from addressing issues of poverty and social exclusion by its two-speed growth pattern. Work-place credit unions, whose members are employed and enjoy higher average incomes, are growing much faster, in terms of assets and membership, than community credit unions.[53] Thus, credit unions serving people in society who need it the most are growing at a slower rate, while credit unions that serve members who need it least are growing at a faster rate. The irony is that a number of community credit unions are uncomfortable about growth, preferring to remain very small. They do not aspire to the growth rate of some of the most successful Community Development Credit Unions in the United States and Canada.[54] Remaining small may have advantages in terms of members' direct engagement in an organisation where most people know each other, but such a strategy fails to address the extensive need for financial services of those excluded from mainstream service providers or paying heavily for equivalent services from money-lenders and others.

While the access provided by credit unions to affordable savings and borrowing facilities in disadvantaged areas is therefore widely acclaimed, few community credit unions nationally have more than 500 members; few have sufficient assets to employ paid staff; and few are readily able to expand to open up services to several thousand members in their service areas without appropriate developmental support, training, and technical assistance.

Conaty and Mayo[55] argue that to address social needs more effectively, community credit unions will have to grow in number and size, without losing their strong value-base, such as their commitment to their members and their roots within their local communities. This will require a new Credit Union Act, currently under review by the government, which grants credit unions powers to offer new services and provides more opportunities for those focusing on disadvantaged areas to draw on external resources, for example from churches or social investors.[56] It will also require the following:

- new organising strategies;
- a more proactive role on the part of organisations such as settlements, Citizens' Advice Bureaux, and development trusts in acting as local 'social incubators' for community credit unions;[57]
- a national resourcing and development framework;[58]
- greater collaboration with mainstream financial-service providers such as banks and insurance companies.

Home-contents insurance[59]

In Chapter 2 Ben Rogaly reported that most home-insurance products are inappropriate and too costly for those on low incomes. Like those without current or savings accounts, those without home-contents insurance often suffer from multiple disadvantages: unemployment, low incomes, no bank accounts, deprived neighbourhoods. Since two-thirds of uninsured households are headed by unemployed or economically inactive individuals, they do not have access to insurance cover provided through trade unions and public-service employers: an example of how exclusion from the labour force can lead to social and financial exclusion.

Some local authorities and housing associations, however, act as intermediaries, through which insurance companies can provide home-contents insurance to a potentially wide pool of low-income tenants. In many cases this involves *Insure with Rent* schemes, whereby premiums are paid along with rent payments. In other cases, tenants have to pay the insurance company directly, for example through the Post Office.

Through their postal survey, Whyley et al identified 130 such schemes, covering some 200,000 tenants. About half of local authorities and one-fifth of housing associations run such schemes. The products provided are more appropriate to low-income households than those provided directly by insurance companies. For example, the economies of scale involved allow a reduction of up to one-third on premiums. The schemes offer a range of payment options, including regular cash instalments. And they allow those insured to make the type of small claim that is often typical of low-income households. Some schemes are also accompanied by improvements to home security, in order to reduce risks on the part of the social-housing providers.

Through their national associations, credit unions also have access to home-contents insurance appropriate to low-income households. The main drawback is the limited coverage of community credit unions in particular, as suggested in the previous section. Some charities, such as Age Concern, also offer insurance services.[60]

The consequences of not having home-contents insurance can be severe, with low-income households that are burgled, or suffer fire or flood, turning to money-lenders for credit, running up debts (for example through rent arrears), relying on the Social Fund, or simply doing without: in other words not replacing their stolen or damaged goods. In this way a crisis drives such households further into poverty. Whyley et al argue that this is unnecessary, that potentially 6 million low-income customers could be protected from such consequences through appropriate home-contents insurance, especially if it were offered through an intermediary such as a housing association.

Local exchange trading systems (LETS)[61]

LETS allow members in a local area to trade services and goods, using a local currency rather than the national currency. The currency consists not of coins or notes, but of credits and debits which are recorded against members' accounts. A directory contains descriptions of what members wish to trade, and transactions are recorded in a central accounting system. The credit and debit balances that result can in effect be regarded as micro-savings and overdrafts. As interest is neither paid nor levied on these balances, members have access to credit without interest and collateral.

LETS have the potential to address many of the issues of poverty and social exclusion outlined in Chapter 2. For example, Barnes et al argue that 'LETS has considerable potential for low income communities. Through LETS, people have access to goods and services they might not otherwise have been able to afford in the cash economy. They are able to improve their skills and sense of self-worth by offering services that other people value, and pay for in local currency.[62] The number of people they are in regular contact with expands, making it easier to hear of jobs and get personal support when needed.' Social networks are enhanced not just through contacts made while trading, but also by reducing or removing cash costs that may deter those on low incomes from taking part in community life.

Specific groups may benefit in particular, such as the unemployed and women. Barnes et al. observe that 'Unemployed people are more likely to join LETS than people with jobs, and do more trading than other members.' 'Women appear to be active in LETS trading. ... The large pay differentials for different tasks in the formal economy are not replicated in LETS trading. Indeed, many systems have reported that traditional low-paid work in the formal economy, such as childcare, is paid higher in LETS.'

By boosting local money-flows — as the local currency can be spent only on local businesses — LETS may also contribute to local economic development.

However, even though there were over 300 LETS in the UK in 1995 (there are now 450), Barnes et al could identify only seven in low-income neighbourhoods. The five of these that they studied were all struggling, and were not experiencing very active trading. Some of the causes identified arise from poverty, unemployment, and social exclusion: lack of confidence and self-esteem among potential members; crime; fears about losing benefits and hindering undeclared work for cash in the informal economy. This suggests there are distinct limits to the extent to which LETS can address poverty and social exclusion, especially without greater and more strategic promotional and development inputs.

Some would even argue that if LETS are given special treatment within the benefits system, for example, they may be marginalised as something for poor people on benefits. In the words of one of the early promoters of LETS, 'it won't do those in greatest need much good if their local money is exempt from assessment, if by that diversion we isolate them from the mainstream economy, and that is what this approach may do'. However, granted the growth of LETS in middle-class areas, they are unlikely to become identified with people on benefits, and the opportunities for work and social networks that LETS provide are more likely to allow them to re-enter the mainstream economy than isolate them from it.

Access to personal financial services: a summary

As described in chapter 2, the poor not only have low incomes, but they are also vulnerable to fluctuations in their income. Such vulnerability is caused by an increasingly 'flexible' labour market, and by crises which the poor may not have adequate incomes and assets to combat. Such factors contribute significantly to 'churning', whereby individuals may move in and out of income poverty. These dynamics of poverty suggest that microfinancial services which help poor people to protect themselves against such vulnerability are critical.

In their 'flight to quality', the banks have largely failed to provide basic banking products that might be appropriate to enable poor people to manage their money better, even though banks could do so with little risk to themselves (although such products are unlikely to be very profitable). The banks have also often failed to provide appropriate assistance to customers who fall on hard times. Instead, poor people turn to the Post Office, for example for cashing benefit cheques and for paying bills, and to the Social Fund, money-lenders, pawnbrokers, cheque-cashers, and mail-order firms for cash loans or for goods bought on credit. As we have seen in this chapter, licensed money-lenders provide credit to at least three million customers. However, there are major problems in using money-lenders: they charge very high interest rates, which poor people can ill afford, and may push them into over-indebtedness, potentially resulting in ever more serious consequences if they cannot repay. Moreover, even licensed money-lenders avoid the most disadvantaged neighbourhoods, especially if they perceive them to be dangerous — and such areas may not have a post office either.

There is clearly room for alternative, socially responsible providers of microfinancial services. The objective should be to widen the range of options that poor people can choose from in managing their money, so that they can develop the most appropriate mix of services for their individual needs.

Among community finance initiatives, credit unions, LETS, and most recently 'time money'[63] have the potential to address some of these needs, for example providing small affordable loans (in pounds, local currency, or time) to pay for essential goods and services or to smooth income fluctuations. Such initiatives not only provide more appropriate services (for example giving members incentives to save as well as access to loans), but also, through their mutuality, develop social networks, the absence of which is one of the main characteristics of social exclusion. LETS and time money also provide opportunities for unemployed members to develop work experience. However, the number of such community finance initiatives (CFIs) which have low-income members is still small. Indeed, their mutuality requires a degree of networking and community organisation that may be absent in the most disadvantaged neighbourhoods. This suggests that such CFIs can be appropriate for low-income individuals, although they need to be accompanied by additional interventions to address multiple disadvantages. In the most disadvantaged neighbourhoods, other interventions may be a prerequisite for the launch of such CFIs.

CFIs must also avoid the problem of 'ghettoisation', of becoming initiatives for low-income households with little potential for development or growth, but taking the pressure off mainstream financial-service providers to meet the needs of such households. Such a strategy risks increasing inequality by marginalising the already disadvantaged still further from the mainstream economy. The failure of a number of credit unions set up in the USA in the 1960s as anti-poverty vehicles under President Johnson's 'War on Poverty' Programme is instructive. Many community development credit unions in the USA now have a mixed membership of low-income and moderate-income savers, while the Community Reinvestment Act places social responsibilities on mainstream financial-service providers.

CFIs must also take care to provide secure and high-quality services for those on low incomes; they cannot be run in an informal or unprofessional manner. Deposits in particular must be safeguarded. More sophisticated financial products, such as insurance services, require significant financial expertise.

In some cases such services can be provided in collaboration, for example between credit unions which retail the product and insurance companies which service the product with actuarial and other expertise. This is certainly an option with home-contents insurance. A minority of low-income households have such insurance, which could protect them from the effects of burglary, floods, and other crises. Such crises often lead to a loss of assets, and hence a fall in wealth, which the poor are least able to afford and can often not replace. Insurance coverage provided through social landlords, credit unions, and others appear promising options here, as already demonstrated by a significant number of local authorities and housing associations.

Finally, this section on access to personal financial services has focused on services that meet the needs of day-to-day money management and short-term credit. Only insurance products looked beyond immediate needs. However, products to provide long-term financial security are equally essential, such as term and life insurance to provide security for families, and pensions to provide security in old age. Kempson and Whyley found that such financial products were considered extremely important by those on low incomes, but that current provision for them is highly inadequate.[64] This is not least the case in the face of a continuing decline in State pension provision, which is contributing significantly to the long-term financial risks faced by those on low incomes.

LOANS TO MICRO-BUSINESSES AND SMALL BUSINESSES[65]

So far this chapter has considered protective microfinancial and money-transaction services. The other important mechanism through which initiatives providing microfinancial services seek to address poverty and social exclusion is to use financial services (primarily credit) to promote employment, thereby integrating individuals into the labour force and, if the conditions of work are reasonable, enhancing their incomes and self-esteem. As suggested in the previous chapter, in the South the focus has largely been on self-employment for the poor. In the North, for example in the community-finance traditions in Britain and the USA, initiatives have also sought to promote enterprises that may hire workers and contribute to the development of the local economy.

There are various potential markets for micro-loans to businesses, which are set out in Table 5.2.[66] However, note that international experience, described in Chapter 4, suggests that micro-credit consists of a range of distinct and specialised financial products, not just the provision of occasional micro-loans.[67] For example, micro-credit initiatives may operate 'stepped lending' programmes, allowing micro-businesses to grow by providing ever-larger loans as soon as the previous loan is repaid on schedule. Or they may lend to 'peer groups' of micro-entrepreneurs who guarantee each other's loans, thereby significantly reducing transaction costs to the lender. As we shall see, there are very few initiatives in the UK that offer such distinct micro-credit products. The main providers of business credit are the banks, public-sector entities, and various types of community finance initiative.

Table 5.2: Potential markets for business micro-credit

Clients	Their needs in addition to micro-credit	Current practice
Unemployed	Business support (pre- and post-loan). Waivers to ensure that benefits are not removed while setting up in business.	The Prince's Trust for young unemployed. Self-employment option under New Deal.
Welfare recipients and those on very low incomes	Motivation and training to learn about different options (e.g. self-employment or further education) before taking loans. Benefit waivers for self-employment option. On-going business support.	Enterprise Rehearsal Ventures that allow some trial trading while on benefits. Three initiatives being developed for women: Full Circle Fund, Norwich; the Glasgow Women's Micro-credit Project; and Sustainable Strength, Birmingham. On-going negotiations on benefit waivers. Coverage of this market still very limited.
Micro-business start-ups	Business support (pre- and post-loan)	Gaps remain in spite of banks' business start-up programmes; public grants and loan-funds; community finance initiatives; Business Links, Enterprise Agencies, etc.
Micro-businesses beyond their start-up phase	Business support	The initiatives above could potentially service such businesses, but in practice very little finance and support are available, particularly for micro-businesses just beyond their start-up phase, but not yet conventionally bankable.
Businesses operating in the 'grey economy'	Integration into mainstream economy to allow them to access finance and business support. Integration within tax system.	In some cases the former Enterprise Allowance Scheme allowed people in the 'grey economy' to launch legitimate businesses. Individual loans from CFIs continue to demonstrate that there is a market here, but none explicitly targets it.

Bank loans to small businesses

Banks lend extensively to small and medium enterprises, usually in the form of overdrafts and term loans, although increasingly also for factoring and leasing.[68] Bank performance in this area has been carefully monitored by the Bank of England since the early 1990s, although there has in fact been a decline in bank lending to the sector since that time. The minimum loan size for small business lending is often £1,000 (the average is £7,000) suggesting that banks are a significant source of micro-loans for businesses. A major problem faced by banks in making such small loans is the high transaction costs and risks (many start-ups fail). As a result, banks have tended to ration such lending rather than increase interest rates to compensate for higher transaction costs and risks (as many initiatives providing microfinancial services in the South have done).[69] However, none of the banks has sought to develop distinct micro-credit products, such as 'stepped and peer lending', which provide alternative mechanisms for reducing transaction costs and risks.

The banks do not provide disaggregated data on their small-business lending which would allow a more careful analysis of the extent to which they are supporting businesses in the more disadvantaged areas. However, (i) the closure of bank branches in those areas, reducing opportunities for relationship banking and understanding of the local economy, (ii) the increasing use of centralised credit scoring, which often identifies disadvantaged areas as more risky than others, and (iii) the demand for loans received by community loan funds in those areas all suggest that the banks are not adequately meeting the needs of such businesses.[70] Of equal importance to an agenda of poverty and social exclusion, 'the small business literature does not deal with access to finance for people without any capital or credit history at all'.[71]

> *Micro and small businesses in disadvantaged communities are [therefore] most likely to face credit rationing: they are suffering more from bank branch closures; and the size of loans requested generally lies well below the average, while perceived risks may be above the average. This applies in particular to the smallest enterprises and start-ups in disadvantaged communities. These are most commonly lifestyle and family businesses, rather than enterprises with growth potential; they may lack detailed business accounts; and there will often be significant social and cultural gaps preventing clear communication and mutual understanding between bankers and potential borrowers.*[72]

The government has sought to encourage banks to lend to viable business propositions which lack security through the Small Firm Loan Guarantee Scheme (SFLGS), set up in 1981. However, demand from banks for the scheme has been poor: fewer than 7,000 loans a year, or on average just over one loan per bank branch per year. Moreover, all retail businesses, most services, and many crafts and arts businesses are excluded — the very types of lifestyle and retail business that ACCION, for example, has supported in the USA (see Chapter 4). Finally, while originally intended also for start-ups, the SFLGS is focusing increasingly on growth and high-tech firms, often medium-sized established firms. A special scheme for inner-city Task-force and City Challenge areas, which guaranteed loans of as little as £500, has been withdrawn, because take-up by the banks was too low. The minimum loan now guaranteed under the SFLGS is £5,000.

The overall evidence therefore suggests that the banks are not meeting the credit needs of business in the most disadvantaged areas, which could potentially address issues of poverty and social exclusion through generating employment and income. In disadvantaged areas in particular, there are of course likely to be constraints on the demand side as well as on the supply side, with many micro-entrepreneurs lacking the capacity to grow their businesses through effective use of credit that might be available to them. In such areas it is therefore critical to link the provision of micro-credit with effective non-financial business-support services.

Public-sector grant and loan funds[73]

In order to fill the gaps in micro-credit for businesses in disadvantaged areas, many local authorities have, since the 1980s, established loan funds to support small businesses, including start-ups as well as worker co-operatives. Many of these met with relatively little success, and their capital was quickly depleted. [74] The same thing happened to the majority of soft loan funds, typically around £500,000, to assist workers formerly employed in steel works, mines, and other declining industries to set up in business, following the changes in the structure of the labour market described in Chapter 2.

Revolving funds for small businesses have nevertheless become common practice. As many as one-quarter of local authorities have loan funds of various kinds. In the 1990s a new generation of funds has evolved under City Challenge and Single Regeneration Budget programmes, or through Training and Enterprise Councils and Business Links. The record of sustainability among these new funds has not been much better: almost one-fifth of such funds surveyed by Kingston University in 1993 had been closed by 1994.[75]

A few of the public-sector loan funds established in the 1980s have survived, especially when handed over to CFIs such as the Glasgow Regeneration Fund, Greater London Enterprise, Hackney Business Venture, and ICOF to manage (see the following section). In Northern Ireland, there are currently proposals to pass over responsibility for public-sector loan funds to the nascent Ulster Community Investment Trust.

The conclusion from the evidence to date suggests that the public sector obviously has a key role to play in addressing poverty and social exclusion through supporting employment generation, but in terms of financial-service provision this is best achieved in partnership with private actors and not typically as a direct lender. For existing public-sector funds, greater sustainability must be a higher priority, so that more of them survive to continue to serve their disadvantaged target areas or groups.

Micro-credit funds

There are few specialised micro-credit funds in Britain. The Prince's Trust (see Case Study A) is the largest provider of micro-loans, and seeks to address the needs of unemployed youth, which Chapter 2 identified as an important group among those who may be poor and socially excluded.

CASE STUDY A: PRINCE'S TRUST

The Prince's Trust is the largest micro-loan and business start-up agency in the country (there is also a separate trust for Scotland). Since its launch in 1983, the Trust has helped more than 40,000 unemployed or under-employed 18–30 year olds — including people from ethnic communities, disabled people, and ex-offenders — to start more than 35,000 businesses. The survival rate of these businesses after three years is higher than 60 per cent. Among those whose businesses do not survive, more than half go into further education, training, or employment.

The Trust extends loans up to £5,000 (average £2,500) to start up a business, repayable with 3 per cent interest over three years. The Trust also offers bursaries of up to £1,500 (£3,000 for groups) to almost half the businesses it supports. In 1997 the Trust gave loans totalling £7.2 million to 3,408 start-up businesses, and bursaries of £4.7 million.

Every new business is allocated a business mentor, a volunteer from the local business community who devotes a few hours each month to advise the new entrepreneur, calling in other expert help if necessary. ('This on-going available support is the one thing that contributes most to the high survival rates; it is probably more important than the money. Starting up a business is very lonely, and mentors provide a shoulder to cry on, or a kick up the backside.') Evaluations show that many of the young entrepreneurs value their mentors highly. As banks become more familiar with the Trust, they are also becoming more willing to lend to applicants, once they have a good business plan and access to a mentor.

In 1996-97 the Trust received grants of more than £12 million, had investments of around £12 million, and loans outstanding (after making provisions for potential loan write-offs) of £5.7 million. The Department for Education and Employment pays £2,500 for each person started in business still trading after 15 months. In 1996 a partnership between the government and the four main clearing banks was launched, generating a further £12 million over three years. In June 1999 The Prince's Trust launched a campaign to raise £100 million to create 30,000 new businesses by the year 2005, to which the government has pledged £50 million.

The Trust therefore has access to significant grant finance and voluntary support, itself awarding grants and providing for about 40 per cent of its loans outstanding. Nevertheless, in 1996-97 the total expenditure (including write-offs and provisioning) of the Trust amounted to less than £3,700 per young person supported, compared with the average of £8,500 a year that an unemployed claimant costs the Exchequer.

(Source: Trust documents and interview in 1998 with Roger Benson, Director of Public Sector Operations, The Prince's Trust)

However, none of the providers of micro-loans reviewed so far provides distinct micro-credit products, drawing on international experience, especially in the South. This challenge has been taken up by very recent initiatives, three targeted at low-income women and one proposed initiative (Street UK) which draws on Polish experience.

The three initiatives (the Full Circle Fund in Norwich (see Case Study B), the Glasgow Women's Micro-credit Project, and Sustainable Strength in Birmingham) are seeking to establish micro-credit funds targeted in particular at low-income women, including those living on welfare benefits, who wish to become self-employed. All intend to draw on the experience of the Grameen Bank and other initiatives in the South, by organising women into groups to guarantee each other's loans, and in some cases to pool their savings.

CASE STUDY B: THE FULL CIRCLE FUND

The Full Circle Fund was established by WEETU (Women's Employment, Enterprise, and Training Unit), which has worked for 12 years with low-income women in Norfolk. The Full Circle Fund sees itself as 'a national pilot for micro-credit through peer lending'. It is targeted at women in Norfolk who cannot obtain start-up or expansion money for their businesses from conventional lenders.

The Full Circle Programme comprises training (in three stages), access to loans, support from other women, help with child-care and travel costs, and social-policy initiatives, for example on benefit waivers. Women form 'lending circles' of three to six members who meet fortnightly. While they do not guarantee each other's loans fully, 5 per cent of any loan is put in an emergency fund kept in reserve in case of a default within the group.

Since May 1998, 150 participants have started the training component of the programme. Of these, 62 per cent are claiming benefits, 34 per cent are lone parents, 7 per cent are disabled or have long-term sickness, and 5 per cent are from ethnic minorities. Five lending circles have been started since the beginning of 1999.

The Full Circle Fund believes that current benefit waivers are inadequate for participants to develop sustainable businesses. 'Benefits are the main obstacle to the women we work with who want to set up in enterprise.' The Fund is proposing a two-year 'protected benefits' period.

(Source: presentation by Erika Watson and Jane Bevan of the Full Circle Fund, 1999)

These initiatives do not promote self-employment as a universal or easy solution for women on low incomes. They recognise the need for significant additional inputs such as training, confidence-building and support, and for providing a range of economic opportunities, whether employment, further education, or training. Ruth Pearson of WEETU comments: 'The enterprise route is only a possibility for a minority of welfare recipients, rather than being a magic solution for all those in poverty or facing unemployment or redundancy. However it does not preclude the probability that it might have potential for a significant number of people and should be explored in combination with other employment-creation, education, and training policies.'

The Prince's Trust and the three funds for women gain added significance in complementing the self-employment option under the New Deals (described in some detail in Chapter 3, under the heading *Active labour markets*).[76] This option was a late addition to the New Deals, and did not adequately consider the need for credit for the unemployed to become self-employed. There remains the issue of benefit waivers, with WEETU, for example, arguing that they are not large or sustained enough to allow women on benefits to test whether they really can be self-employed.[77]

A proposed new micro-credit initiative, Street UK, draws on the experience of the most prominent micro-credit initiative in the North, Fundusz Mikro in Poland. Street UK will promote group lending among micro-entrepreneurs, many of them on low and insecure incomes (although they are unlikely to be among the poorest). Street UK will not make soft loans or grants, and will target micro-businesses either just beyond their start-up phase or operating in the 'grey economy', drawing the latter into the mainstream economy.[78]

Community loan funds and social banks

There are several community loan funds and social banks in Britain,[79] serving the small business, social and community enterprise, housing, and charity sectors. These organisations seek to address the needs of disadvantaged neighbourhoods and groups. As David Brown of the Glasgow Regeneration Fund (GRF) comments, GRF lends to businesses in 'eight designated regeneration areas, which house 44 per cent of Glasgow's resident population and 66 per cent of its long-term unemployed. People within these areas suffer multiple deprivation; their exposure to enterprise is the corner shop.' GRF, established in 1993, has invested more than £2 million in 230 businesses, half of them start-ups, in these eight regeneration areas. These investments have created more than 1,400 jobs and saved a further 400 jobs at risk. Over 80 per cent of these assisted businesses trade beyond their first year.[80]

The loan funds thus lend not only for self-employment, but also to businesses which are likely to employ local people in disadvantaged areas, as well as to enterprises and charities that seek to provide social and community services, such as child-care and training for the unemployed. In so doing, they emphasise the need to generate paid employment, not just self-employment, in order to regenerate disadvantaged neighbourhoods and local economies. They also recognise that business is not sufficient to tackle the complex issues of poverty and social exclusion, and that social services which directly address non-economic needs are just as important. The Local Investment Fund, specifically targeted at charities, is described in Case Study C.

CASE STUDY C: THE LOCAL INVESTMENT FUND (LIF)

LIF is a charitable loan fund, established in 1994, which lends to charities that are unable to obtain all the funds they need from a bank. The Fund's capital totals £3 million, of which the then Department of the Environment gave £1 million, NatWest Bank £0.5 million, and about 30 other private companies £1.5 million. This is substantial capital for a pilot project, but 'to earn enough revenue, you just can't do this kind of work without a big head of steam'.

LIF has agreed 15 loans, totalling £1.4 million. Some examples of projects include:

- a community construction company which trains unemployed youth on probation;
- two social entrepreneurs providing care services to local black youth;
- an agency established by residents in inner-city Nottingham to provide computer and IT training for the long-term unemployed, ethnic minorities, and parents returning to work;
- premises purchased and refurbished by a Mencap[81] organisation.

'In real terms, and without double counting, we've created 303 jobs, preserved 65 jobs, and generated 550 training places.'

(Based on interview in 1999 with Roger Brocklehurst, Director, LIF)

Other examples of such finance providers are described below.

- **Triodos Bank,** an ethical bank which aspires 'to be seen as the bank for the social economy', operating in the Netherlands, Belgium, and Britain. The Bank lends only to 'value-led projects' with social and environmental objectives. In Britain projects in renewable energy, organic agriculture, social housing, and charities (such as schools, complementary medicine, and community hospitals) are prominent. An example is the Southdown Housing Association in Sussex, providing housing and support for people with special needs and learning difficulties.

- **Hackney Business Venture,** an independent Enterprise Agency established 14 years ago, managing five loan funds for small businesses in the borough, including one fund established under a City Challenge Area. Between June 1995 and June 1997 these funds provided £841,200 in loans and attracted a further £1.2 million in support from banks to just over 100 small businesses. About one-third are managed by women.

- **The Aston Reinvestment Trust (ART)**, seeking to attract and recycle investment funds in inner-city Birmingham to finance projects in housing, small business, community enterprise, social business, and energy efficiency. Examples of projects include a £7,000 loan, along with public grant support, which allowed an Aston painting and plating business to expand and hire five more workers; and a £5,000 loan which enabled a charity helping people recovering from alcohol and drug addiction to buy a second-hand van for furniture renovation and sales work.

However, these CFIs have also struggled with the transaction costs and risks of micro-loans. ART, for example, calculated that it could not lend below £2,000 and still cover its costs. None has yet followed international experience in stepped lending, abandoning the classic banking model of preparing a business plan to provide very small amounts and gradually increasing the size of subsequent loans depending on the repayment history of the borrower. The danger of this strategy is that it can lead borrowers to take on credit beyond their capacity to repay (see Chapter 4).

Mutual-guarantee societies and business credit unions

In Britain the existing initiatives in this category are still too few and too recent to allow a considered judgement of their success. There are currently eight pilot mutual-guarantee societies, although most members are likely to be small and medium-sized enterprises. Business credit unions, of which there are currently three, may be a more suitable vehicle for the smallest businesses.[82] The North London Chamber and Enterprise Credit Union has made loans of £250,000 since 1994, and also has a small fund to make loans of £500 to micro-businesses in trouble. It has made 14 such loans so far, and believes that 'all these people would have been foreclosed' without these loans.[83]

Promotional lending for micro and small enterprise: a summary

Protective microfinancial services do not allow the poor to enhance their incomes and assets (unless small loans are used for purchasing consumer-durables, for example). For this, poor people may require promotional microfinancial services, especially for micro-businesses. Chapter 2 identified changes in employment patterns as a critical factor contributing to poverty and social exclusion. In this chapter, it has thus been suggested that micro-credit which supported employment generation might contribute towards integrating excluded individuals into the workforce. Evidence suggests that since 1979 micro-enterprises have indeed generated more jobs than any other size of enterprise, and that around one million businesses are accounted for by sole traders and the self-employed.[84]

The extent to which micro-enterprises, and micro-credit to serve them, address poverty and social exclusion depends, in part, on perspectives on self-employment. Much self-employment among poor people is precarious, for which strong evidence is adduced in Chapter 3. On the other hand, self-employment can serve as a refuge from discrimination in the workplace, and part-time self-employment might be suited to women's greater needs for flexibility in employment. Self-employment may also serve as a stepping-stone to employment, as CFIs like The Prince's Trust have discovered. At a broader level, as James Robertson argues, 'It is unrealistic to assume that conventional jobs can provide useful work and livelihoods for everyone.'[85]

The challenge for microfinancial service initiatives is to support the potential gains of self-employment without pushing individuals into low-paid low-quality work. In particular, micro-credit for micro-enterprise is inappropriate for the very poorest, who cannot afford to take on the additional risks of business. On the other hand, it may be a viable option for some poor people, if not the poorest, and those who suffer social exclusion on grounds other than income poverty. Evidence from developing countries and the United States suggests that micro-credit for micro-enterprise can lead to substantial rises in income.[86] This will not be a viable option, however, without changes in the benefit system: not reductions, but greater flexibility to guard against early failure and to cover needs during initial periods of low returns before any micro-enterprise is likely to succeed.

The banks are often failing to address the financial needs of micro-businesses set up by poor or socially excluded individuals (in contrast to the extensive services provided to the small-business sector as a whole). They are also withdrawing services from the most disadvantaged areas. Public-sector loan funds have provided start-up capital in such areas, but have often experienced high rates of loan failure and not been able to sustain their services. Neither the banks nor public-sector loan funds have addressed the often critical need of micro-enterprises for second- and third-round financing, beyond start-up finance but before such an enterprise is likely to have become bankable.[87]

Various types of CFI, on the other hand, seek to lend to disadvantaged groups, such as the unemployed, or to regenerate disadvantaged neighbour-hoods. In the latter case they lend not only for self-employment, but also to businesses that can employ local workers and enhance money-flows within the neighbourhood. Community loan funds, along with social banks, also support enterprises, often charities, providing social services, such as training, rehabilitation, and child-care, which can potentially address wider problems of poverty and social exclusion in their neighbourhoods.

Granted that such initiatives are still young, the available evidence on their success is largely confined to the number of jobs generated, their survival rates, and the number of social enterprises supported. The figures for The Prince's Trust and the Glasgow Regeneration Fund given above are significant, suggesting that CFIs can contribute to regeneration strategies. To achieve this, they have had to be innovative, often rooted within their local neighbourhoods, so that they adapt to the changing needs of local residents.

However, evidence on the wider impact beyond employment and enterprises supported is not yet available. Just as public-sector regeneration initiatives have often been fragmented and isolated, and have therefore failed to address the complexities of disadvantaged neighbourhoods,[88] the same challenge faces community finance initiatives. Their overall impact will depend to a significant extent on what other strategies are being pursued in their area, and to what extent these are co-ordinated.

FINANCIAL PERFORMANCE AND SUSTAINABILITY OF CFIs

Most of the community finance initiatives reviewed here are too recent to enable a firm judgement on their financial performance and sustainability. The range extends from organisations that are highly dependent on grants, such as The Prince's Trust at one end, to a modestly profitable bank, Triodos.

Some within the sector do not believe that CFIs should be self-sustaining and profitable. The Prince's Trust makes provisions in its accounts for about 40 per cent of its outstanding loans, and makes few apologies for this. It has a target of reducing write-offs by five percentage points.

Others seek to preserve their loan capital, but recognise that they cannot cover their full administrative costs and overheads, especially if they devote so much time to non-financial services, such as business planning, training, and support. One community loan fund manager has suggested, 'It's about doing stuff where in a commercial environment you just couldn't justify the cost of this kind of treatment.'

Others recognise that they must at least break even. Funding from members, depositors, and social investors, rather than grants, clearly demands both good financial stewardship and discipline. For UK credit unions, bad-debt write-offs represent an average 2.9 per cent of total assets. However, this is predominantly consumer credit, rather than unsecured micro-enterprise finance.

The need for initiatives providing microfinancial services to be financially sustainable has become a highly contested issue within international debate on microfinance, especially in relation to the ability of microfinancial services to address poverty. There are those who argue that an initiative providing microfinancial services must become financially sustainable, and the best way to achieve this is by reducing costs[89] and scaling up its operations.[90] Others argue that pursuing such goals will distance the initiative from the poorer clients, for example by providing larger loans which reduce financial costs but are inappropriate for the poorest, and by putting commercial considerations before local needs.[91]

This debate is of critical concern to the British context also. As suggested above, money-lending companies can generate significant profits from serving low-income households, while community finance initiatives in the UK range from being highly dependent on grants to being modestly profitable.

Clearly, if an initiative providing microfinancial services is to continue to offer such services to its members or users in the long term, it needs to be organisationally and financially sustainable. Financial services are not something that should be here today and gone tomorrow. If providing them is to make a significant contribution to combating poverty and social exclusion, a long-term approach is needed.

However, the emphasis on financial sustainability needs to be dealt with carefully, for four reasons. First, financial sustainability will depend on the primary purpose of the initiative. Three potential purposes stand out:

- *reducing poverty*: addressing many aspects of poverty and social exclusion, as suggested in earlier chapters, including a focus on the poorest, who often need protective rather than promotional services;
- *generating employment*: promoting micro or small businesses which can overcome exclusion from the labour force, a primary component of social exclusion;
- *developing financial markets*: in Southern countries, in particular, it is of considerable importance to establish viable financial services for the millions of people, many of them poor, who have no bank account.

The first of these purposes is likely to lead to the least financially sustainable initiatives, the last to the most sustainable. The major exceptions are some initiatives that are focused on the first purpose, which depend on their savings for capital. Chapter 4 gave examples such as SEWA Bank in India and URAC in Mexico, both of which raise adequate capital for their lending through deposits, rather than grants or subsidies. The closest parallel in the British context (although many do not serve the poor) is the credit unions, which lend out of capital accumulated through member shares (savings), just as the previous generation of mutual societies did.[92]

Clearly, deposits provide means of achieving greater financial sustainability without necessarily undermining the attempt to address poverty and social exclusion. However, accepting savings is not appropriate to all initiatives that provide microfinancial services, since depositors, especially those who are poor, require adequate protection, and it is therefore often not possible to use deposits for more experimental and risky lending.

Secondly, even within each of the three purposes set out above, there will be major differences among the various target groups or markets. For example, it is vital to distinguish between the needs of different groups of poor people, not least between *poor* individuals and the *poorest* among them. In the latter case, protective financial services are clearly the most critical, while promotional micro-credit for micro-business is likely to be inappropriate, even dangerous.

Table 5.2 set out the various potential markets for micro-credit in the UK. Micro-credit that reaches the unemployed and those on benefits effectively is highly unlikely to generate returns to cover its costs, while initiatives serving existing micro-enterprises, including those operating in the 'grey economy', should.[93] For policy-makers, careful consideration of the different users and markets addressed by different initiatives is therefore critical in determining the potential for their financial sustainability.

Thirdly, in the British context, the last purpose mentioned above — to develop financial markets — may seem less relevant. Widespread exclusion from financial services is far less prevalent in the UK than in the South.[94] On the other hand, with the increasing withdrawal of banks and other financial-service providers from disadvantaged neighbourhoods in the UK, establishing viable financial markets in these neighbourhoods is becoming ever more important.[95]

Fourthly, an exclusive emphasis on financial sustainability diverts attention from other issues. In particular, the multiple dimensions of poverty and social exclusion described in Chapter 2 make it clear that the *quality* and *effectiveness* of the services in meeting the needs of poor people are critical.

The emphasis on financial sustainability also diverts attention from other factors of *organisational* sustainability, such as management and governance, organisational structure and culture.[96] The financial sustainability of initiatives will in fact vary across different stages of their organisational development. A clear lesson from international experience is that new and young initiatives (including those that draw on deposits for their lending capital) are very unlikely to be able to survive and grow without grants and subsidies. Even those with a strong commitment to reaching financial sustainability may take five or even ten years to achieve this. Since almost all CFIs in the UK are still young, widespread financial sustainability within the sector is unlikely to be achieved for some time, certainly not within typically limited policy horizons.[97]

The case for subsidies in addressing issues of poverty and social exclusion thus remains strong, and it would be inappropriate to demand that all CFIs must become self-sustaining financially. Much depends on their objectives in addressing the needs of disadvantaged neighbourhoods and groups. Even in the case of the least financially sustainable initiative reviewed in this chapter, The Prince's Trust, total expenditure (*after* write-offs and provisioning of around 40 per cent) amounts to no more than £3,700 per young person supported. Moreover, two-thirds of Trust-supported businesses survive, and half of those whose businesses fail do not return to unemployment. This compares favourably with the average of £8,500 a year they would receive from the government if they remained unemployed (assuming of course that the new businesses provide sustainable and fairly paid employment). These figures demonstrate the true value for money that some CFIs have achieved.

TRANSFORMATIVE STRATEGIES

One of the three questions set out in the Introduction to this book was whether microfinancial services primarily strengthen people's ability to cope in poverty and social exclusion, to manage the *effects* of structural change on their lives, or whether such services can also address the underlying structural *causes* of poverty and social exclusion. The pragmatic reality described in this chapter makes clear that microfinancial services in Britain are concerned more with the former than with the latter. This is all the more evident when set against the complexities of poverty and social exclusion, and their causes at the national and global levels, described in Chapters 2 and 3. It would be foolish to suggest that one tool alone could resolve such complexities and deep-seated injustices.

In particular, Chapter 2 set out growing inequality within Britain as the major dimension of poverty and social exclusion in the last 20 years. To the extent that financial exclusion, which in Britain is closely correlated with other indicators of disadvantage, contributes to such inequality, addressing such exclusion through the provision of microfinancial services could contribute to greater equality. To the extent that inequalities *among* the poor in Britain, a much smaller group than in the South, is less of an issue, there is also less of a danger that microfinancial services will enhance inequalities among the poor. However, it is quite obvious from the evidence cited in this chapter, including the limited outreach of community finance initiatives, that microfinancial services by themselves cannot make a significant dent on inequality, rooted as it is in the types of economic and social change described in Chapter 2.

However, microfinancial services should never be considered in isolation. Alongside the primary protective mechanisms of social security benefits and workplace regulations, and along with other services including health-care and education, they can have an important role. Given the realities of poverty and social exclusion, such a role, even as a palliative alongside other measures, is significant and should not be underestimated.

To achieve greater impact, the provision of microfinancial services in the UK needs to be integrated with wider strategies for social change and economic improvement. In an era of economic risk and uncertainty, in particular in relation to livelihoods, microfinancial services could form part of a broader strategy, involving public, private, and voluntary actors, to address the needs of disadvantaged neighbourhoods and to enable more people to develop their own autonomy.

More integrated strategies, focusing on broader concerns than just financial services, are in line with international experience, for example initiatives like URAC and SEWA Bank (see Chapter 4). In the latter case, the bank services are complemented by a union that fights for the legal rights and other rights of its poor members, a trust to work on improving housing conditions, an academy to undertake relevant research, and so on.

Can initiatives providing microfinancial services contribute to tackling poverty and social exclusion beyond enabling people to cope better, and beyond being part of more integrated strategies? International experience suggests that microfinance initiatives do indeed strive to have a more transformative role, seeking to influence underlying structures, or at least the ideologies that support them. The Grameen Bank prides itself that it has demonstrated, against all conventional banking wisdom at the time when it was established, that poor people are bankable. SEWA Bank, which provides basic social security provision to its members, has argued that this demonstrates that such provision for self-employed people in the informal sector is a viable option for the Indian government to promote nationally. SEWA Union has also used its experiences to enhance the visibility, at the national and international levels, of the economic contribution made by workers, especially women, in the informal sector.[98]

Likewise in Britain, some community loan funds seek not only to mitigate the predominant economic trends which cause the decline of neighbourhoods, but also to challenge the dominant economic paradigms that underlie those trends, and thus contribute to political debate. The same applies to credit unions. Are these only a convenient way for people to save, or are they part of a social movement based on co-operation and a radical vision of how society can be organised?

One answer is that, if they are not the first, they will find it hard to be the second. According to John Turner,[99] microfinancial services need to be understood as tools. These tools, in turn, must address *pragmatic* needs in order to have an effect. Some tools, however, can also play a *transformative* role if they are part of an integrated approach that can change the paradigm of how a society or economy is organised.

This is surely in line with realistic expectations of social change. Microfinancial-service providers cannot achieve more transformative goals, unless they are part of wider strategies for social change and economic transformation, as suggested above, or if they are able to act as 'beacons' of change, to project a vision of alternative ways of organising society and demonstrate that such alternatives are feasible.[100] Evidence suggests that such a role is not impossible.

In Ireland, for example, the credit union movement was founded and established by women as a pragmatic response to financial discrimination and exclusion, but it also played a significant transformative role in helping to promote the principle of gender equality in the Irish economy. In the United States, a few leading community development finance initiatives have provided an essential complement to the Community Reinvestment Act (CRA) by demonstrating the feasibility of lending within run-down neighbourhoods, and contributing to their economic regeneration.[101]

However, such initiatives still remain small, relative to the extent of the need. Their effect on poverty and social exclusion must be reviewed constantly, and their strategies renewed in the light of such reflection. This book seeks to caution against exaggerating the potential of microfinancial services, a danger clearly seen in the international 'microfinance movement', which sometimes promotes microfinance as an easy remedy to poverty, and, given that capital circulates between financial institution and user, apparently at little cost. Such naivety is clearly dangerous, particularly as it risks diverting resources from other pressing needs, such as health-care and education.

However, there seems little alternative to a process of evolutionary change promoted by innovation and demonstration, both practical and inspirational, which has been the hallmark of many microfinancial initiatives. The challenge, therefore, for microfinancial-service providers in the UK is threefold: first and foremost, alongside other essential services, to address effectively the financial needs of poor and socially excluded people among their users; second, to integrate microfinancial services within wider strategies for social change and economic improvement; and third, to pursue deliberate moves to amplify the difference they make to the wider structures, social and economic, that underlie the stark realities of poverty and social exclusion.

CONCLUSIONS

This chapter has reviewed the wide range of microfinancial services, both protective and promotional, and their providers in Britain which have the potential to address poverty, financial exclusion, and social exclusion. Poor and socially excluded individuals often draw on a range of such microfinancial services to meet their particular needs.

They need microfinancial services to *protect* themselves against the effects of a low income, and against fluctuations in that income, and to manage their limited resources more effectively. Mainstream financial-service providers have largely failed to provide basic products to meet these needs. Instead poor people turn not just to the Post Office but also to the Social Fund, money-lenders, pawnbrokers, cheque-cashers, and mail-order firms, in spite of the often high costs and unequal power relations involved.

There is clearly room for alternative socially responsible providers of protective microfinancial services. Among community finance initiatives, credit unions, LETS, social landlords and other intermediaries have the potential to address some of these needs. However, the number of such CFIs which have low-income members is still small, and they need to be accompanied by additional interventions to address multiple disadvantages.

To enhance their incomes and assets, poor people may require *promotional* micro-credit for micro-businesses. There is evidence that such micro-credit can raise incomes and contribute towards integrating excluded individuals into the workforce. The challenge is to support the potential gains of self-employment without pushing individuals into low-paid, low-quality work. In particular, micro-credit for micro-enterprise is inappropriate for the poorest, who cannot afford to take on the additional risks of business.

Mainstream financial-service providers are often failing to address the financial needs of micro-businesses set up by poor or socially excluded individuals, and they are withdrawing from disadvantaged neighbourhoods, while public-sector funds have often proved unsustainable.

Micro-credit funds and community loan funds seek to fill the gaps, lending not only for self-employment but also to businesses which can employ local workers, as secure employment is often preferable to self-employment. However, there is so far no evidence on the impact of such CFIs beyond employment and enterprises supported.

Thus, although finance alone is rarely an answer to complex and multi-faceted patterns of social exclusion, CFIs are potentially able to address a wide range of economic needs and opportunities. For example, credit unions can mobilise local savings and loans; community loan funds may mobilise increased inward investment; and micro-credit can create opportunities for starting up and sustaining micro-enterprises.

To the extent that such initiatives address financial exclusion, they can also contribute to greater equality, although they cannot influence the many other causes of inequality. Indeed, community and microfinance initiatives need to avoid the creation of financial mechanisms that in effect ghettoise poor people outside mainstream financial markets; it is just as important to induce the latter to adapt their services to low-income users. Otherwise such initiatives risk contributing to even greater inequality.

The organisational and financial sustainability of community and microfinance initiatives depends on a diverse range of factors, and will vary according to the purposes that an initiative pursues, the markets it targets, and the stages in its organisational development. Impact must clearly remain the paramount criterion for judging success in addressing poverty and social exclusion.

Chapter 2 set out the complex realities and causes of poverty and social exclusion. It would be naive to believe that the provision of microfinancial services alone could address these complexities. Nevertheless, it is clear that access to microfinancial services, if accompanied by other forms of action, can enable people to cope better with poverty and social exclusion. The role of microfinancial services includes enabling people to manage their money and protect themselves through savings and insurance in times of change; providing finance for self-employment for those who wish to choose this route; and making loans to small enterprises likely to increase employment and regeneration. Above all, the *process* involved is critical. Organising local-level financial services can offer the opportunity to empower those involved to increase their confidence and their social networks. The bottom line for microfinancial services should be greater control for the users over their lives.

Microfinancial-service projects can achieve more transformative goals only if they are integrated into wider strategies for social change and economic transformation, or if they are able to project, as some microfinance initiatives in other countries have sought to do, a vision of alternative ways of organising society — and demonstrating that such alternatives are feasible. Only then will they fully satisfy the ideals and ambitions of the many microfinance practitioners seeking to combat poverty and social exclusion.

6 Conclusion

THOMAS FISHER, ED MAYO, AND BEN ROGALY

OVERVIEW

THIS book began by asking three questions:

- First, what are the dimensions of poverty and social exclusion in Britain, and what role can microfinancial services play in combating them?

- Secondly, from international experience of using microfinance as an approach to tackling poverty and social exclusion, which lessons are relevant in the British context?

- Thirdly, are microfinancial services able to address the underlying structural causes of poverty and social exclusion? Or do they primarily strengthen people's ability to manage the effects of structural change on their own lives?

The analysis of poverty and social exclusion and their structural causes in Britain, presented in Chapter 2, suggests that a significant number of people lack access to affordable and appropriate financial services.

The main benefit of financial services is to enable people to match the money they have to the vagaries and risks of life, and this applies in particular to those living in poverty. Savings, insurance, and credit can all be matched against needs that arise, from school uniforms to funerals. This, the primary role of financial services in relation to poverty and social exclusion, is termed a 'protective' effect.

Financial services, such as a current account enabling bill payment and cheque cashing, can also make life easier and reduce costs. However, for those on very low incomes, money management with such services may be more difficult than managing a cash budget, so that one response to losing a job, for example, may be to close an account.

Another way in which financial services may be useful in tackling poverty and social exclusion is 'promotional', rather than 'protective'. Promotional financial services involve the use of credit, aimed at enabling poor people to promote themselves out of income poverty. Examples of such promotional services include loans for starting up or expanding micro-enterprises, or to support group enterprises aimed at improving local services. However, such promotional services are not relevant to all poor and socially excluded people, particularly not for the very poorest, for whom the costs, and risks, associated with establishing an enterprise may be too great. On the other hand, even the poorest may benefit if loans are given to local businesses which generate decent employment and services for them.

As described in Chapter 5, there is a wide range of mainstream and informal providers of microfinancial services in Britain, including banks, post offices, and licensed and unlicensed money-lenders. Three million people use licensed money-lenders. Some have no choice, others are choosing the convenience and apparent benefit of the service; but the cost of money is often so high, and the profit margins so considerable, that the relationship is exploitative. This concern has been raised by advice bureaux and the Office of Fair Trading. Buying a financial service is a complex matter, as is recognised in the way financial services are regulated. It is often hard to compare services, and the 'financial literacy' of the consumer should not be assumed.

The main potential of initiatives that address poverty and social exclusion in Britain through the use of financial services is to offer protective services that strengthen people's ability to cope through life. These services include not just those, such as basic banking services, that meet the needs of day-to-day money management, but also those that provide long-term financial security, such as life insurance and pensions, and medium-term financial security, such as home-contents insurance.[1]

By themselves, such services will not, however, address the causes of poverty and social exclusion, which are predominantly structural. Promotional financial services, which generate enterprise and employment, may contribute to addressing poverty caused by exclusion from the labour market, and develop the capacity of neighbourhoods to retain wealth and build local demand. While such a strategy cannot address the root causes of poverty and exclusion at the national and international levels, it may, in combination with other initiatives, be able to deal with some of the more local or regional causes.

ANALYSING THE POTENTIAL OF FINANCIAL SERVICES TO ADDRESS POVERTY AND SOCIAL EXCLUSION

How does the potential of financial services to address poverty and social exclusion, summarised above, compare with what international and British experience suggests can in reality be achieved? The main intended effects of such initiatives are analysed below, drawing where appropriate on the conclusions of previous chapters.

Access to financial services

Widespread exclusion from financial services is far less prevalent in the UK than in many countries in Africa, Latin America, and many parts of Asia. Indeed, only a decade ago the UK was dubbed 'the indebted society' by researcher Janet Ford, in view of the significant proportion of people who did not merely have access to financial services but also (for a range of reasons, including mis-selling and the collapse of property prices) ended up in debt. The risks of taking on excessive and expensive debt are particularly acute for the poorest people, and encouraging debt through ever-larger personal and micro-business loans, as has often happened in the South, should therefore not be done without due care. This suggests that in Britain the *appropriateness* and *affordability* of financial services may be more of an issue than access *per se*, in contrast to countries with much higher levels of financial exclusion.

Exceptions to this generalisation include home-contents insurance for those living on low incomes in areas where premiums have been pushed up by high levels of crime. Another exception is the significant number of people who have acquired a bad credit rating, for example for defaulting on loans or for having County Court judgements outstanding against them. If initiatives were more flexible in relation to credit history, they might enable people to build up a good credit rating and re-enter the market for mainstream financial services.

Credit unions in the UK stress that they offer a highly competitive rate for borrowers, and this appears to be an important attraction for members. So too is the insistence on regular saving and the convenience of doing this. On the other hand, much larger numbers of people rely on licensed money-lenders and mail-order credit, in spite of their very high costs, partly because such arrangements are convenient and impose fewer restrictions on borrowing, but also because poor people lack choices. In these cases, access is an issue for poor people, and they often have to pay above market rates for using such financial services. Greater access to alternatives might have an impact on the structure of local informal markets for microfinancial services, making them more competitive. The high profit-margins of money-lenders point to the current absence of any such competition.

Reducing vulnerability through protective financial services

The key need for poor and socially excluded people is often financial services that can protect them from fluctuations in income or the costs of emergencies, and can enhance and protect their limited wealth. Greater access to personal financial services can make a difference by enabling them to protect their incomes and avoid indebtedness (thereby retaining credit-worthiness), to manage money, to build up assets such as savings and pensions, and also to maintain wider social networks. Services such as reasonably priced home-contents insurance, micro-deposit facilities, and loans for 'getting by' can have a protective impact, for example by reducing people's vulnerability to losses through burglary and at times when they have little or no income.

As described in Chapter 4, many initiatives in the South offer savings facilities and flexible micro-loans, both of which can serve protective purposes, although insurance services are still rare.

The opportunities for providing accessible and cost-effective savings are considerable in the UK. Indeed, it was noted in Chapter 5 that customers of money-lenders may in fact be using the weekly collection as a form of saving. Given the very high cost of this (implying a significant negative interest rate, if the aim is to maintain the habit of saving rather than borrowing), there must be significant opportunities for initiatives such as credit unions to provide more effective competition to money-lenders.

With the growth of credit-scoring in Britain, mainstream insurance companies increasingly discriminate against high-risk groups, including many socially excluded people, because, for example, their neighbourhoods typically suffer from high rates of crime. Given such risks, a major challenge is to keep costs down while offering insurance. The involvement of registered social landlords, acting as intermediaries between households and insurance companies, has in some cases made contents insurance accessible and affordable to low-income households, even in disadvantaged neighbourhoods.

Credit unions that encourage savings, provide small 'consumption' loans, and now offer household insurance through their federations also have a role to play. However, few credit unions currently have many members who are poor and socially excluded.

Enhancing employment and income through promotional financial services

Many initiatives offering microfinancial services in the South focus on promotional rather than protective financial services. Most lend to the self-employed, and few seek to support small enterprises managed by entrepreneurs which might generate employment for poor people. In fact, evidence for significant job creation through micro-credit in the South is limited. However, such credit can help poor self-employed people working in the informal sector to stabilise or somewhat expand their micro-businesses. The evidence of impact studies suggests that micro-loans in the South do have a positive effect on incomes from business. However, the size of the effect is directly proportional to the starting point of the borrower. In other words, the less poor the borrower, the more he or she can benefit in terms of income from such loans. Conversely, the very poorest generally benefit very little from promotional micro-credit, which subjects them to greater business risks than they can afford.

The review of international experience in Chapter 4 further demonstrated some of the unintended consequences of micro-enterprise credit: for example in Bangladesh, the transfer of control over the loan between household members (particularly from women to men) and the widespread use of business credit for immediate personal needs (for getting by) or for repaying money-lenders. The latter consequences are not necessarily negative. However, they point to the need for initiatives providing microfinancial services, including those in Britain, of understanding the ways in which their users manage money, their daily lives, and the kinds of social relations, including gender relations, in which they are involved.

The opportunities in Britain for initiatives which use credit to promote income from micro-businesses, particularly among poor and socially excluded people, are more limited and will need to be developed carefully. In terms of numbers of borrowers, the scale of international initiatives such as the Grameen Bank, which makes no attempt to identify who is suited to business and who is not, is not appropriate in Britain. There are a number of reasons for this.

First, the marginal rate of return on offer to micro-entrepreneurs in many parts of the South, i.e. the difference between getting their goods to market to sell and not doing so, is likely to be far higher than in Britain. One reason for this is the UK benefits system, which provides a safety-net for income, but may discourage enterprise if income gains from business are offset by benefit losses.

Secondly, the opportunities for generating income through micro-business are more limited in Britain. Whereas self-employment within the informal economy is often the only option for the majority of workers in many Southern countries, and credit for working capital in particular can therefore prove helpful, in Britain the informal economy is far weaker, partly due to laws and standards which effectively make it illegal.

Thirdly, the enterprise culture within Britain is weaker than in many other countries. Even in the USA, however, micro-credit schemes tend to target people carefully. Rather than seeking a broad coverage, which may be the intention of some initiatives in Southern countries, they target people who have chosen to be micro-entrepreneurs and often show at least some evidence of being successful.

With these three factors in mind, initiatives in Britain which target microfinancial services at those in receipt of social-security benefits often warn that micro-business is an option for only a few of them, who may require other support services, such as mentoring, even more than loan finance. In particular, they will often need benefit waivers for a much longer period than they are currently offered by the government's New Deal scheme, to guard against early failure and to cover their needs during initial periods of low returns before they can establish themselves successfully in business.[2]

An additional factor which may limit the role of micro-credit in enhancing incomes is the larger loan size often required to start a business in Britain, compared with many countries in the South. For even larger business loans, there is competition among mainstream lenders, and a wide range of grant and loan facilities offered by the public sector.

However, this does not mean that promotional financial services are of no value for addressing poverty and social exclusion. If some people are helped off state benefits into self-employment, perhaps as a stepping stone to employment,[3] they may well have benefited from micro-enterprise credit. If initiatives, including those providing protective microfinancial services, also offer opportunities for involvement by users and members, for example in mutual-support groups, they may enable people to build up social networks and other resources and skills which enhance their employability and their potential for social citizenship.

Credit can also be of value to micro-entrepreneurs who are poor and socially excluded, particularly those with some business experience and some assets of their own (i.e. not the poorest). Previous chapters have given a range of perspectives on self-employment among poor and socially excluded people. Self-employment can serve as a refuge from discrimination in the workplace, and part-time self-employment might be suited to women's greater needs for flexibility in employment. However, evidence in Chapters 2 and 3 makes clear that self-employment is a precarious and inappropriate option for a majority of poor people in Britain; as demonstrated in Chapter 2, the proportion of self-employed people among the lowest-earning workers in Britain has been steadily rising. The challenge for microfinancial service initiatives is to support the potential gains of self-employment without pushing individuals into low-paid, low-quality work. The experience of providing micro-credit to millions of self-employed workers in the informal sector in the South is thus not something to emulate in the UK.

The tradition of 'community finance' or 'community development finance' in the North,[4] in contrast to that of microfinance in the South, has often sought to promote small businesses, rather than micro-businesses in disadvantaged neighbourhoods, thereby generating employment for residents in those neighbourhoods. This may involve promoting entrepreneurs already living there, or attracting inward investment. Indeed, community loan funds often use the number of jobs supported by businesses that have taken their loans in such neighbourhoods as the main indicator to measure their performance.

Supporting group and social enterprises

There has historically been a strand of initiatives in the South offering financial services to group enterprises such as co-operatives. However, this approach has been marginalised in much recent international debate on micro-credit, which emphasises lending for individual self-employment.[5]

In continental Europe, there is a strong tradition of providing loan finance for niche-group enterprises such as worker and producer co-operatives, which are often excluded by mainstream financiers. In Britain, the community loan fund established by Industrial Common Ownership Finance (ICOF) started, in the 1970s, offering loans to co-operatives and then diversified, in the early 1990s, to cover a wider range of 'social enterprises'.[6] In the USA, a focus for 'community development finance initiatives' (CDFIs) has been group enterprises, known as community development corporations, financing housing and regeneration. The shift by CDFIs into the small-business sector has been a more recent phenomenon.

In Britain, neighbourhood-level social enterprises such as development trusts can provide essential services, such as child-care or training, for people in poverty. On the other hand, leaving aside the wider voluntary sector which relies on grants, the social-enterprise sector remains relatively small. It is argued by Thomas Fisher in Chapter 5 that the opportunities for expanding finance to it will depend on its ability to scale up. One of the key factors behind this is the withdrawal or reorganisation of public funding. The housing sector, for example, has recently seen a very significant injection of mainstream finance, with the substantial assets owned by registered social landlords serving as collateral, and with the state in effect providing a secure stream of income through housing benefit. The expansion of loan finance from community finance initiatives, however, cannot be assumed to be beneficial if it reflects the withdrawal of grant finance from the state.

Inequalities among the poor

We have focused above on both protective and promotional financial services. For the poorest people, the most urgent need is clearly protective services. Neither British nor international experience suggests that promotional enterprise credit is typically appropriate for them. In fact, it may be damaging if it introduces a final straw for those who can least afford the risk of enterprise failure and debt. Not surprisingly, therefore, many poor borrowers in the South who take the enterprise loans on offer use them in practice for personal purposes to deal with income shortfalls or household crises, or even for repaying more expensive loans from money-lenders.

It seems clear, however, that even internationally many initiatives, especially those that offer enterprise loans, do not reach the very poorest groups in society. In Britain, while the need among these groups for protective services is apparent, to meet this need will require British initiatives to succeed where others have often failed. The difficult history of credit unions in the poorest neighbourhoods, for example (particularly those initiated by outside bodies, as in the US 'War on Poverty'), has in practice led to an emphasis on creating a mixed membership of low- and moderate-income savers.

In such cases in the South there have sometimes been concerns that initiatives offering microfinancial services may be exploited by people on relatively better incomes. Even where this is not so, the effect of success among people outside the very poorest groups is to increase inequalities between different groups of poor people. This may be less of an issue in Britain if the focus is on socially and financially excluded people, who form a much smaller group in Britain than in the South. However, there is a constant danger of initiatives being captured by middle-class users or staff, as with any regeneration initiative.

Inequalities between men and women

As reviewed in detail in Chapter 4, the gender-related dimension of microfinancial services in the South is complex. Many initiatives, particularly those in Asia, focus exclusively on women. However, even such targeting does not necessarily address gender discrimination. For example, loans provided for micro-enterprises in Bangladesh have enabled millions of women either to make productive investments or to smooth consumption. However, many women may pass control over their loans to male members of their household. Yet even for such women there may be benefits in terms of their status and autonomy within the household. The process of women organising collectively into savings and credit groups can also enable them to take greater control over other aspects of their lives.

Among initiatives providing microfinancial services in the UK, only three recent initiatives, the Full Circle Fund in Norwich, the Glasgow Women's Micro-credit Project, and Sustainable Strength in Birmingham, explicitly seek to address gender discrimination. Each seeks to organise women into groups in which they provide mutual guarantees for each other's loans, and at least one of them enables its users to save. Each recognises the need for non-financial services, such as training and advice on available options.

Financial literacy

Few initiatives providing microfinancial services in the South have a strong focus on financial literacy, but it is reasonable to believe that using financial services successfully can develop the knowledge and experience of those involved. Education, about finance or other matters such as health, is an explicit focus in a number of initiatives which operate group lending. In the UK, some credit unions and Local Exchange and Trading Schemes (LETS) aim to educate members or volunteers and enable them to learn and develop skills and knowledge. But there is little hard evidence of the impact of these initiatives on financial literacy. Money-advice agencies, on the other hand, specialise explicitly in financial literacy, at least for people in debt, and constitute a valuable complement to the provision of financial services.

ASSESSING CURRENT PRACTICE IN BRITAIN

The context in Britain is therefore very specific. Gaps in financial services that exist in other countries may be filled in Britain by mainstream providers or other agencies. Or the gaps that do exist, for example in the provision of long-term financial security for those on low incomes, may not be best filled by the models on offer from international experience. The challenge of using microfinancial services to address poverty and social exclusion in the UK is therefore far from straightforward. At least, it will require the same degree of energy, application, creativity, and willingness to admit and learn from errors that has characterised much international experience. How well does the fledgling British experience of community finance initiatives so far compare with international experience?

Outreach

The first point to emphasise is that British experience is indeed still in its infancy. Not only are there few initiatives providing microfinancial services, but far fewer still reach a significant scale of people served. In part this may be due to the success of mainstream financial-service providers in reaching large numbers of users, thus leaving a smaller, more specialist role for community finance and microfinance initiatives. However, some initiatives in the South aim to grow to a size at which they can benefit from economies of scale and reduce the otherwise high transaction costs of providing microfinancial services. If the potential in Britain for microfinancial services is limited to a specialist role, then the adaptation of some models is likely to be limited.

Innovation

Britain nevertheless has a remarkable history of innovation in the field of financial services for those, including poor people, who have been excluded from existing mainstream service providers. The building-society movement, the National Savings Bank, the penny banks of the Victorian era, indeed the development of retail banks are all remarkable achievements which have done an enormous amount to spread the use and benefit of financial services. It may be that this endowment helps to explain the late arrival in Britain of initiatives such as credit unions, which have a much longer history elsewhere in Europe.

However, there is not yet sufficient diversity in British experience of community finance, nor is there sufficient experimentation, to pilot appropriate methods of meeting the many financial needs of poor and socially excluded individuals. There are nevertheless some major innovations, of which the following are significant examples.

- The Prince's Trust, the largest micro-credit provider in Britain, which has helped more than 40,000 unemployed or under-employed youth to start more than 35,000 businesses, of which 60 per cent survive for at least three years. Among those whose businesses do not survive, more than half go into further education, training, or employment.[7]

- WEETU, which has long supported women on low incomes through training and skill development, and is now adapting international experience in credit for micro-businesses to the British context as one of a range of possible options for disadvantaged women. The innovation consists in particular in integrating micro-enterprise development within the context of a benefits system, which also involves on-going advocacy for supportive changes in that system.[8]

- Some parts of the charity sector, serviced by loan funds such as that of the Charities Aid Foundation and social banks like Triodos Bank, which are also being innovative in their use of finance and enterprise to meet their social objectives. Along with developments in the USA, new experience and models are emerging which address the critical issue of enterprise development, trading, and loan finance within the voluntary sector. Part of the reason for this, again, is the wider national context of the withdrawal of the state from service provision, increasingly contracting out such provision to both non-profit and profit-oriented organisations.

- Also within the charity sector, some registered social landlords have not only successfully drawn on mainstream finance for their development, made possible because of housing benefits to their low-income tenants, but also acted as intermediaries for such tenants to gain access to banking services and home-contents insurance. Some of the Development Trusts have also been experimenting with the integration of financial and other services into their housing and business-support activities.

- There are also a number of community loan funds, such as the Aston Reinvestment Trust, the Glasgow Regeneration Fund, and Hackney Business Venture, which seek to regenerate disadvantaged neighbourhoods through lending to enterprises. However, their experience is still limited, compared with similar initiatives in the United States. ICOF, on the other hand, was a very early loan fund targeting workers' co-operatives and, more recently, social enterprises.

- Credit unions and some mutual community loan funds such as the Aston Reinvestment Trust aim to build capacity among members through a strong emphasis on promoting self-help and mutual aid.

- A number of mainstream banks, such as the Bank of Scotland and NatWest, are now active in testing and developing innovative approaches to finance for regeneration.

There is much insight to be gained from international experience that appears to be relevant for Britain. This includes the capacity to provide full and affordable basic banking facilities appropriate to the poor; new approaches to safe and convenient savings facilities; alternatives to borrowing from money-lenders; and repeat loans of increasing size, if successfully repaid, without recourse to credit-scoring. Other innovations include a secondary market for loans to be sold on, so that the primary lender of micro-loans can make additional loans; and the reinsurance of insurance products. The success of some community development credit unions in the USA in serving poor neighbourhoods with microfinancial services is something that currently only a handful of the most successful community credit unions in Britain could aspire to. Similarly, only a handful of recent initiatives, such as the case of the Full Circle Fund mentioned above, have begun to experiment with organising low-income and socially excluded individuals into groups or membership-based organisations for the provision of microfinancial and other services.

Moreover, many of the existing initiatives in Britain have needed to test and try new approaches with considerable energy before finding their niche. The Aston Reinvestment Trust, for example, has taken eight years to move from drawing-board to reality, changing course at many points on the way. Such a creative approach, including the willingness to learn and change, will be critical to success for any initiatives in Britain. Top-down approaches with rigid ideas are guaranteed to fail.

Cost-effectiveness

There is not yet sufficient evidence to be able to compare British initiatives with international experience in relation to cost-effectiveness. Credit unions are an exception in typically being self-reliant, because they depend on savings, and having a low average rate of loan losses. However, the experience of credit unions in Britain also demonstrates two paradoxes.

The first is that initiatives may be slowest to take off where there is most need. This is evidenced by the slow rate of growth among community credit unions, compared with the rapid acceleration of work-place credit unions. The reasons for this have been the subject of intense discussion and debate within the British credit-union movement over recent years.

The second paradox is that non-profit initiatives, while potentially cost-effective and self-sustaining, grow more slowly in terms of capital base, because they do not necessarily aim for the accumulation of profit or surpluses. This is a critical long-term challenge to initiatives that, in Britain more so than the USA, have found it hard to attract external funds to develop a capital base.

There are certainly exceptions to this rule, but they offer two lessons for public policy. First, as many local authorities have found, it is costly and certainly not simple to promote credit unions or other community finance initiatives in poor neighbourhoods.

Second, as Britain lacks such large funding bodies as have provided funding to capitalise initiatives in the USA and in the South, the public sector has a key role to play in providing part of the capital base and revenues for some initiatives to succeed. As an example, The Prince's Trust is supported by the public sector, which contributes funds for each borrower who does not return to the dole queue. The Trust is far from self-sustainable from its own revenues, making provisions for some 40 per cent of its loans. However, in 1996-97 its total expenditure (including write-offs and provisioning) amounted to less than £3,700 per young person supported, in comparison with the average of £8,500 a year that an unemployed claimant costs the national exchequer. (This assumes, of course, that the new businesses provide sustainable and fairly paid employment.)

Measuring impact

The connections between microfinancial services on the one hand and poverty and social exclusion on the other are complex. This is important to bear in mind when forming judgements on the usefulness of microfinance interventions, because one must assess a mix of impacts across a range of indicators. Given the recent history of excessive personal debt in Britain, which is a major cause of stress for people on low incomes in particular, encouraging debt through micro-business or ever-larger personal loans, even with the potential benefits suggested above, should not be done without due care.

International experiences also suggest that, within the context of addressing poverty and social exclusion, the scale and self-sufficiency of an institution are certainly not the only or even primary criteria of success, especially if increasing the size and returns of their operations distances them from their poorer users.

Clearly, the extent to which particular initiatives can be financially self-sufficient will depend on their objectives — whether focusing primarily on reducing poverty along many dimensions, generating employment, or developing financial markets — and on the contexts in which they operate.

Above all, the real impact on poverty and social exclusion must remain the paramount criterion for judging success, and for this initiatives will have to assess and evaluate themselves constantly , and remain open to change, innovating and adapting in the light of the results. Finally, as public funding is scarce, there should not be an assumption that public money is better spent on microfinancial services than on other services such as health care and education. As with all such expenditure, the test is the extent to which it reduces social exclusion, improves people's quality of life, or achieves other public-policy goals.

ADDRESSING THE CAUSES OF POVERTY AND SOCIAL EXCLUSION

Above we suggested that some community finance initiatives may be able to contribute to addressing more localised causes of poverty and social exclusion, for example by developing the capacity of a neighbourhood to retain wealth and build local demand, or to attract capital from socially responsible investors. Community and microfinance initiatives could also, perhaps, have a political impact, enabling people to build personal confidence and organise collectively through networks that are able to challenge decision-makers, and power structures that are in a position to affect the local causes of social exclusion. Examples such as SEWA Bank in India and community organising networks in the USA are, however, not common in Britain.

Some commentators have expressed the fear that people who use alternative financial services also become locked into an alternative economy, which limits their opportunities. Yet it seems clear that the best practice serves to expand the options open to disadvantaged groups. While many initiatives in Britain have been inspired by co-operative ideals, there has also been much pragmatic reflection: in the case of credit unions, the withdrawal of banks has left a hole to fill; in the case of community loan funds, there is an imperative to move beyond increasingly scarce public funds in order to make some regeneration activities an investment proposition, thus putting them in a position to tap private capital markets. In a number of cases in other countries, a secondary market has emerged, enabling, for example, loans to be packaged into securities and refinanced. Ultimately, far from being an alternative economy, this places community finance and microfinance firmly within the global financial system and subject to the same rules and the same shocks that may occur. Yet some such initiatives have proved that they can become strong, durable institutions serving poor people.

It is clear that microfinancial services in Britain serve to help people to cope with poverty and social exclusion, rather than changing their underlying structural causes. Alongside the primary protective mechanisms of social-security benefits and work-place regulations, and along with other services including health and education, microfinancial services can play a significant role. By themselves, however, they are not likely to be able to change the primary causes of poverty, which lie in structural changes at the national and global levels.

The provision of microfinancial services could potentially contribute to an integrated strategy by enabling more people to manage their money and protect themselves through savings and insurance in times of rapid economic change; through finance for self-employment and micro-businesses, though not for the poorest; and through loans given by community finance initiatives to small enterprises likely to increase employment. The process of organising local-level financial services could also enable those involved to increase their social networks and gain greater control over their lives.

To maximise impact, therefore, the cutting edge of microfinancial services in the UK must be integrated within wider strategies for social change and economic improvement. In an era of economic risk and uncertainty, microfinancial services could form part of a broader strategy involving public, private, and voluntary actors, to enable people to build their own autonomy.

Notes

CHAPTER I

1   See Richard Wilkinson, 1998, 'What health can tell us about society', *IDS Bulletin*, 29 (1).

2   John Hills, 1998, *Income and Wealth: The Latest Evidence*, York: Joseph Rowntree Foundation, p11.

3   See Justice, 1997, 'Poverty Undermines Rights in the UK', Joint submission to the United Nations Committee on Economic, Social and Cultural Rights.

4   Tony Blair: 'In Britain today, millions are still trapped in a cash economy; vulnerable, extorted, prey to loan sharks. In Britain today, that is not acceptable', *Observer*, 31 May 1998. Social Exclusion Unit, 1998: *Bringing Britain Together: A National Strategy for Neighbourhood Renewal*, London: HMSO. The latter report sets out a rapid policy-development programme to report by December 1999. Three of the 18 action teams focus wholly or partly on aspects of microfinance. These concern 'business', 'financial services', and 'shops'.

5   Micro-enterprises are usually defined formally as enterprises with either fewer than ten or fewer than five employees. In many of the contexts discussed in this book, micro-enterprises are one-person operations, often using labour contributed by family members.

6   This definition of social exclusion is adapted from the editors' introduction to Part One of *Social Exclusion in European Cities: Processes, Experiences and Responses*, edited by Ali Madanipour, Goran Cars and Judith Allen, London: Jessica Kingsley Publishers, 1998.

7   Elaine Kempson and Claire Whyley, 1999, *Kept Out or Opted Out? Understanding and Combating Financial Exclusion*, Bristol: The Policy Press and York: The Joseph Rowntree Foundation.

8   See E. Mayo, T. Fisher, P. Conaty, J. Doling and A. Mullineux: *Small is Bankable: Community Reinvestment in the UK*, York: Joseph Rowntree Foundation and London: New Economics Foundation, 1998.

9   Social and community enterprises are enterprises that are run for social purposes, or by members of a community for the benefit of themselves or their wider community. Such enterprises seek to be financially sustainable, but may not seek to generate significant profits.

10 A. Leyshon and N. Thrift: *Money/Space: Geographies of Monetary Transformation*, London: Routledge, 1997. Many of those without current

accounts in a High Street bank, for example, have not applied for them, in some cases because they expected to be refused, but mostly because of the lack of an appropriate type of account. This applies equally to many other financial products, for example insurance and pensions (see Kempson and Whyley 1999, op cit, and Elaine Kempson and Claire Whyley, 1998, *Access to Current Accounts: A Report to the British Bankers' Association*, London: BBA).

11 This was the central message of *Microfinance and Poverty Reduction*, by Susan Johnson and Ben Rogaly (Oxford: Oxfam, 1997).

CHAPTER 2

1 See Anne E. Green, 1994, *The Geography of Poverty and Wealth*, University of Warwick: Institute of Employment Research.

2 See Wilkinson, 1996, *Unhealthy Societies: the Affliction of Inequality*, London: Routledge.

3 John Hills, 1998, *Income and Wealth: The Latest Evidence*, York: Joseph Rowntree Foundation, p11.

4 Martin Evans, 1998, 'Behind the rhetoric: the institutional basis of social exclusion and poverty', *IDS Bulletin*, 29 (1), pp 42–9.

5 Judith Allen, Goran Cars, and Ali Madanipour, 1998, Introduction, pp18–19, in Ali Madanipour, Goran Cars and Judith Allen (eds), *Social Exclusion in European Cities: Processes, Experiences and Responses*, London: Jessica Kingsley.

6 Arjan De Haan draws on Hilary Silver's work to distinguish between French models of social integration based on the maintenance of social bonds, and British and US models where inclusion is used to refer to access to markets and infrastructure ('Social exclusion in policy and research: operationalising the concept', forthcoming in J. Figueiredo and A. De Haan (eds), *Social Exclusion: The Way Forward in Policy and Research* (working title), Geneva: International Institute for Labour Studies).

7 Melvin Oliver and Thomas Shapiro, 1995, *Black Wealth White Wealth: A New Perspective on Racial Inequality*, New York and London: Routledge, p177.

8 'It is not possible to define poverty, and in particular trends in poverty, in any meaningful way without some reference to the prevailing living standards in society as a whole' (Alissa Goodman, Paul Johnson and Steven Webb, 1997, *Inequality in the UK*, Oxford: Oxford University Press, p231). In much of the literature on poverty in Britain, the reference group has been the population of the whole country. This practice is followed here. However, a more general approach would define 'the poor as disadvantaged ... because the amount of resources at their disposal is insufficient for socially acceptable conditions of life in a *particular historical community*' (Enzo Mingione, 1997, 'Enterprise and Exclusion', *Demos Collection*, 12, emphasis added).

9 Financial literacy involves, among other things, knowledge of sources of credit, knowledge of rights in relation to specific creditors, budgeting skills, and an understanding of basic financial terminology.

10 Madanipour et al, op cit, introduction to Part One: 'Processes and Dimensions of Social Exclusion'.

11 Reference here is to those social relationships, which 'mean that "living in a place" contributes to human flourishing' (Judith Allen, Goran Cars and Ali Madanipour, Introduction to Madanipour et al, op cit).

12 Ingrid Palmer in H. Afshar and C. Dennis (eds), *Women and Adjustment Policies in the Third World,* Basingstoke: Macmillan, 1992.

13 Tariq Modood, 1997, 'Conclusion: ethnic diversity and disadvantage', in Tariq Modood, Richard Berthoud, Jane Lakey, James Nazroo, Patten Smith, Satnam Virdee and Sharon Beishon, *Ethnic Minorities in Britain: Diversity and Disadvantage,* London: Policy Studies Institute.

14 See John Hills, 1998, *Income and Wealth: The Latest Evidence,* York: Joseph Rowntree Foundation, p36.

15 'Fear of crime' or 'feeling unsafe' are top of the list of residents' major dislikes in areas of multiple deprivation. Social Exclusion Unit, 1998, *Bringing Britain Together: A National Strategy for Neighbourhood Renewal,* London: HMSO, p14.

16 Thomas Acton, quoted in the *Economist,* 30 May 1998, p29. See also Ian Daley and Jo Henderson (eds), 1998, *Static – Life on the Site,* Yorkshire Art Circus.

17 See Judith Butler, 1997, 'Merely cultural', *New Left Review* 227, pp33–48; and Nancy Fraser, 1998, 'Heterosexism, misrecognition and capitalism: a reply to Judith Butler', *New Left Review* 228, pp140–9. I am grateful to Cecile Jackson for drawing my attention to this debate.

18 Green, op cit, p99.

19 Although it has often been left out of analysis, the multidimensional experience of poverty is not a new concept (see, for example, Ken Coates and Richard Silburn, 1970, *Poverty: The Forgotten Englishmen,* Harmondsworth: Penguin, Chapters 1 and 2). It is illustrated very clearly by the data presented in Social Exclusion Unit, 1998, op cit.

20 De Haan, forthcoming, op cit.

21 Although see Modood et al, 1997, op cit, for evidence of diversity as well as disadvantage among the ethnic minorities.

22 Mingione, op cit, p12.

23 This is therefore a measure of relative rather than absolute poverty.

24 Dorothy Wedderburn, 1974, 'Introduction' in Dorothy Wedderburn (ed), *Poverty, Inequality and Class Structure,* Cambridge: Cambridge University Press, p5.

25 Peter Townsend, 1979, *Poverty in the United Kingdom: A Survey of Household Resources and Standards of Living,* Harmondsworth: Penguin, p921.

26 The increase, however, was not great: from 5.8 per cent of all pupils in the UK in 1979–80 to 6.3 per cent in 1994–95 (Howard Glennerster, 1998, 'Education: reaping the harvest', in Howard Glennerster and John Hills (eds.), *The State of Welfare: The Economics of Social Spending* (2nd edition), Oxford: Oxford University Press).

27   Will Hutton, 1996, *The State We're In* (revised edition), London: Vintage.

28   *Guardian*, 1 September 1998.

29   See Goodman et al, op cit, *Inequality in the UK*.

30   R.G. Wilkinson, op cit. Elsewhere Wilkinson has shown that mortality is more closely related to relative income within countries than to differences in absolute income between them (R.G. Wilkinson, 1997, 'Socio-economic determinants of health — health inequalities: relative or absolute material standards?', *British Medical Journal*, 314: 591–5).

31   Goodman et al, op cit, Chapter 8.

32   Carey Oppenheim and Lisa Harker, 1996, *Poverty the Facts* (3rd Edition), London: CPAG Ltd, pp52ff.

33   Sarah Jarvis and Stephen P. Jenkins, 1998, 'Low income dynamics in 1990s Britain', *IDS Bulletin*, 29 (1).

34   Oppenheim and Harker, op cit, pp39–41.

35   Peter Townsend, 1996, *A Poor Future: Can We Counter Growing Poverty in Britain and Across the World?*, London: Lemos and Crane.

36   Robert Walker and Jennifer Park, 1998, 'Unpicking poverty', in Carey Oppenheim (ed), *An Inclusive Society: Strategies for Tackling Poverty*, London: Institute for Public Policy Research, pp36–7.

37   John Hills, 1998, 'Does income mobility mean that we do not need to worry about poverty?' in A.B. Atkinson and John Hills (eds), *Education, Employment and Opportunity*, London School of Economics, Centre for Analysis of Social Exclusion, Paper 4.

38   *Tackling Poverty and Extending Opportunity: The Modernisation of Britain's Tax and Benefit System no. 4*, HM Treasury, 1999; also see *Persistent Poverty and Lifetime Inequality: The Evidence*, CASE Report 5/HM Treasury Occasional Paper 10, 1999, an accompanying research document published jointly by the Centre for Analysis of Social Exclusion (London School of Economics) and HM Treasury.

39   Perri 6, 1997, 'Social Exclusion: Time to Be Optimistic', *Demos Collection*, 12, p5.

40   Townsend, op cit, p61.

41   Amartya Sen, 1997, *Inequality, Unemployment and Contemporary Europe*, Development Economics Research Programme No 7 (New Series), Suntory and Toyota International Centres for Economics and Related Disciplines (STICERD), London School of Economics.

42   Ibid, pp 11–16.

43   See Lydia Morris, *Dangerous Classes: The Underclass and Social Citizenship*, London: Routledge, 1994, p104.

44   See Elaine Kempson and Claire Whyley (1998), *Access to Current Accounts: A Report to the British Bankers' Association*, London: BBA, pp13–14.

45   Elaine Kempson, 1996, *Life on a Low Income*, York: Joseph Rowntree Foundation, p55.

46   Ibid, p65.

47 Goodman et al, op cit. 'The proportion of children growing up in households with below half the average income grew from 10 per cent in 1979 to 32 per cent in 1994–95' (Social Exclusion Unit, op cit, p20).

48 Ibid, p28.

49 Ibid.

50 Eithne McLaughlin, 1998, 'Taxes, benefits and paid work', in Carey Oppenheim (ed) *An Inclusive Society: Strategies for Tackling Poverty*, London, IPPR, p96.

51 Anne Power and Rebecca Tunstall, 1995, *Swimming Against the Tide: Polarisation or Progress on Twenty Unpopular Council Estates, 1980–1995*, York: Joseph Rowntree Foundation. Poor areas or neighbourhoods have been the focus of much recent central government analysis (see the discussion of the work of the Social Exclusion Unit in the following chapter).

52 Green, op cit, p.xii. See also Chris Philo (ed), 1995, *Off the Map: The Social Geography of Poverty in the UK*, London: CPAG Ltd.

53 See Cameron and Davoudi in Madanipour et al, op cit.

54 Green, loc cit.

55 Food poverty is partly about not being able to afford a diet considered to be adequate in both quantity and quality by wider society (see E. Dowler and C. Calverty, 1995, *Nutrition and Diet in Lone-Parent Families in London*, London: Family Policies Studies Centre). It can also be experienced as a form of relative deprivation: in particular through the increasing trend towards building out-of-town supermarkets, which constrain those without cars. Moreover, for those who visit these supermarkets to buy a few unbranded ordinary products — a loaf of bread, some tea bags, etc — and see others with trolleys piled high with evidence of a varied, high-quality, and *expensive* diet, a sense of low social status may be perpetuated (Michelle Harrison and Tim Lang, 'Running on Empty', *Demos Collection* 12, pp25–7).

56 Morris, op cit, pp100ff.

57 Perri 6, op cit, p6.

58 Michael Simmons, 1997, *Landscapes of Poverty: Aspects of Rural England in the Late 1990s*, London: Lemos and Crane, p29.

59 Ibid, pp22–3.

60 Ibid, p26.

61 Goodman et al, op cit.

62 See, for example, David Webster, 1997, 'Promoting jobs could reduce lone parenthood', in *Working Brief*, Unemployment Unit/Youthaid, October, pp20–22.

63 Goodman et al, op cit, p106.

64 Low Pay Unit, 1996, *Out of Poverty Towards Prosperity: A Report on Poverty, Low Pay and the Minimum Wage*, London: Public Services, Tax and Commerce Union (PTC), pp5–6. The differential has declined, however. The median earnings of women in full-time employment were 62 per cent of the median earnings of men in full-time work in 1979 (Hills, 1998, op cit, p28).

65 Office for National Statistics, cited in *Guardian*, 16 October 1998, p2.

66 Hutton, op cit, p108.
67 Patsy Healey, 1998, 'Institutionalist theory, social exclusion and governance', in Madanipour et al, op cit, p56.
68 Peter A. Hall, 1997, 'Social Capital: A Fragile Asset', *Demos Collection*, 12, p36.
69 Morris, op cit, pp100ff.
70 It is generally acknowledged that the income of the self-employed is more difficult to assess accurately.
71 A number of axes of discrimination operate to exclude particular groups of people from employment more than others. The passing of anti-discrimination legislation, such as the Disability Discrimination Act, and its recent strengthening in the area of employment along with the Race Relations Act, show that discrimination on the grounds of race and disability was considered significant enough to require action by both the previous Conservative government and the present Labour administration. The same could be said for the Sex Discrimination and Equal Pay Acts with regard to gender-based discrimination.
72 Frank Vandenbroucke, 1998, *Globalisation, Inequality and Social Democracy*, London: Institute for Public Policy Research, p15. Vandenbroucke's argument draws on P. Krugman, 1995, 'Growing world trade: causes and consequences', *Brookings Papers on Economic Activity*, 1, pp327–77.
73 Bob Deacon with Michelle Hulse and Paul Stubbs, 1997, *Global Social Policy: International Organisations and the Future of Welfare*, London: Thousand Oaks/New Delhi: Sage, p2.
74 Hutton, op cit, p167.
75 Vandenbroucke, op cit, pp21–2. Trends in income inequality were also found in another study to differ between countries facing similar global pressures. In Britain the proportion of 'workless' households increased from 9 to 20 per cent between 1979 and the mid-1990s, at the same time that inequality within work was also rising (Hills, 1998, op cit, p8).
76 Coats and Silburn, op cit.
77 The term 'workless', increasingly used to refer to being without paid employment, is unsatisfactory in that it implies that people not in paid employment do not work. As noted elsewhere, it is important to recognise explicitly the social contribution made by unpaid caring work, for example, which is usually performed by women. The term is used here because it has become customary in many writings about Britain, but inverted commas are retained to acknowledge its problematic nature; it is interchanged in places with the term 'jobless'.
78 Many other people also benefit from state transfers: social security is not for poor people alone.
79 Ruth Cohen, Jill Coxall, Gary Craig and Azra Sadiq-Sangster, 1992, *Hardship Britain: Being Poor in the 1990s*, London: CPAG Ltd.
80 Hills, op cit, p33.
81 See Bob Holman with Carol, Bill, Eric, Anita, Denise, Penny and Cynthia, 1998, *Faith in the Poor*, Oxford: Lion Publishers.

82 See Hills, 1998, op cit, p15.
83 See analysis in Social Exclusion Unit, op cit.
84 Kevin Watkins, 1995, *Oxfam Poverty Report*, Oxford: Oxfam, p33.
85 Hills, 1998, op cit, p46. Analysis of trends in public services in this depth has not yet been extended to 1994/95.
86 See, for example, Janet Ford, 1988, *The Indebted Society: Credit and Default in the 1980s*, London: Routledge; Janet Ford, 1991, *Consuming Credit: Debt and Poverty in the UK*, London: CPAG Ltd; Elaine Kempson, Alex Bryson and Karen Rowlingson, 1994, *Hard Times? How Poor Families Make Ends Meet*, London: Policy Studies Institute; Alicia Herbert and Elaine Kempson, 1996, *Credit Use and Ethnic Minorities*, London: Policy Studies Institute; Kempson, op cit, 1996, *Life on a Low Income*.
87 Kempson, op cit, Chapter 3.
88 Ibid, p25. The 'choice' comes down to going without essentials to avoid borrowing, or borrowing and juggling bills to avoid going without essentials. A later study, not confined to low-income families, suggested that there is in fact no simple dichotomy of approaches; it divides different ways of managing money according to the following typology: moral planners, pragmatic planners, flexible planners, muddlers, and pay-as-you-go (Claire Whyley, Elaine Kempson and Alicia Herbert, 1997, *Money Matters: Approaches to Money Management and Bill Paying*, London: Policy Studies Institute).
89 Kempson et al, op cit, p144.
90 Ford, 1991, op cit, p78.
91 Kempson et al, op cit, p138.
92 A more recent study, based mainly on in-depth interviews conducted with 31 couples in spring 1997, aimed to examine how the management and control of money inside households was influenced by the levels of social-security benefits and the way in which they were paid. The study showed much difference in the ways in which money was managed, controlled, and distributed, according to age and life-cycle stage. Women's experiences, attitudes, and activities were found to influence couples' decisions greatly, as did their relation to the labour market and the way social-security benefits were paid (Jackie Goode, Claire Callender and Ruth Lister, 1998, *Purse or Wallet? Gender Inequalities and Income Distribution Within Families on Benefits*, London: Policy Studies Institute, pp3–4 and 102–3).
93 Attitudes which Ford reminds us may be structurally determined by, for example in relation to home ownership in the 1990s, 'ideological pronouncements that presented private ownership not only as non-problematic but as positively beneficial' (1988, op cit, p180).
94 Financial literacy, and in particular familiarity with and access to information technology, could reduce the threat of exclusion represented by the 'rise of the cashless society' (David Birch, 1997, 'Do You Take Cash? The Rise of the "Cashless Society" Threatens to Exclude Those Who Cannot or Will Not Relinquish Hard Currency', *Demos* 12).

95 Ford, loc cit. See also Tom Bentley and Ben Jupp, 1997, 'Future Financial Literacy: Why Social and Economic Development Will Increase People's Need for Financial Literacy', Demos, November, mimeo.

96 The Social Fund provides emergency loans without interest for people in receipt of benefits. Repayments are deducted at source from benefit payments.

97 Simmons, op cit, p26.

98 See Ford, 1991, op cit. Whereas low-income households are less likely than others to take credit *per se*, they are more likely to be in debt.

99 Ibid, pp65–68 and 81.

100 Debt enquiries are the second-largest work area of the Citizens' Advice Bureaux (see their annual report for 1997–98).

101 National Consumer Council (1997), *In the Bank's Bad Books: How the banking code of practice works for customers in hardship*, pp3, 66, 70.

102 A. Leyshon and N. Thrift, 1997, *Money/Space: Geographies of Monetary Transformation*, London: Routledge.

103 Kempson and Whyley, op cit, pp1–2, 14 and 17.

104 Claire Whyley, James McCormick, and Elaine Kempson, 1998, *Paying for Peace of Mind: Access to Home Contents Insurance for Low-Income Households*, London: Policy Studies Institute.

105 Social Exclusion Unit, op cit.

106 Elaine Kempson, 1998, *Benchmarking in Micro-Lending Country Report – UK*, University of Bristol: Personal Finance Research Centre.

107 Whyley et al, op cit.

108 Kempson et al, op cit, p143.

109 Ibid, p139.

110 Ibid, p171.

111 Ibid, p170.

112 R. Berthoud and E. Kempson, 1992, *Credit and Debt in Britain, the PSI Report*, London: Policy Studies Institute. Cited by Oppenheim and Harker, op cit, p76.

113 Herbert and Kempson, op cit.

114 Op cit, p36.

115 Kempson et al, op cit, pp251ff.

116 Ford, op cit, p87.

117 Andrew Leyshon, Nigel Thrift and Jonathan Pratt (1998), 'Reading financial services: texts, consumers, and financial literacy', *Environment and Planning* 16, pp40–41.

118 The author of an in-depth study of 15 of the largest banks in the world comments that 'the percentage of profitable customers is very small — 5 per cent. Your competitors don't worry about the 95 per cent of your customers that are unprofitable. But if they take the other 5 per cent of your customers, you go out of business.' Quoted in Pat Conaty and Ed Mayo, 1997, *A Commitment To People and Place: The Case for Community Development Credit Unions*, London: New Economics Foundation, p2.

119 Leyshon and Thrift, op cit, p234.

120 Data from British Bankers' Association. Only Midland Bank (HSBC) has recently adopted a strategy of refocusing on branches; see Leyshon et al (1998), op. cit, p47.

121 Banking based on building up knowledge of customers and their credit-worthiness through continuity of interaction with particular bank staff.

122 Rowlingson (1994), op cit.

123 Lynch and Haidar (1997), *The Social Responsibility of Credit Institutions in the EU: UK executive summary and country report*, Malcolm Lynch Solicitors.

124 Leyshon, Thrift and Pratt (1998), op. cit.

125 See, for example, Conaty and Mayo, op cit.

126 Leyshon and Thrift, op cit, p254.

127 Leyshon et al (1998), op cit, pp48–50.

128 Ibid, pp29, 47, 50–51.

129 Leyshon and Thrift assert that the term 'community' is a 'highly contentious concept'. The US Community Reinvestment Act operates in a country where the banking system is much more localised than it is in Britain (1997, op cit, p251).

CHAPTER 3

1 'In the UK more of the unemployed are means-tested and means-tested earlier than in continental European countries' (Eithne McLaughlin, 1998, 'Taxes, benefits and paid work', in Carey Oppenheim (ed) *An Inclusive Society: Strategies for Tackling Poverty*, London: Institute for Public Policy Research, p99).

2 Social-security spending reached £100 billion in 1998, around one-fifth of government spending (*Economist* 28 March 1998).

3 However, for many people, the availability of income support and housing benefit has not been enough to prevent homelessness and in some cases sleeping rough. See, for example, Angela Evans, 1996, '*We Do Not Choose to be Homeless ... '*, Report of the National Inquiry into Preventing Youth Homelessness, London: CHAR. Devising proposals for preventing people having to sleep rough was one of the three priorities set for the new Social Exclusion Unit when it was set up by the Labour government in 1997. This is discussed in more detail below.

4 On this, see McLaughlin (op cit).

5 Derek Fraser, 1973, *The Evolution of the British Welfare State*, Basingstoke: Macmillan, cited by Nicholas Timmins, *The Five Giants: A Biography of the Welfare State*, London: Fontana, p28, 1995.

6 Jochen Clasen et al., 1997, *Long-term Unemployment and the Threat of Social Exclusion*, Bristol: The Policy Press.

7 Elizabeth Abbott and Katherine Bompas, 1943, *The Woman Citizen and Social Security*, Women Freedom's League, cited by Ruth Lister, 1994, '"She has other duties" – women, citizenship and social security', in Sally Baldwin and Jane Falkingham (eds), *Social Security and Social Change: New Challenges to the Beveridge Model*, Hemel Hempstead: Harvester Wheatsheaf, p32.

8   Heather Joshi and Hugh Davies, 1994, 'The paid and unpaid roles of women: how should social security adapt?', in Baldwin and Falkingham (eds), p254.

9   *Guardian*, 16 December 1998.

10   Ruth Lister, 1994, op cit, p40.

11   The discussions referred to here have taken place between HM Treasury and the Full Circle Fund of the Norwich-based Women's Employment, Enterprise and Training Unit.

12   Timmins, op cit, p513.

13   Ibid, p514.

14   Susan Johnson, 1998, 'Microfinance North and South: contrasting current debates', *Journal of International Development*, 10 (6).

15   For a critique of this promotion, see Ben Rogaly, 1996, '"Microfinance evangelism", "destitute women", and the hard-selling of a new anti-poverty formula', *Development in Practice*, 6 (2).

16   Many of these reforms became law as part of the Employment Relations Act, July 1999, after this chapter was written.

17   See Department of Trade and Industry White Paper, *Fairness at Work*, 1998 and the Department for Education and Employment's *Employment Action Plan*, 1998.

18   See Ruth Pearson, 1998, 'Micro credit meets social exclusion: learning with difficulty from international experience', *Journal of International Development*, 10 (6). See also Perri 6, 1997, 'Social Exclusion: Time to Be Optimistic', *Demos Collection*, 12.

19   James McCormick, 1998, 'Brokering a New Deal – the design and delivery of welfare-to-work', in James McCormick and Carey Oppenheim (eds), *Welfare in Working Order*, London: IPPR.

20   Stephen Nickell, 1997, 'Unemployment and labour market rigidities: Europe versus North America', *Journal of Economic Perspectives*, 11 (3). F Blau and L Kahn, 1996, 'International differences in male wage inequality: institutions versus market forces', *Journal of Political Economy*, 104 (4), pp791–837.

21   Stuart Hall, 1998, 'The great moving nowhere show', *Marxism Today*, Special Issue November–December, p11.

22   Lucy Anderson, 1998, 'Family friendly: does it work for the low paid?', *Family Policy*, Autumn Issue, p6. This potential problem has been acknowledged by the present government.

23   Although levels of benefit for children, especially young children, and pensioners have been increased by the present government.

24   This view is expressed by Rosalind Bayley in a discussion on 'Pension reform and the family', *Family Policy Bulletin*, Autumn 1997, p2.

25   See Chapter 5, note 77.

26   G. Mulgan, op cit. William Plowden, who was involved in a comparable cross-departmental unit in the 1970s – the Joint Approach on Social Policy — has warned that the present government must heed lessons from the past if its plans for tackling social problems are to succeed after the euphoria of the launch

(*Guardian*, 7 January 1998). Mulgan, who at the time of writing was the Prime Minister's Special Adviser on Inequality and Social Exclusion, claims that the design of the Social Exclusion Unit reflects exactly those lessons.

27   The Social Exclusion Unit's consultation letter on 'deprived neighbourhoods' expressed a desire to find a different language, because the Unit recognised that the label 'worst estates' was stigmatising; by implication, it was not satisfied with 'deprived neighbourhoods' as an alternative. The report on this topic was published in September 1998 and eventually entitled *Bringing Britain Together: A National Strategy for Neighbourhood Renewal* (London: HMSO).

28   In 1998, the government also set up a separate Task Force to investigate the potential role of credit unions.

29   Angela Evans, op cit. The National Inquiry into Preventing Youth Homelessness defined homelessness to include street sleeping, temporary accommodation such as bed and breakfasts and hostels, and the situation of people living with friends and relatives unable to put them up for long periods.

30   Anne Power, 1994, 'Area-Based Poverty, Social Problems and Resident Empowerment', London School of Economics, STICERD, Welfare State Programme, Discussion Paper, p3. Social housing includes properties owned by councils and housing associations. Between 1979 and 1994 the number of homes owned by housing associations doubled from 500,000 to 1,000,000. However, according to Power, housing associations have not turned out to be the sensitive, locally controlled organisations that some had assumed. As they grew, they began to replicate some of the mistakes made by local-authority landlords (op cit, p5).

31   Ibid.

32   Ibid, p9.

33   See the discussion of Community Development Projects in the 1960s and 1970s in the following section.

34   An influential exponent of this ideology is American writer Charles Murray.

35   Sean Damer, 1989, *From Moorepark to 'Wine Alley': The Rise and Fall of a Glasgow Housing Scheme*, Edinburgh: Edinburgh University Press.

36   As a reviewer of the first draft of this book observed, there are more poor people living outside areas of concentrated poverty than there are poor people living in them.

37   Indeed, Geoff Mulgan holds that '[i]n the government's first year of office almost every domestic department has reframed its agenda around poverty and social exclusion' (Mulgan, 1998, op cit, p259).

38   David Donnison, 1997, 'Getting jobs to the places economic growth can't reach', *Family Policy Bulletin*, Autumn, p6.

39   G. Mulgan, 1998, 'Social exclusion: joined up solutions to joined up problems', in Oppenheim (ed), op cit.

40   Cathy Pharoah (ed), 1996, *Dimensions of the Voluntary Sector*, Charities Aid Foundation.

41   G. Mulgan and C. Landry, 1995, *The Other Invisible Hand: Remaking Charity for the 21st Century*, London: DEMOS.

42   This point is made by David Donnison in his writing on the role of local authorities.

43   The phrase is David Donnison's.

44   Pete Alcock, 1997, *Understanding Poverty*, Basingstoke: Macmillan, p248. Yet, also during the 1990s, several local authorities in Britain began to reveal the results of entrenched power.

45   Robin Murray, 1991, *Local Space: Europe and the New Regionalism*, Manchester: Centre for Local Economic Strategies.

46   Alcock, op cit, p248.

47   Ed Mayo, Stephen Thake and Tony Gibson, 1997, *Taking Power: An Agenda for Community Economic Renewal*, London: New Economics Foundation, p12.

48   Ibid, p14.

49   Ibid, p15.

50   Adrian Harvey, 1999, *A Strategic Approach: The Local Government Response to Poverty and Social Exclusion*, London: Local Government Anti-Poverty Unit.

51   Pete Alcock, 1997, *Understanding Poverty*, Basingstoke: Macmillan.

52   This section implies that the neighbourhood renewal work to be carried out in 17 pathfinder areas and co-ordinated by the Social Exclusion Unit could make a significant difference to people's capacity to cope with poverty and social exclusion.

53   Power, op cit, p21.

54   Ibid, p33.

55   Ibid, pp36, 48.

56   Chris Church, Adam Cade and Adrienne Grant, 1998, *An Environment for Everyone: Social Exclusion, Poverty and Environmental Action*, Community Development Foundation, summary. See http://www.cdf.org.uk/environ4everyone.htm.

57   Agenda 21, arising out of the Rio Earth Summit, lays emphasis on the role of local action for sustainable development in consultation with locally resident people.

58   Church et al, op cit.

59   Moraene Roberts, 1998, 'Fighting Poverty and Social Exclusion: The European Experience', UK Coalition Against Poverty/ATD Fourth World, mimeo.

60   Bob Holman with Carol, Bill, Erica, Anita, Denise, Penny and Cynthia, 1998, *Faith in the Poor*, Oxford: Lion Publications.

61   For the case of co-operative microfinance institutions, see Ben Rogaly, 1998, 'Combating financial exclusion through co-operatives: what role for external assistance?', *Journal of International Development*, 10 (6), pp823–36.

62   Annette Rimmer, 1997, 'Power and dignity: women, poverty and credit unions', *Gender and Development*, 5 (3).

63   Margaret Nolan, 1997, 'Pebbles in the Pond', paper to the National Poverty Consultation, Manila to Manchester: Globalisation and Local Poverty, November.

64   Personal Finance Research Centre, 1998, *Benchmarking in Micro-lending: Country Report – UK*, University of Bristol.

65   Ibid.

66   Nigel Meager, Gill Court and Janet Moralee, 1996, 'Self-employment and the distribution of income' in J. Hills (ed), *New Inequalities: The Changing Distribution of Income and Wealth in the United Kingdom*, Cambridge: Cambridge University Press.

67   Ibid, pp222–7.

68   Personal Finance Research Centre, op cit.

69   Ibid; Robert Gavron, Marc Cowling, Gerald Holtham and Andrea Westall, 1998, *The Entrepreneurial Society*, London: IPPR.

70   Gavron et al, op cit, p105.

71   Personal Finance Research Centre, op cit.

72   Ibid.

73   Gavron et al, op cit, Chapter 5.

74   Pearson, op cit.

75   This is of course only one reason for self-employment among Asians. There is also much divergence between the extent, causes, and types of self-employment among Bangladeshis, Pakistanis, and Indians as well as among South Asians and other ethnic minorities. See Hilary Metcalf, Tariq Modood and Satnam Virdee, 1997, *Asian Self-Employment: The Interaction of Culture and Economics in England*, London: Policy Studies Institute.

76   See Gavron et al, op cit, and Department for Education and Employment, 1998, 'Review of Business Start-Up Activities Under the Single Regeneration Budget', June.

77   Meager et al, op cit, p234.

78   Susan Johnson, 1998, 'New Economics: A Gender Perspective', paper prepared for the New Economics Foundation, mimeo. Indeed, an ethnographic investigation of one micro-enterprise programme in the USA in the mid-1990s found that 'while microenterprise may suffice as an alternative to traditional labor market participation for a small number of women with sufficient access to resources, business experience, and entrepreneurial skills, in general, microenterprise produces a host of latent consequences that are ultimately more damaging than productive for women' (Tracy Bachrach Ehlers and Karen Main, 'Women and the false promise of microenterprise', *Gender and Society*, 1998, 12 (4), p426).

79   See Pearson, op cit.

80   S. McKay, R. Walker and R. Youngs, 1997, *Unemployment and Jobseeking Before Jobseeker's Allowance*, Department of Social Security Research Report 73, London: HMSO, cited by J. Hills (op cit, 1998, p23).

81   Op cit, p18.

82 Alex Bryson, Reuben Ford and Michael White, 1997, *Lone Parents, Employment and Well-Being*, Joseph Rowntree Foundation Social Policy Research Findings 129, cited by Rosalind Bayley, 'Breaking the cycle of disadvantage', *Family Policy Bulletin*, Autumn 1997.

83 'An eye on the future: Blair's radical rethink of welfare provision is about a move to private insurance and self-reliance', *Guardian*, 28 May 1998.

84 S. McKay et al, op cit.

85 John Given, 1998, 'A local anthropology of exclusion', in Iain Edgar and Andrew Russell (eds), *A Local Anthropology of Exclusion*, London and New York: Routledge. See also Damer, op cit, on how the other residents of greater Govan, Glasgow did just this in perpetuating the image of 'Wine Alley' for the Moorepark housing scheme.

86 Duncan Fuller, 1998, 'Credit union development: financial inclusion and exclusion', *Geoforum*, 29 (2), p155

87 Pia Christensen, Jenny Hickey, and Allison James, 1998, '"You just get on with it": questioning models of welfare dependency in a rural community', in Edgar and Russell (eds).

88 A.P. Cohen, 1985, *The Symbolic Construction of Community*, London: Routledge.

89 See, for example, Christine McCourt, 1998, 'Concepts of community in changing health care: a study of change in midwifery practice', in Edgar and Russell (eds), op cit.

90 Tony Gibson, 1998, *The Power in Our Hands: Neighbourhood Based World Shaking*, Charlbury, UK: Jon Carpenter, p60.

91 Mai Wann, 1998, 'Building social capital', in Jane Franklin (ed), *Social Policy and Social Justice*, Cambridge: Polity Press.

92 P. Kropotkin, 1972, *Mutual Aid: A Factor of Evolution*, Harmondsworth: Allen Lane, cited in Wann, op cit. In a similar but more contemporary vein, see Jonathan Freedland, 1998, 'Sweet liberty', *Marxism Today*, Special Issue November–December.

93 Rogaly, 1998, op. cit.

94 Kevin Watkins, 1995, *Oxfam Poverty Report*, Oxford: Oxfam, p33.

95 Johnson, 1998, op cit.

96 Geoff Mulgan and Charles Landry, 1995, *The Other Invisible Hand: Remaking Charity for the 21st Century*, London: DEMOS, pp48–9.

97 See, for example, J. Rossiter (ed), 1997, *Financial Exclusion: Can Mutuality Fill the Gap?*, London: New Policy Institute/UK Social Investment Forum.

CHAPTER 4

1 Andrew Leyshon and Nigel Thrift, *Money/Space: Geographies of Monetary Transformation*, London: Routledge, 1997.

2 J. Rossiter (ed.), *Financial Exclusion: Can Mutuality Fill the Gap?*, London: New Policy Institute and UK Social Investment Forum, p8.

3   Susan Johnson, 1998, 'Microfinance North and South: contrasting current debates', *Journal of International Development*, 10 (6).

4   As we shall see later in the chapter, however, full financial sustainability is out of the reach of all but a handful of microfinancial-service providers.

5   S. Rutherford, 1996, *A Critical Typology of Financial Services for the Poor*, ActionAid Working Paper, cited in Susan Johnson and Ben Rogaly, 1997, *Microfinance and Poverty Reduction*, Oxford: Oxfam, pp1–2.

6   World Bank, 1996, *A Worldwide Inventory of Microfinance Institutions*, Sustainable Banking with the Poor Project, Washington, DC: World Bank, pp7–8.

7   Ibid.

8   See Chapter 5.

9   Linda Mayoux has attempted a typology of 'organisational models' of microfinance, which, though confined to grassroots organisations and NGOs, illustrates the extent of the diversity. Linda Mayoux, 1998, *Women's Empowerment and Micro-Finance Programmes: Approaches, Evidence and Ways Forward*, Development Policy and Practice Working Paper No 41, Milton Keynes: Open University.

10 This strategy is being adopted by a growing number of NGOs in India, with the support of the National Bank for Agriculture and Rural Development, which is encouraging banks to lend to 'self-help groups' of borrowers who distribute and retail the bank loan to their members. The national Indian NGO PRADAN has been particularly active in assisting such groups to gain access to bank loans.

11 World Bank, op cit.

12 Despite the evidence from anthropological studies that poor rural women are not without social networks: see, for example, Sarah White, 1992, *Arguing with the Crocodile: Gender and Class in Bangladesh*, London: Zed Press, and 'Bangladesh', chapter in Roger Riddell and Mark Robinson (eds), *NGOs and Rural Poverty Alleviation*, Oxford: Oxford University Press, 1995.

13 Institutions differ in size as well as orientation, so that many do not involve users in their management or operations. Many users are also likely to be far too busy to spare the time for such engagement and are more interested in the outputs.

14 This section relates to the period before the South-East Asian economic crisis of the late 1990s. It draws details from Stephanie Charitonenko, Richard Patten and Jacob Yaron, 1998, 'Indonesia: Bank Rakyat Indonesia Unit Desa 1970–1996', Washington, DC: World Bank: *Sustainable Banking for the Poor, Case Studies in Microfinance*.

15 Hans Dieter Seibel and Uben Parhusip, 'Attaining outreach with sustainability: a case study of a private micro-finance institution in Indonesia', *IDS Bulletin*, 29 (4) pp81–90.

16 This section draws liberally on Syed M Hashemi and Lamiya Morshed, 1997, 'Grameen Bank: a case study', in Geoffrey D. Wood and Iffath Sharif (eds), *Who Needs Credit? Poverty and Finance in Bangladesh*, New York and London: Zed.

17 Strictly, the criteria are that the potential borrower's household must own 'less than 0.5 acres of cultivable land or assets with a value equivalent to less than 1 acre of medium quality land' (ibid, p218).

18 Including the recitation of the 'sixteen decisions', to which members of the Grameen Bank are expected to be committed.

19 Pankaj Jain, 1996, 'Managing credit for the rural poor: lessons from the Grameen Bank', *World Development*, 24 (1) pp79–89. A centre consists of six to eight groups of five.

20 See David Hulme and Paul Mosley, 1996, *Finance Against Poverty*, London and New York: Routledge, and its adaptation in Johnson and Rogaly, op cit, p36, table 3.1.

21 Stuart Rutherford, 1996, *A Critical Typology of Financial Services for the Poor*, ActionAid Working Paper, London: ActionAid.

22 See Imran Matin, 1997, 'The renegotiation of joint liability: notes from Madhupur', in Wood and Sharif (eds) (op cit), p270.

23 Hashemi and Morshed, op cit, pp219–20.

24 See Graham Wright, Mosharrof Hossain and Stuart Rutherford, 1997, 'Savings: flexible financial services for the poor (and not just the implementing organisation)', in Wood and Sharif (eds), op cit, p318.

25 Ibid, pp321–2.

26 See, for example, Helen Todd (ed), 1996, *Cloning Grameen Bank: Replicating a Poverty Reduction Model in India, Nepal and Vietnam*, London: IT Publications.

27 *Financial Times*, 1 October 1998, p4.

28 Those with the largest assets are workplace credit unions, many in the North. Using data from the World Council of Credit Unions, the World Bank (1996, op cit, p19) calculated that in 1994 loans totalling US$2.5 billion were recorded by credit unions in the South. While the volume of loans outstanding from credit unions is important, even more notable is the ratio of depositors to borrowers, which at 2.9 reverses the position of NGOs, whose depositor-to-borrower ratio was 0.7 (ibid, p21). The major role of credit unions in providing microfinancial services is often underestimated.

29 Community development credit unions (CDCUs), like community credit unions in Britain, are those with a common bond based on residential location rather than on workplace or association. The details of CDCUs are taken from Pat Conaty and Ed Mayo, 1997, *A Commitment to People and Place: The Case for Community Development Credit Unions*, London: New Economics Foundation. For the impact on poverty and social exclusion of the different types of credit union, see Ben Rogaly, 1998, 'Combatting financial exclusion through co-operatives: is there a role for external assistance?', *Journal of International Development*, 10 (6).

30 See the case study of URAC in Johnson and Rogaly (op cit) on which this section draws.

31 Alana Albee and Nandasiri Gamage, 1996, *Our Money Our Movement: Building a Poor People's Credit Union*, London: IT Publications.

32 Peter Fidler, 1998, *Assessing the Performance of Banco Solidario, S.A. As a Provider of Micro-Finance*, Washington, DC: World Bank, table 2.

33 All the data on SEWA Bank in this section were provided by Thomas Fisher of the New Economics Foundation.

34 This section draws on Pat Conaty and Thomas Fisher (1999), *Micro-credit for Micro-Enterprise*, London: New Economics Foundation.

35 Tracy Ehlers and Karen Main, 1998, 'Women and the false promise of micro-enterprise', *Gender & Society*, 12 (4).

36 Malcolm Harper, comment in panel discussion, in Imran Matin and Saurabh Sinha with Patricia Alexander (eds), 1998, *Recent Research on Micro-Finance: Implications for Policy*, University of Sussex: Poverty Research Unit, Working Paper No 3.

37 E-mail from Thalia Kidder (November 1998), policy adviser to Oxfam GB in Managua, Nicaragua.

38 Alicia Herbert and Elaine Kempson (1996), *Credit Use and Ethnic Minorities*, London: Policy Studies Institute, pp54–56.

39 Kidder, op cit.

40 Op cit. Another study found that micro-enterprise loans were effective for those who already had experience of running businesses.

41 Mark Schreiner, 1998, 'The Context for Micro-enterprises and Micro-enterprise Programs in the United States and Abroad', draft report for the Ford Foundation, New York, p37.

42 Op cit, p14; Tracy Ehlers and Karen Main, op cit. Changes in some of the determinants of the business environment, such as welfare and regulation, may of course not be desirable for addressing poverty and social exclusion. Schreiner (p14) writes, 'The safety net should not be lowered just so that micro-enterprise sector can grow. After all, the goal is not to have a big micro-enterprise sector but rather to improve human welfare in the best way.'

43 Schreiner, op cit, p15.

44 R. Spalter-Roth, E. Soto and L. Zandniapour, 1994, *Micro-enterprise and Women. The Viability of Self-employment as a Strategy for Alleviating Poverty*, Washington DC: Institute for Women's Policy Research, quoted in Ehlers and Main, op cit, pp429–30.

45 See, for example, the studies by Hassan Zaman and Syed Hashemi (of BRAC and Grameen Bank respectively) in the section of Wood and Sharif (eds) (op cit) entitled 'Problems of reaching the poorest'; and Sergio Navajas et al, 1998, 'Micro-credit and the Poorest of the Poor: Theory and Evidence from Bolivia', paper presented at the Latin American and Caribbean Economic Association, October 22–24, Universidad Torcuato Di Tella, Buenos Aires, Argentina. Also, Rachel Marcus et al, 1998, *Money Matters: Microfinance and Save the Children Fund*, London: Save the Children Fund (UK).

46 See ACCION, 1997, *US Network Annual Report*, Somerville, Massachusetts.

47 Elaine Kempson and Claire Whyley, 1998, *Access to Current Accounts*, London: British Bankers' Association.

48 Hassan Zaman, 1998, 'Can mis-targeting be justified? Insights from BRAC's micro-credit programme', *IDS Bulletin*, 29 (4) pp59–65.

49 Hulme and Mosley, op cit, p201. No qualifications were made in Hulme and Mosley about the possible negative impacts of additional labour on household members working most intensively.

50 Small enterprises are (usually) defined in the UK as enterprises with fewer than 50 employees. In this book we follow the same convention, using 'small business' and 'small enterprise' interchangeably. In practice, the small businesses discussed in this book are at the lower end of the scale.

51 Hulme and Mosley op. cit, p.103.

52 Of the 415 credit recipients surveyed, 23% of those with 1–2 employees generated one or more new jobs, 56% of those with 3–6 employees, 77% of those with 7–13 employees, and 71% of those with more than 14 employees. Quoted by Kidder, op cit, from a preliminary report for CEPAD, Nicaragua (October 1996).

53 See Imran Matin, 1998, '"Mistargeting"' by the Grameen Bank: a possible explanation', *IDS Bulletin*, 29 (4) pp51–8.

54 Zaman, op cit.

55 Ehlers and Main, op cit, p438.

56 Saurabh Sinha and Imran Matin, 1998, 'Informal credit transactions of micro-credit borrowers in rural Bangladesh', *IDS Bulletin*, 29 (4), pp66–80.

57 Ibid.

58 B. Ackerly, 1995, 'Testing the tools of development: credit programmes, loan involvement and women's empowerment', *IDS Bulletin*, 26 (3), pp56–68, cited by Johnson and Rogaly (op cit, p13). This paragraph and the next draw heavily on Johnson and Rogaly.

59 Linda Mayoux, 1998, *Women's Empowerment and Micro-Finance Programmes: Approaches, Evidence and Ways Forward*, Development Policy and Practice Working Paper No 41, Milton Keynes: Open University, pp15, 20, 24.

60 A. Goetz and R. Sen Gupta, 1996, 'Who takes the credit? Gender, power and control over loan use in rural credit programmes in Bangladesh', *World Development*, 24 (1) pp 45–63.

61 See also A. Rahman, 1999, 'Micro-credit initiatives for equitable and sustainable development: who pays?', *World Development* 27 (1) pp67–82.

62 Helen Todd (ed), 1996, *Cloning Grameen Bank: Replicating a Poverty Reduction Model in India, Nepal and Vietnam*, London: IT Publications, p22.

63 S. M. Hashemi, S. R. Schuler, and A. Riley, 1996, 'Rural credit programs and women's empowerment in Bangladesh', *World Development*, 24 (4).

64 Lutfun N. Khan Osmani, 1998, 'Impact of credit on the relative well-being of women: evidence from the Grameen Bank', *IDS Bulletin* 29 (4) pp31–8.

65 This was one of the studies undertaken for and published in Johnson and Rogaly, op cit.

66 Interviews were carried out by Martha Romero.

67 See Dichter, 1996, 'Questioning the future of NGOs in microfinance', *Journal of International Development* 5 (3): 259–71.

68 Marcus et al, op cit.

69 M. Zeller et al, 1997, *Rural Finance for Food Security for the Poor: Implications for Research and Policy*, Food Policy Review No. 4, Washington DC: IFPRI.

70 Shahidur Khandker, 1998, 'Micro-credit programme evaluation: a critical review', *IDS Bulletin* 29 (4) pp11–20.

71 This section is adapted from chapters 3 and 4 of Johnson and Rogaly, op cit.

72 A. S. Yenni Suryani, 1998, 'Micro-Credit Programme from a Gender Perspective: Targeting Women Versus Meeting Practical and Strategic Gender Needs', unpublished MA dissertation, School of Development Studies, University of East Anglia.

73 See, for example, Fuad Al-Omar and Mohammed Abdel-Haq, 1996, *Islamic Banking: Theory, Practice and Challenges*, London and New Jersey: Zed Press. Note also, however, that the largest-scale success stories in microfinancial services do involve interest payments on loans and have evolved among largely Islamic populations in Indonesia and Bangladesh. There is wide diversity of legal approaches to banking in countries with majority Muslim populations.

74 Susan Johnson, 1998, 'Microfinance North and South: contrasting current debates', *Journal of International Development*, 10 (6).

75 See, for example, Aidan Hollis and Arthur Sweetman, 1998, 'Micro-credit: what can we learn from the past?', *World Development*, 26 (10), pp1875–91.

76 Hulme and Mosley, op cit, p206.

77 This paragraph draws on comments made by Susan Johnson on an earlier draft.

78 BASIX, a microfinance institution based in Hyderabad, India, which uses its non-banking finance company for its lending operations, has been at the forefront of lending to the poor through traders and commission agents.

79 For the role of groups in microfinance, see Johnson and Rogaly, op cit, pp38–43.

80 Hollis and Sweetman, op cit, p1876.

81 Ibid.

82 See, for example, N. McNamara and S. Morse, 1998, *Developing Financial Services: A Case Against Sustainability*, Cork, Ireland: Onstream.

83 Hollis and Sweetman, op cit, p1888.

84 See the editors' introductory chapter in Geoffrey D. Wood and Iffath Sharif (eds), op cit.

85 Hulme and Mosley, op. cit., p200.

86 *Financial Times*, 1 October 1998.

CHAPTER 5

1   For example through legislation such as the Community Reinvestment Act in the United States. See chapter 4 in E. Mayo, T. Fisher, P. Conaty, J. Doling, and A. Mullineux, 1998, *Small is Bankable: Community Reinvestment in the UK*, York: Joseph Rowntree Foundation and London: New Economics Foundation. This chapter draws extensively on this report.

2   Provided by Citizens' Advice Bureaux (CABx), members of the Money Advice Association, the Consumer Credit Counselling Service, and some local authorities. 'In 1995 the major UK agencies dealt with well over a million money advice cases' (National Consumer Council, 1997, *In the Bank's Bad Books: How the Banking Code of Practice Works for Customers in Hardship*, London).

3   See the annual report of the National Association of CABx for 1997–98. Compare also comments at the beginning of the section of this chapter headed 'Access to personal financial services'.

4   See E. Kempson and C. Whyley, 1999, *Kept Out or Opted Out? Understanding and Combating Financial Exclusion*, Bristol: The Policy Press and York: The Joseph Rowntree Foundation; and A. Leyshon, N. Thrift and J. Pratt, 1998, 'Reading financial services: texts, consumers, and financial literacy', *Environment and Planning* 16.

5   In Chapter 2, Ben Rogaly quotes from the National Consumer Council report (op cit), which draws extensively on the experience of money-advice services helping individuals to deal with the banks. Below I cite the example of the Citizens' Advice Bureaux supporting the development of credit unions.

6   African-Caribbean, Pakistani, and Bangladeshi; A. Herbert and E. Kempson, 1996, *Credit Use and Ethnic Minorities,* London: Policy Studies Institute.

7   For details of what a basic banking product might look like, see Kempson and Whyley, op cit; M. Lynch and L. Haidar, 1997, *The Social Responsibility of Credit Institutions in the EU: UK Executive Summary and Country Report*, Leeds: Malcolm Lynch Solicitors; and Office of Fair Trading, 1999, *Vulnerable Consumers and Financial Services*, London.

8   Social and community enterprises are enterprises that are run for social purposes, or by members of a community for the benefit of themselves or their wider community. An example mentioned in this chapter is a construction company that trains local youth on probation. Such enterprises seek to be financially sustainable, but may not seek to generate significant profits.

9   Such as 'time money', which is now being promoted in the UK by the New Economics Foundation; for various existing alternative currencies see D. Boyle, 1999, *Funny Money: In Search of Alternative Cash*, HarperCollins.

10 For details of community finance initiatives in the UK, see Mayo et al, op cit.

11 The building societies established as mutual societies are of course much older and could be described as an earlier wave of community finance initiatives. The first building society was established in 1775 (Jenny Rossiter, ed., 1997,

Financial Exclusion: Can Mutuality Fill the Gap?, London: New Policy Institute and UKSIF, p7). Likewise, the international history of credit unions is much older than in Britain (see section on credit unions later in this chapter).

12   Analysed in greater detail later in this chapter.

13   Data from LETSLINK UK in Portsmouth.

14   See note 9 above.

15   The Full Circle Fund in Norwich, the Glasgow Women's Micro-credit Project, and Sustainable Strength in Birmingham. The extent to which The Prince's Trust and these three funds can be described as providing distinctive 'micro-credit' products is reviewed later in this chapter.

16   Street UK; see P. Conaty and T. Fisher, 1999, *Micro-credit for Micro-enterprise*, London: New Economics Foundation.

17   Such as the Ulster Community Reinvestment Trust in Northern Ireland. There are also funds, such as Shared Interest, which focus on supporting economic initiatives to address poverty in the South.

18   See note 1.

19   These figures exclude British initiatives, like Shared Interest and Opportunity Trust, which are targeted overseas.

20   Social investors invest funds in financial institutions with a social purpose (such as a community loan fund). While the investors may earn a financial return on their investments, it is often lower than what they could expect to earn through standard financial investments.

21   E. Kempson, 1994, *Outside the Banking System: A Review of Households Without a Current Account*, Social Security Advisory Committee Research Paper 6, London: HMSO.

22   J. Ford and K. Rowlingson, 1996, 'Low-income households and credit: exclusion, preference, and inclusion', *Environment and Planning*, 28(8), pp1345, 1349. I have been unable to find equivalent data that are more recent.

23   National Consumer Council, op cit, p2.

24   E. Kempson and C. Whyley, 1998, *Access to Current Accounts*, London: British Bankers' Association. For more details from this study, see Ben Rogaly's comments in Chapter 2 ('Where finance fits').

25   See S.P. Kaur, S. Lingayah and E. Mayo, 1997, *Financial Exclusion in London*, London: New Economics Foundation.

26   See note 7.

27   National Consumer Council, op cit; for more details of this report, see under the heading 'Money management, poverty, and social exclusion' in Chapter 2.

28   Both quotations from Leyshon et al, op cit, p49.

29   Kempson, 1994, op cit. See also Leyshon et al, op. cit, p49.

30   Quoted in Social Exclusion Unit, 1998, *Bringing Britain Together: A National Strategy for Neighbourhood Renewal*, London: The Stationery Office, p31.

31   See Kempson, 1994, op cit, p28.

32   Op cit.

33   Leyshon et al, op cit, p49.

34   Kempson and Whyley, 1999, op cit, p35.

35   See Lynch and Haidar, op cit.

36   Quoted in Lynch and Haidar, op cit.

37   K. Rowlingson, 1994, *Money-lenders and their Customers*, London: Public Studies Institute, p2. The cost of using pawnbrokers is equally high. 'One woman pawned a bracelet for £20 and it cost her £40 to redeem. Another raised a loan of £34, for which she was charged £2.40 a month — a total charge of nearly £15 over the six-month term of the pawn. At least two of the seven people who had pawned possessions said they had been unable to find the money to redeem them' (Kempson and Whyley, 1998, op cit, p28).

38   Rowlingson, op cit.

39   Ibid, pp4, 55.

40   Kempson, 1994, op cit, p23.

41   Others, on the other hand, stop using money-lenders, if they can, to avoid paying so heavily for such services; see Kempson and Whyley, 1999, op cit.

42   Ford and Rowlingson, op cit.

43   'One of the strongest influences on the use of money-lenders rather than an overdraft or credit card (where these were available) was the access to cash which the recipients could then physically hand over for goods or to settle bills. Non-cash transactions were rejected as unsafe and less controllable. ... For many respondents ... a loan from a money-lender was seen as a cash rather than a credit transaction' (Ford and Rowlingson, op cit, p1354).

44   This can significantly reduce transaction costs for borrowers. Transaction costs have become a very important issue in assessing microfinancial services in the South (in part to justify the high interest rates charged), but they seem to receive far less consideration in the literature on microfinancial services in the North. An important reason, for example, why micro-businesses may prefer to draw on their credit cards rather than take small business loans, even though the latter are cheaper, is that a business loan requires drawing up a business plan, which involves high transaction costs for the borrower.

45   Rowlingson, op cit, p6. Most customers of money-lenders 'welcomed the fact that they could determine how much to borrow and arrange for the money to be repaid in installments they felt they could afford. They also welcomed the flexibility of lenders if they were short of money one week and could not afford to make the repayment. Few, if any, of them considered how much the loan was costing them' (Kempson and Whyley, 1998, op cit, p27).

46   See Ford and Rowlingson, op cit, pp1355–7 for examples.

47   Lynch and Haidar, op cit.

48   It had an annual turnover of £5 billion by the early 1990s; Ford and Rowlingson, op cit, pp1351, 1354.

49   Kempson and Whyley, 1998, op cit, p25.

50 For some of the characteristics that such an initiative would require, see D. Khudabux and R. Simpson, 1995, 'Umbrellas and Safety Nets: The Borrowing Needs of People on Low Incomes', a draft report, not finalised, for The National Consumer Council. Effective competitors would need to learn from existing money-lenders, and introduce measures such as providing regular door-to-door collection services. Compare SEWA Bank's strategy (described in Chapter 4), which includes learning from pawnbrokers by lending against gold and jewellery deposited at the Bank.

51 This section draws on P. Conaty and E. Mayo, 1997, *A Commitment to People and Place: The Case for Community Development Credit Unions*, London: New Economics Foundation.

52 See annual report of the National Association of CABx for 1997–98, pp9, 15. (CABx are also supporting LETS schemes.) An experimental contingency fund managed by the Parks and Walcot Credit Union in Swindon helps members in serious hardship to secure a loan for emergencies, or prospective members to pay off a money-lender or other expensive credit agreement.

53 Workplace credit unions are growing faster for several reasons: payroll deductions of credit-union share and loan payments by the employer sponsor; higher average income and therefore savings of members; and explicit or implicit gifting of employee staff time to work on developing and helping to service the credit union.

54 Self-Help in North Carolina and VanCity in Vancouver are the best-known cases, but there are many others. For example, since 1991 the North Carolina Minority Support Center has been supporting the growth of 14 other Community Development Credit Unions in the state: their combined assets have risen from $20 million to $47 million since 1991.

55 Op cit.

56 In the USA, access to non-members' deposits from social investors has proved critical for the growth of designated 'low-income' credit unions, over half of whose members live on low incomes.

57 As the citation on credit unions taken from the annual report of the National Association of Citizens' Advice Bureaux suggests, CABx are already responding to this agenda. Settlements in Britain are multi-purpose community-development centres in urban areas. The first settlement was Toynbee Hall in London. Similarly, development trusts are 'community-led enterprises with social objectives and are actively engaged in the economic, environmental and social regeneration of an area' (*Community Works! A Guide to Community Economic Action*, London: New Economics Foundation, p25). Many development trusts are involved in housing and managed workspace.

58 The New Economics Foundation is currently conducting a feasibility study, funded by Lloyds TSB, for a national Credit Union Growth Fund.

59 This section draws on C. Whyley, J. McCormick and E. Kempson, 1998, *Paying for Peace of Mind: Access to Home Contents Insurance for Low-Income Households*, London: Policy Studies Institute.

60   Age Concern Insurance Services (ACIS), a wholly owned trading company of Age Concern, 'endeavours to offer some of the best value policies available while ensuring that these products are designed to meet the *specific needs of older customers*'. It was set up in 1982; 'at the time, general insurance was an area in which over-55s had been ill-served for a long time.' ACIS now provides home, contents, travel, motor, motor breakdown, and pet insurance (ACIS Factsheet, London: Age Concern).

61   Information taken from H. Barnes, P. North and P. Walker, 1996, *LETS on Low Income*, London: New Economics Foundation.

62   While changes in labour markets, as described in Chapter 2, mean that many who are poor or socially excluded may no longer have marketable skills demanded by modern businesses, LETS can in fact provide opportunities for members to use and develop their skills within a localised market.

63   See Boyle, op cit.

64   Kempson and Whyley, 1999, op cit.

65   This section draws heavily on Mayo et al, op cit.

66   Micro-loans are also suitable for house repairs and property alterations (for example, to conserve energy). With the reduction of local council grants, and the reluctance of commercial lenders to extend mortgages due to high transaction costs, there is currently very little finance available for such purposes (see Mayo et al, op cit).

67   See Conaty and Fisher, op cit.

68   In factoring, a specialised company buys invoices for money owed to firms (or acts as agent to collect the money). The firms thus benefit from receiving payment earlier, although of course at a discount or for a percentage fee. Leasing is a form of rental agreement whereby a firm can hire equipment by paying a regular lease payment. The lease agreement may also provide for the purchase of the equipment.

69   This section draws on Lynch and Haidar, op cit.

70   Mayo et al, op cit., chapter 1.

71   Malcolm Lynch Solicitors, 1998, *Microfinance in Industrialised Countries: Enterprise Creation by the Unemployed; Stocktaking Exercise April–May 1998*, London: International Labour Organisation.

72   Mayo et al, op cit, p10.

73   Ibid, p29

74   For reasons for this lack of success, see Mayo et al, op cit, p29.

75   M. Klett, 1994, *A Directory of Soft Loan Schemes, 1993, 1994*, Small Business Research Centre, Kingston University.

76   For 18–24 year olds; for 25+; for Lone Parents; for the Disabled; for Partners of the Unemployed (Social Exclusion Unit, op cit).

77   WEETU argues that women using the Full Circle Fund should be able to build up their business for two years while continuing to claim welfare benefits. 'The New Deal period of "Enterprise Rehearsal" extends to only a maximum of 6 months, and could undermine the trust and confidence built up by Full Circle participants. I.e., their business is "owned" by the training

organisation, not by themselves, and the training organisation is responsible for maintaining their business records. For women long-term dependent on a range of primary and secondary benefits, especially lone parents, the New Deal period of enterprise rehearsal is insufficient to enable them to build a viable alternative income to benefits' (*Full Circle Policy Briefing No 1*, 24 May 1998, Norwich: WEETU).

78 For both Fundusz Mikro and Street UK, see Conaty and Fisher, op cit.

79 Such as the Aston Reinvestment Trust, Investors in Society, Enterprise Ventures Limited, Glasgow Regeneration Fund, Greater London Enterprise, Hackney Business Venture, Industrial Common Ownership Finance, Local Investment Fund, Merseyside Special Investment Fund, Radical Routes, Scottish Community Enterprise Investment Fund, and Triodos Bank (see Mayo et al, op cit, for details).

80 The figures are taken from a 1998 briefing note of GRF, and its 1998–99 Annual Review. GRF has also provided significant support (including the loan capital) to the Glasgow Women's Micro-credit Project reviewed in the previous section.

81 Mencap is the Royal Society for Mentally Handicapped Children and Adults.

82 Although the size and term of loans are limited by legislation. Wellpark in Glasgow is planning a new business credit union for women.

83 For more details, see Conaty and Fisher, op cit.

84 See Conaty and Fisher, op cit.

85 James Robertson, 1998, *Transforming Economic Life*, Totnes, Devon: Schumacher Society and London: New Economics Foundation, p34.

86 See Conaty and Fisher, op cit.

87 Ibid.

88 Social Exclusion Unit, op cit.

89 Some of the mechanisms typically used by micro-credit lenders, for example, help to reduce their costs: peer lending groups to screen proposals and guarantee loans; strong incentives for borrowers to repay; mandatory savings; high interest rates; and lending through intermediaries (see Conaty and Fisher, op cit, and Chapter 4 above).

90 For example, a recent survey of micro-credit interventions in Latin America argues: 'It is commonly believed that the more [microfinance institutions] aim for financial sustainability, the less their impact on poverty reduction will be ... However, the evidence provided by numerous studies does not support this conclusion. It is unclear whether there is a trade-off between an institution's emphasis on financial sustainability and its willingness or ability to reach the poorest. There is a positive correlation, however, between achieving financial sustainability and reaching *many* poor people: well-run financial institutions of all types are able to reach greater numbers of poor people' (Hege Gulli, 1998, *Microfinance and Poverty: Questioning the Conventional Wisdom*, Washington DC: Inter-American Development Bank). These proponents therefore set out different levels of sustainability, from initiatives dependent on grants and subsidies through to those that can

provide a market return on capital employed, and suggest that over time initiatives must move from the first towards the last (see ACCION International, *Ventures*, Winter 1998, Somerville, Massachusetts; for alternative degrees of sustainability, see Conaty and Fisher, op cit; and R. Christen, E. Rhyne, R. Vogel and C. McKean, 'Maximizing the Outreach of Microenterprise Finance: An Analysis of Successful Microfinance Programs', USAID Program and Operations Assessment Report No.10, Agency for International Development, Washington DC. However, very few initiatives providing microfinancial services in the South have been able to generate market returns.

91   This has been one of the causes of the decline of neighbourhoods in Britain and the United States, as banks and other financial-service providers have refused to reinvest in their locality or have withdrawn from disadvantaged areas altogether.

92   Moreover, as Chapter 4 suggests, because of their ownership structure, local membership-based financial institutions are more likely to recycle capital locally than to invest it outside the neighbourhood. Some community loan funds, such as the Aston Reinvestment Trust, have also attracted social investments (on which investors earn below-market returns).

93   Street UK, a proposed micro-credit initiative to serve existing enterprises, including those operating in the 'grey economy', aims to earn a return of 5 per cent, still below full market returns (Conaty and Fisher, op cit).

94   Indeed, only a decade ago the UK was dubbed 'the indebted society' (see remarks in Chapter 6). Susan Johnson made the following comments on the draft manuscript of this book: 'There is ... potentially more of an argument for subsidy in the UK context than in the case of some international MFIs [microfinance institutions]. Internationally many MFIs are finding technologies to serve the vast unbanked population (and these are not necessarily poor) and in some cases are increasingly moving away from the poor in order to be profitable. The reason why they have not been served is not necessarily because the clientele are not profitable, but that a range of factors, including broad institutional ones, have meant that banking services have not yet reached them. In the UK, poor people may lose access because market segmentation has got to a degree which makes these segments of the population unprofitable.'

95   Some community (development) finance initiatives in the US, such as Shorebank, which is mentioned in Chapter 4, see their role in terms of 'community capitalism', stabilising or restoring markets to prevent the collapse of the local economy, and allowing it to grow again through a variety of private and community initiatives.

96   For example, staff need not only the appropriate financial skills, but also honesty, integrity, and accountability to users or members; see D. Hulme and P. Mosley, 1996, *Finance Against Poverty*, 2 vols, London: Routledge, and Johnson and Rogaly, op cit. A governance structure that is not accountable to the users or members of the organisation is unlikely to continue to address

their particular needs. The organisational form, which can be highly diverse, as seen in this chapter about the UK and in the previous chapter on international experience, is a significant design element for achieving the long-term sustainability of initiatives providing microfinancial services. As Ben Rogaly argues in Chapter 4, the nature and structure of the organisation, and its sensitivity to the local environment, may be the most critical factors in ensuring its longevity.

97 An issue that arises, therefore, is to what use subsidies should be put. For micro-credit for micro-enterprises, Conaty and Fisher (op cit) argue that subsidies are best targeted at reducing the transaction costs and risk to the lender, rather than subsidising interest payments, which can distort markets, displace existing enterprises which do not have access to subsidies, and promote businesses that are unsustainable once the subsidies run out. However, the high interest rates often charged by providers of micro-financial services in the South are clearly inappropriate for Britain, especially in an economic context where returns to self-employment and micro-business are generally much lower than in developing economies.

98 Compare other Indian initiatives with which I work. PRADAN, a non-government organisation in India which promotes small savings and credit groups among rural women, not only values the potential *social* impact of such organising, as explored in Chapter 4, but also pursues a strategy of educating bankers throughout the country to change their dismissive attitudes towards the poor. A practical outcome of this strategy is that many of their groups are linked with local mainstream banks. Likewise, the Cooperative Development Foundation, which promotes credit unions in rural India, sees these as potential vehicles for enhancing local democracy. And BASIX, a group of financial companies, not only provides an integrated package of services for promoting rural livelihoods, but has also drawn on this experience to project itself effectively into national policy arenas, where it has successfully championed significant changes in relevant financial regulation.

99 Of Hastings Development Trust.

100 As Rolf Lynton, a leading practitioner and thinker on social change, argues, 'innovative institutions aim to make a difference beyond themselves. *What* difference precisely and how, and how much it mattered in the light of history many forces will influence, as also the deliberate moves [made by those innovative institutions]' (Rolf Lynton, 1998, *Social Science in Actual Practice*, New Delhi, Thousand Oaks and London: Sage, p229). Opposing forces, such as global capital, will of course pursue similar strategies of seeking to alter paradigms, as well as appropriating other paradigm-changing events for their own ends.

101 Such demonstration, and its projection on to the policy level, has been critical, for example for regulators to press the demands of the CRA on banks, knowing that such lending is profitable and hence will not undermine the financial performance of the banks.

CHAPTER 6

1   E. Kempson and C. Whyley, 1999, *Kept Out or Opted Out? Understanding and Combating Financial Exclusion,* Bristol: The Policy Press, and York: The Joseph Rowntree Foundation.

2   See Chapter 5, note 77.

3   This is one of the motivating rationales behind the training and loans for low-income women entrepreneurs provided by the Full Circle Fund in Norwich (Ruth Pearson, 1998, 'From micro-credit to social exclusion', *Journal of International Development,* 10 (6)).

4   This tradition is referred to as 'community development finance' in the USA and as 'community finance' in Britain; see E. Mayo, P. Conaty, J. Doling, and A. Mulllineux, 1998, *Small is Bankable: Community Reinvestment in the UK,* York: Joseph Rowntree Foundation, and London: New Economics Foundation.

5   For the ideological underpinnings of this recent emphasis in the South on self-help through micro-business, see Susan Johnson, 1998, 'Microfinance North and South: contrasting current debates', *Journal of International Development* 10 (6), where she contrasts it with the ideology that gave rise to many community (development) finance initiatives in the North.

6   Social enterprises and community enterprises are run for social purposes, or by members of a community for the benefit of themselves or their wider community. Such enterprises seek to be financially sustainable, but may not seek to generate significant profits.

7   See Case Study A in Chapter 5.

8   See Case Study B in Chapter 5.

Suggestions for further reading

Barnes, H., P. North and P. Walker, 1996, *LETS on Low Income*, London: New Economics Foundation

Boyle, David, 1999, *Funny Money: In Search of Alternative Cash*, London: HarperCollins

Conaty, Pat and Thomas Fisher, 1999, *Micro-credit for Micro-enterprise*, London: New Economics Foundation

Conaty, Pat and Ed Mayo, 1997, *A Commitment to People and Place: The Case for Community Development Credit Unions*, London: New Economics Foundation

Damer, Sean, 1989, *From Moorepark to 'Wine Alley': The Rise and Fall of A Glasgow Housing Scheme*, Edinburgh: Edinburgh University Press

Dichter, T., 1996, 'Questioning the future of NGOs in microfinance', *Journal of International Development*, 5 (3)

Edgar, Iain and Andrew Russell (eds), 1998, *A Local Anthropology of Exclusion*, London and New York: Routledge

Ehlers, Tracy and Karen Main, 1998, 'Women and the false promise of microenterprise', *Gender and Society*, 12 (4)

Ford, J. and K. Rowlingson, 1996, 'Low-income households and credit: exclusion, preference, and inclusion', *Environment and Planning* 28 (8)

Goetz, A. and R. Sen Gupta, 1996, 'Who takes the credit? Gender power and control over loan use in rural credit programmes in Bangladesh', *World Developmment*, 24 (1)

Goodman, Alissa, Paul Johnson and Steven Webb, 1997, *Inequality in the UK*, Oxford: Oxford University Press

Gulli, Hege, 1998, *Microfinance and Poverty: Questioning the Conventional Wisdom*, Washington DC: Inter-American Development Bank

Herbert, A. and E. Kempson, 1996, *Credit Use and Ethnic Minorities*, London: Policy Studies Institute

Hills, John, 1998, *Income and Wealth: The Latest Evidence*, York: Joseph Rowntree Foundation

Hollis, Aidan and Arthur Sweetman, 1998, 'Microcredit: what can we learn from the past?', *World Development*, 26 (10)

Holman, Bob with Carol, Bill, Eric, Anita, Denise, Penny and Cynthia, 1998, *Faith in the Poor*, Oxford: Lion Publishers

Hulme, David and Paul Mosley, 1996, *Finance Against Poverty*, London and New York: Routledge (2 vols).

Hutton, Will, 1996, *The State We're In* (Revised edition), London: Vintage

Johnson, Susan and Ben Rogaly, 1997, *Microfinance and Poverty Reduction*, Oxford: Oxfam GB

Kempson, Elaine, 1994, *Outside the Banking System: A Review of Households without a Current Account*, Social Security Advisory Committee Research Paper 6, London: HMSO

Kempson, Elaine, 1996, *Life on a Low Income*, London: Policy Studies Institute

Kempson, Elaine, Alex Bryson and Karen Rowlingson, 1994, *Hard Times? How Poor Families Make Ends Meet*, London: Policy Studies Institute

Kempson, Elaine and Claire Whyley, 1998, *Access to Current Accounts*, London: British Bankers' Association

Kempson, Elaine, and Claire Whyley, 1998, *Benchmarking in Micro-lending Country Report – UK*, Bristol: Personal Finance Research Centre

Kempson, Elaine and Claire Whyley, 1999, *Kept Out or Opted Out? Understanding and Combating Financial Exclusion*, Bristol: The Policy Press and York: The Joseph Rowntree Foundation

Leyshon, Andrew and Nigel Thrift, 1997, *Money/Space: Geographies of Monetary Transformation*, London: Routledge

Leyshon, Andrew, Nigel Thrift, and Jonathan Pratt, 1998, 'Reading financial services: texts, consumers, and financial literacy', *Environment and Planning* 16, pp29-55

Lister, Ruth, 1994, '"She has other duties" — Women's citizenship and social security' in Sally Baldwin and Jane Falkingham (eds), 1994, *Social Security and Social Change: New Challenges to the Beveridge Model*, Hemel Hempstead: Harvester Wheatsheaf

Lynch, M. and L. Haidar, 1997, *The Social Responsibility of Credit Institutions in the EU: UK Executive Summary and Country Report*, Leeds: Malcolm Lynch Solicitors

Madanipour, Ali, Goran Cars and Judith Allen (eds), *Social Exclusion in European Cities: Processes, Experiences and Responses*, London: Jessica Kingsley

Mayo, E., T. Fisher, P. Conaty, J. Doling, and A. Mullineux, 1998, *Small is Bankable: Community Reinvestment in the UK*, York: Joseph Rowntree Foundation and London: New Economics Foundation

Modood, Tariq et al, 1997, *Ethnic Minorities in Britain: Diversity and Disadvantage*, London: Policy Studies Institute

National Consumer Council, 1997, *In the Bank's Bad Books: How the Banking Code of Practice Works for Customers in Hardship*, London: National Consumer Council

Office of Fair Trading, 1999, *Vulnerable Consumers and Financial Services*, London: Office of Fair Trading

Oliver, Melvin and Thomas Shapiro, 1995, *Black Wealth White Wealth: A New Perspective on Racial Equality*, New York and London: Routledge

Oppenheim, Carey (ed), *An Inclusive Society: Strategies for Tackling Poverty*, London: Institute for Public Policy Research

Pearson, Ruth, 1998, 'Microcredit meets social exclusion: learning with difficulty from international experience', *Journal of International Development*, 10 (6)

Rahman, A., 1999, 'Microcredit initiatives for equitable and sustainable development: who pays?', *World Development*, 27 (1)

Rogaly, Ben, 1996, 'Microfinance evangelism, "destitute women", and the hard-selling of a new anti-poverty formula', *Development in Practice*, 6 (1)

Rowlingson, K., 1994, *Money-lenders and their Customers*, London: Policy Studies Institute

Schreiner, Mark, 1998, 'The Context for Micro-Enterprise and Micro-Enterprise Programmes in the United States and Abroad, Report on Ford Foundation funded research', available from the author at Center for Social Development, George Warren Brown School of Social Work, Washington University in St Louis, St Louis, MO, 63130-4899, USA or schreiner@gwbmail.wust1.edu

Social Exclusion Unit, 1998, *Bringing Britain Together: A National Strategy for Neighbourhood Renewal*, London: HMSO

Timmins, Nicolas, 1995, *The Five Giants: A Biography of the Welfare State*, London: Fontana

Townsend, Peter, 1979, P*overty in the United Kingdom: A Survey of Household Resources and Standards of Living*, Harmondsworth: Penguin

Vandenbroucke, Frank, 1998, *Globalisation, Inequality and Social Democracy*, London: Institute for Public Policy Research

Whyley, C., J. McCormick and E. Kempson, 1998, *Paying for Peace of Mind: Access to Home Contents Insurance for Low-Income Households*, London: Policy Studies Institute

Wilkinson, R. G., 1996, *Unhealthy Societies: The Affliction of Inequality*, London: Routledge

Wood, Geoffrey D. and Iffath Sharif (eds), 1997, *Who Needs Credit? Poverty and Finance in Bangladesh*, New York and London: Zed

Index

ACCION, USA 63, 71–3, 77, 114
Africa, microfinance 62
Age Concern 107
Age Concern Insurance Services 168n60
agricultural loans 60
aid donors: *see* donors
Anglican Church 44
anti-poverty: international action 49; Labour
    1, 8; local strategies 47; microfinance
    initiatives 58; national action 56; NGOs
    1; Oxfam iv; policy-making 4, 32–3; trade
    unions 44
ASA, Bangladesh 66
Asia, microfinance 62, 90
associational credit unions 96
Aston Reinvestment Trust 120, 141, 142,
    169n79, 170n92
ATD 4th World 49

Badan Kredit Desa, Indonesia 64
BancoSol, Bolivia 69, 73, 78, 89
Bangladesh: ASA 66; BRAC 79; fungibility of
    loans 135; land-ownership 77–8; loans for
    women 62–3, 81, 90, 138; micro-credit
    loan providers 80; micro-enterprise loans
    77–8; savings 61; *see also* Grameen Bank
Bank Rakyat Indonesia 63, 64–5, 83, 87, 99
banks: appropriate accounts 60; basic
    product 99, 164n7; branch closure 25,
    28, 41, 99, 113; current accounts 25, 131,
    145–6n10; debt handling 24; financial
    exclusion 28, 51; flight to quality 4, 27,
    58, 109, 152n118; intermediaries 87;
    micro-businesses 113, 121; microfinancial
    services 94; peer pressure 65; penny banks
    105, 140; rural areas 60; small businesses
    113; social roles 29; supermarkets 101
Barnes, H. 108
BASIX, India 163n78, 171n98
benefits bank 100; *see also* welfare benefits
Berthoud, R. 26
Bevan, Jane 117
Beveridge, William 14, 34

bill payment: management of money 22–4,
    60, 131, 92; Post Office 109; welfare
    benefits 24
Birmingham: Sustainable Strength 116, 139,
    165n15; urban poverty 16
Blair, Tony 145n4
Bolivia, BancoSol 69, 73, 78, 79
borrowing: from friends/family 26, 52;
    National Consumer Council 167n50;
    sustainability 89; *see also* loans
BRAC, Bangladesh 66, 79
Bringing Britain Together, Social Exclusion
    Unit 5, 41
Britain: community loan funds 127; credit
    unions 123–4, 133; enterprise culture 135;
    ghettoisation of poverty 79; housing sector
    42, 46, 137, 155n30; Industrial Common
    Ownership Finance 137; Italy, compared
    11; micro-business opportunities 135;
    microfinancial services 5, 62, 139–43;
    Pakistani remittances 75; poverty 11,
    16–17; SEWA Bank example 71; *see also*
    social security; welfare benefits
Brocklehurst, Roger 119
Brown, David 118
building societies 58, 140; low-income
    customers 100; microfinancial services 94;
    mutual societies 95, 97, 120, 164–5n11
business angels 51
business credit unions 120
Business Links 112, 114

Caisses de Credit Municipal, France 105
Cambridge Building Society Ltd 100
Cambridge Housing Society 100
Canada 106, 167n54
capital flows 19–20
CARUNA, Nicaragua 75
cash transactions 60, 103
cashless society 151n94
Charities Aid Foundation 140
Cheque Act 103
cheque-cashing 42, 109, 131